# WHAT'S IT ALL ABOUT, ALPHA?

&

## *Other Investment Essays from an Incredible Decade*

*Jason DeSena Trennert*

ISBN-10: 0-9978316-2-6

ISBN-13: 978-0-9978316-2-7

Library of Congress Control Number: 2016959700

Published by Willow Street Press LLC Bronx NY
www.willowstreetpress.com

Design: www.fantabulousdesign.com

Printed in the United States of America

*To all of my partners, colleagues, family, friends,*
*and especially the clients who took a chance on Strategas*
*when they didn't have to.*

*A special thanks to Susan Konig,*
*owner of Willow Street Press, who took an interest in*
*this project and made it a reality.*

# CONTENTS

## BEST ESSAYS OF 2008 — 39



## BEST ESSAYS OF 2009 — 54



## BEST ESSAYS OF 2010 — 68



## BEST ESSAYS OF 2011 — 86

## BEST ESSAYS OF 2012 97



## BEST ESSAYS OF 2013 119



## BEST ESSAYS OF 2014 139



## BEST ESSAYS FROM 2015 157

# BEFORE THE BEGINNING

## *So Long*

*(My last essay at ISI—August 14, 2006)*

It was July 4, 1991, and I watched the Yankees beat the Orioles 3-2 from the bleachers under the hot summer sun at the Stadium. I drank cold beer and, between screaming epithets at Segui in right, I pondered my job at a start-up company called ISI to begin the next day. A year out of Georgetown, my major accomplishments on Wall Street to this point were passing the Series 7 and getting the pizza order right for the traders I worked for at Morgan Stanley. Oddly, I started work on a Friday. My notes from the time reveal that I wrote everything in red ink, obviously some vestige of an article in an academic psych journal from college, and that I was totally bewildered by the concepts discussed at our morning research meeting. I could not have been any more green. I scrawled in big block letters across the first page of my first notebook "REVIEW RELATIONSHIP BETWEEN BONDS AND INFLATION."

I shared a small room with my fellow salesmen at ISI and we all became fast friends. Pat Alwell asked me whether I was familiar with a new product called "sunscreen" and Frank Chiodi and Alan Goldman debated at length, without asking for my input, whether my glasses were too big for my face. (It might be hard to believe, but they were.) We were part of something new and exciting and the company was almost immediately successful, which helped. We spent a lot of our off-time together doing what most people in their 20s do and for the most part still do today, the only real difference being that we didn't have to check in with anyone back then and if we did we would had to have found a payphone in one of the bars on the Upper East Side.

And here I write my final essay at ISI, a little more than 15 years later and 15 pounds heavier, married and a father, pondering my future at a new start-up, my own, to start this fall. What would possess men and women with good jobs to leave and start new ventures fraught with risk will remain one of the great mysteries of this country. It might be even more curious in my case because I love my job, am good friends with my co-workers, and respect my bosses. But I am now 38, have a little money in the bank, and can list as my dependents only one wife, my son, and two understanding bartenders. It might be a Fool's Paradise but I hope that starting my own firm will afford me a little less time traveling, a little more time with my family, and more time to write. One of the ironies of the sellside research business is that the more widely your stuff is read the less time you have to do research. Lastly, I became more sensitive to the irony of spending as much time as I do pontificating about the economy and criticizing corporate America without ever having to have met a payroll myself.

I will be forever grateful for the tremendous leaps of faith and misplaced confidences Ed Hyman and Nancy Lazar have placed in me over the years. They have built one of the great franchises in the financial services industry. Jim Moltz is one of Wall Street's true gentleman, possessing the type of class and erudition that one sadly only sees in black and white motion pictures these days. He has been a great mentor and friend.

We're just beginning the process of starting a new business and it appears as if it will be an infinitely more expensive, yet far more useful, MBA. I'm starting the company with Nick Bohnsack and Don Rissmiller, both smarter, more energetic, and better looking than I. We are learning in short order that the word "expedite" may be the most expensive word in the English language and we are all beginning to wonder why children don't have nightmares about lawyers rather than big hairy monsters with one eye and eight arms.

It has been forever thus, but Wall Street remains one of the most dynamic industries in the world. In some ways it's unrecognizable to me from when I started: mutual funds have been replaced by hedge funds as the Street's biggest customers, bulge bracket brokerage firms are acting less and less as agents and more and more as principals, and it appears that the sheer number of players and the democratization of information technology are making the investment world smaller and more efficient. My contrarian instincts tell me that it may be time for good lower cost active managers to reassume their place in the sun after years of competitive pressures from hedge funds and ETFs.

Finally, among the many lessons learned in my tenure at ISI about Wall Street and business in today's flat world is that the only thing you can count on is change and greater levels of competition. On this last day, I am reminded of what I believe to be one the great novels of the 20th Century, Lampedusa's *The Leopard*, as singularly beautiful in English as it is in Italian. (For the purposes of full disclosure, the pulchritude of *La Professoressa* who taught it to me in college may have something to do with feelings about the book.) The novel takes place in Sicily during the Risorgimento, and its main protagonist, Don Fabrizio, a Sicilian prince, is forced to confront what will be the inevitable decline of his influence in a unified Italy. His favorite nephew Tancredi, offers the book's central paradox: "Se vogliamo che tutto rimanga come e', bisogna che tutto cambi." If we wish for everything to stay the same, everything must change.

# *Kitty Genovese, Bystander Apathy, and the Plight of Large Cap Stocks*

*First Essay Published at Strategas—September 15, 2006*

Recently returning to my home town for my 20th high school reunion, I spent a little time helping my Mom clean out the basement of my childhood home. Most of the garbage down there was mine but among the baseball cards and Hot Wheels, I found a number of my old college notebooks. Leafing through them I was amazed at how little I retained from those four years of study. It was sad to see that two semesters and 5,000 years of Chinese history could be reduced to some hazy recollection of Han Fei, the military strategist, and my infantile fascination with eunuchs. But in that musty basement I also found my notes from my freshman psychology class and was reminded of one of the more interesting stories I've ever heard—the sad fate of Kitty Genovese, a young lady who was murdered in Queens in 1964. It's a sad comment about urban life that this fact in and of itself is unremarkable in a large city. But what was interesting about the case was that it became apparent that few who had heard her screams for help did anything to help her. In fact, while 38 people in the neighborhood had reported hearing her pleas for help, the first call to the police came in nearly 35 minutes later. Police were on the scene in less than two minutes. The Genovese case led to scores of articles about urban decay and the insensitivity of people in modern society. But perhaps the most important legacies of this sad story were the findings of a pair of psychology professors who studied the case. In a series of experiments later chronicled in *The Journal of Personality and Social Psychology*, John Darley and Bibb Latane found that Genovese was doomed not because there were not enough witnesses to help her but because there were too many. The diffusion of responsibility led to apathy. Their findings also led to a greater understanding of the importance of the concept of "social proof" or the idea that human beings are social creatures who have a tendency to act as those around them act. This basic need to be connected to others makes human beings highly susceptible to "groupthink" and to being influenced by 'the herd'. Their findings became the basis for the widely accepted psychological theory of Bystander Apathy also known as the Kitty Genovese syndrome.

It may be inappropriate and a stretch to link the passing of a poor young woman 40 years ago to the current malaise affecting large cap stocks and the listless trading of the broader market. It is no secret in the investing business that, despite attempts to have non-consensus ideas, few of us have the courage to wander too far away from the crowd for very long. Keynes' recognized the social pressures inherent in investing when he claimed in *The General Theory of Employment, Interest, and Money* that "worldly wisdom teaches that it is better for one's reputation to fail conventionally than to succeed unconventionally." **In our discussions with institutional investors it seems clear that the least consensus view in the financial markets today is to be very bullish on the outlook for equities.** Even the most optimistic prognosticators feel compelled to concede that, given the current strength of profit margins and the already low-levels of interest rates, the market will have a tough time posting gains in excess of profit growth in the years to come. In *Barron's* roundup of strategists over Labor Day, the most bullish forecast for the S&P 12 months ahead hence was 1480. (That was mine.) The average forecast for the Index twelve months from now is 1379, scarcely 5% higher than where the S&P stands today and only 15.4x the average top-down estimate for 2007 S&P 500 operating earnings of $89.48. Investors' aversion to risk is understandable given the drama that followed the end of the last bull market. And while I have been in the business too long to take seriously the concept of "smart money" it seems odd to me that large cap stocks are languishing while the number of companies going private is soaring. This undoubtedly has something to do with the regulatory burdens of Sarbanes-Oxley, but it increasingly appears to have more to do with valuation. The decline in oil, gold, and bond yields suggests that the Fed should be finished with its tightening campaign. And yet, as the table below indicates, investors appear to fear the largest of the large cap stocks. The top quintile trades at a steep discount to the market as a whole despite having a significantly higher earnings growth rate. (This is still true if one excludes the Energy sector.) While this may be simply a function of the fact that the last bubble was most apparent in mega cap stocks, we also believe, although it would be impossible to prove, that there is significant social pressure among the market's most active traders to pay-up for the small and opaque and sell the large and well known. A good friend of mine put it this way at an idea dinner for hedge fund managers, "Let's face it, for the young hedge fund manager it's difficult to stand up and say I'm worth 1 and 20 if I'm buying Citi." We continue to maintain that there is value in stocks in general and large cap U.S. stocks in particular.

## Executive Pay in Perspective

Perhaps the most fun and most interesting read from my summer reading list was Leigh Montville's *The Life and Times of Babe Ruth*. The Sultan of Swat was, of course, a great character and the stories about his carousing were great fun. But what was perhaps more interesting were his nearly constant salary battles with the Yankees' owners. Although the $80,000 he made in 1931 was a handsome sum at the time, it would be the equivalent of a little more than $1 million today—not bad by any means but peanuts for the most famous athlete and entertainer in the world. This passage from the book puts today's debate about executive pay, and perhaps our own, into perspective.

*A discussion about Babe Ruth's money took place in the third week of March 1933 at the Gold Dust Lodge, a shelter at 40 Corlears Street run by the Salvation Army to house and feed 2,000 homeless, destitute, and jobless men in New York City. The discussion started to get warm, pro and con. The Babe was the last Yankees holdout in St. Petersburg, fighting a major reduction in his $75,000 salary—and adjutant Andrew Laurie, director of the shelter, decided that maybe there should be a vote. If nothing else, it would kill a little time.*

*How much should Babe Ruth earn? More than half of the residents, 1,171 men, voted. The figure they decided was $48,999, an average of all the numbers submitted. One man said the Babe should make a million dollars a year. Another said he should make a dime, and yet another said he should work for free. Some suggested he should be paid by the home run, $1,000 per homer.*

*It was mentioned that once upon a time (two years ago) the slugger had made $80,000 per year. A second vote was taken on whether any person in any job was worth $80,000 per year. This was close: 599 men said yes, and 572 said no.*

*The 599 men who had said yes were then asked who they thought should receive $80,000 per year. Each man had one vote. The results were as follows:*

*1. Any president of the United States (185 votes)*

*2. Babe Ruth (140)*

*3. President Franklin Roosevelt (97)*

*4. Former Governor Al Smith(12)*

*5. Former New York Mayor Joseph McKee and Jack Dempsey(5)*

*6. Herbert Hoover(4)*

*7. Henry Ford, Charles Schwab, and comedian Joe E. Brown (3)*

*A number of candidates received one or two votes. Among the single vote getters were Albert Einstein, William Randolph Hearst, Gene Tunney, Tom Mix, Enrico Caruso, Thomas Edison, Walter Winchell, John D. Rockefeller, and Lou Gehrig. No women were mentioned.*

***The average pre-Depression salary of the 1,171 voters had been $49 per week. The Salvation Army said the cost of keeping each man in the shelter with two meals per day was $1 per week.***

*Two days after the vote, the Babe officially signed a contract in a ceremony in the St. Petersburg sun for $52,000 for the 1933 season, a $23,000 pay cut from 1932. He squealed, but not too loudly. This was 17 days after Roosevelt had declared a bank holiday as a last-gasp effort to save the remaining banks in the country. Kenesaw Mountain Landis has set a precedent for baseball, dropping his own salary $10,000 to $40,000 after lopping off $15,000 a year earlier. Virtually all of the Yankees had taken pay cuts. Lou Gehrig dropped $5,000 to $22,500.*

*"I've had three ambitions," the Babe said. "I've wanted to complete 20 years of baseball and I'll do that this year. I've wanted to play in ten World Series and I realized that ambition last year. And I hope to boost my home run total to 700. I hope to do that by hitting at least 48 this year."*

*"You must hit 61 this year, Root, and give us a new record," Col. Ruppert said. The twentieth season began.*

# *Margins, the Entrepreneur, & the New Economy*

*Originally Published—October 13, 2006*

Among the many justifications and rationalizations I used to leave a high-paying job at a good firm and start my own little company was that the experience of running a business would make me a better strategist and student of the financial markets. After all, I said, Jack Daniels in hand holding forth to my partners at Rothmann's on 54th, nothing focuses the mind like the need to meet a payroll, right? It was, admittedly, a little thin but it was also a necessary part of the emotional and psychological case I needed to do something that was, by all accounts, risky. And so now, here I am, nearly five weeks and untold hours later, and I'm starting to believe that what I thought was the weakest justification for establishing Strategas may have, in fact, been the strongest. *This will hardly come as a revelation to anyone who's started their own business, but you tend to behave differently when it's your own money.* The warm nuts and Cabernets in First Class are long gone and I was, to be honest, a little disappointed when I didn't get a personalized note from the hotel manager with a basket of fruit when I stayed at the Omni in downtown in Los Angeles as I once did when I stayed at the Peninsula in Beverly Hills. I had no driver and relied on taxis, felt a lot more like I did when I started out as a salesman in the business 15 years ago, and for whatever reason I loved it. Our little office in New York consists of a conference room with 8 people and 13 flat panel screens. It's hot and there's no privacy but we're all having fun and are being forced, for the first time in a long-time, to economize on things we once took for granted. What I'm learning as a strategist is that technology may be the small businessman's best friend. E-mail and the Internet are saving us untold sums and headaches as we start. Perhaps one of our greatest discoveries has been the company Salesforce.com (CRM, $40.29). In years past there is no doubt in my mind that we would have had to spend thousands of dollars and have hired small department to manage our mailing list. But Salesforce.com allows us to have an extraordinarily efficient solution to this critical function for literally peanuts. What's perhaps more surprising is that the firm's resident old fart (that would be me, at age 38) can actually use it. I have done little work on CRM and see that it trades at 126x forward earnings so please don't view this as a solicitation to buy the stock. All I can say is that it's a great product and has been a Godsend. And so, I can actually see in practice that technology is clearly a long-term secular bull case for the sustainability of margins. You need revenues to have profit margins, of course, and that's still largely a work in progress. But if we had meaningful revenues our margins would be terrific—and that's a statement that would make Andrew Fastow blush.

# *The Secular Case for Equities as a Source of Yield*

*Originally Published—October 27, 2006*

## Shades of My Old Man

For the better part of a generation I saw my father go through his annual, and in his later years, semi-annual, ritual of ceremoniously cancelling The New York Times. "That's it, Fil," he'd proclaim to my mother standing up from the kitchen table, "the Times will no longer be read in this house!" And then he'd march over to the phone in the foyer and call the circulation switchboard and spend five minutes explaining his decision, loudly and with dramatic flair, to someone who undoubtedly couldn't have cared less. Even a cursory glance at my father's file would have told the person on the other end of the phone not to take his protestations too seriously—he would re-subscribe in matter of days once his sense of indignation passed. The scene became all the more comical to me because my parents, owing to their working class and immigrant roots, were, as late as the 1980s, registered Democrats. The article or editorial that would set my father off could have been on just about any topic—sports, foreign policy, you name it—but were generally due to some disagreement over values or religion.

I recount this story because I felt myself channeling my Dad this week when my friend Larry Kudlow asked me on his eponymous show whether the current bull run could be described as a "Pelosi rally." After all, he baited me, hadn't the markets already discounted a Democratic House? I'm a pretty mild mannered guy but I felt my face flush and I thought, for a moment at least, that I might pass out from pure exasperation. The only thing that was missing was a phone and my most recent copy of the Times. The current rally, I petulantly explained, had nothing to do with someone who had not yet been elected Speaker and everything to do with the fact that the market was behind in discounting the economy's incredible performance over the last few years. Corporate profits are at all time highs, long-term interest rates are below 5%, the unemployment rate is 4.6%, and home ownership is at record levels. How could Nancy Pelosi take credit for that, I whined.

When I calmed down however, I realized that Larry's question was driven by his recent interview with Congressman Pelosi in which she claimed, rather convincingly, that she would not seek to repeal President Bush's tax cuts on dividends and capital gains. Whether this is sincere or election-year posturing I don't know. But further thought about the topic has led me to believe that the aging of the population in the U.S. and in the developed world makes higher tax rates on dividends a big political loser. With nearly 50% of the households in America owning stocks and with the proportion of the world's population over 65 years old scheduled to grow to new heights, it seems unlikely that either party will seek to mess around too much with a potentially enormous source of income for the aging.

**400 YEARS OF AGING**

| Year | % of Total Population over 65 |
|---|---|
| 1700 | 4% |
| 1800 | 4% |
| 1900 | 4% |
| 1950 | 5% |
| 2000 | 7% |
| 2050 | 16% |
| 2100 | 21% |

* Source: Ronald Lee, " The Demographic Transition," JEP 2003

## Are the Natives Restless Enough to Affect Change?

It's hard to claim that dividends will become a third rail of politics the way Social Security has become, but as the table above indicates it's not hard to see why politicians from both sides of the aisle will have an increasingly difficult time increasing the tax rate on dividends and capital gains. The longer the tax cuts stay in place the greater the opposition will be to increase them. More immediately important may be to ask why more companies haven't initiated dividends and why dividend paying stocks have not performed better versus non-dividend paying stocks. There are several plausible explanations for this. The first and perhaps most important may be, in fact, that both retail investors and corporate Treasurers alike are unsure about how permanent the tax cuts really are. The second reason is that an entire generation of portfolio managers were led to believe that paying dividends was a travesty at the altar of growth investing[1]. And the third is that it

1. Asness and Arnott's paper, "Surprise! Higher Dividends = Higher Earnings Growth," from the Financial Analysts Journal largely put the lie to this ill-conceived notion.

seems rather unrealistic for investors to count on dividends as a source of income after nearly 50 years of discriminatory tax treatment against them. But the tide may be changing. As the chart below indicates, companies have more cash on their balance sheets today than they have had at any time in the last 40 years and the amount of private equity money being raised suggests that companies may come to the conclusion that they have to use the cash or it will be used for them.

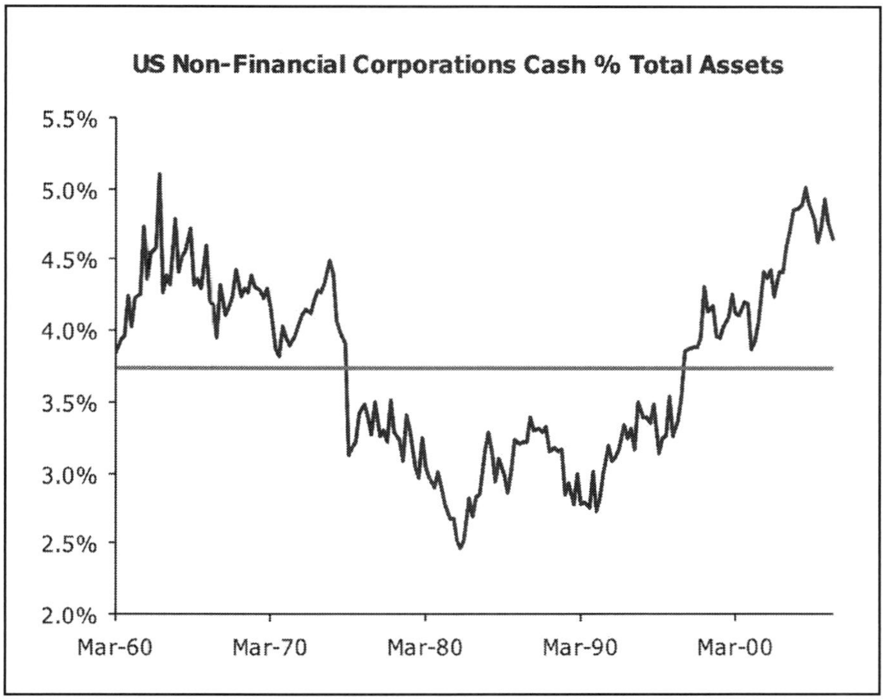


## The Return of Dividends Will Be Secular

While it appears as if the stars seem to be aligning for investors to once again view dividends as an important part of their total return, it would be unrealistic to assume corporate dividend policies and investor attitudes will change overnight. Because corporate treasurers have more than one option when deciding the best way to dispense with cash, there is certainly no guarantee that there will be a stampede toward the tried and true method of enhancing shareholder value through yield. Companies are understandably leery about paying dividends because of their perceived permanence. If share buybacks are dating, dividends are marriage and that can be a pretty scary prospect for more than a few CEOs. M&A is undoubtedly the most fun, replete with dinners in the executive dining rooms of bulge bracket firms and the occasional trip on a G-5. And capital expenditures require hard work and real risk. Only dividends give the investor a certain and permanent enhancement to their total return.

As the population ages, more and more investors may start to view equities as they once did—as a source of yield. Somewhat remarkable to anyone under 60 years old, dividends have accounted for the not-too-inconsequential sum of about 45% of the total return from stocks since 1926. **If one believes, as we do, that stocks are cheaper than bonds on a pre-tax basis (the S&P 500 is trading at about 15x forward earnings while bonds are trading at greater than 20x), equities are clear winners in the valuation sweepstakes on an after-tax basis.** A 15% tax rate on dividends and capital gains compares rather favorably to ordinary income tax rate that must be paid on bonds and that's something both Democrats and Republicans can agree on.

# *The Dawn of the Bernanke Fed the Chairman's "Hybrid" Monetary Policy*

*Originally Published—November 24, 2006*

Buried beneath the perfunctory, perennial, and pleasant stories surrounding the run-up to the Thanksgiving holiday, was a small story on Bloomberg about what some might see as a quiet revolution at the Fed. In "Bernanke's Programs May Dilute Greenspan Intuition," Scott Lanman revealed that a small team of economists at the Fed was testing a forecasting model that condenses as many as 150 economic indicators into several weighted average series with an eye toward shaping monetary policy. This story comes on the heels of the October Fed minutes which indicated that numeric inflation targeting is gaining traction at FOMC meetings and will undoubtedly be discussed again at the next two-day meeting, in January. While it should come as no surprise that economists at the Fed are using quantitative models to divine the future path of economic growth, we do believe these developments signal a major shift at the Fed away from the intuitive and qualitative approach to monetary policy under Greenspan to a more quantitative and model-based approach under Bernanke.

It seems like only yesterday when Greenspan stepped down as Chairman, but February 1st 2007 will mark Bernanke's first anniversary at the helm of the Fed. Perhaps remembering the experiences of both Volcker and Greenspan in their inaugural years as Chairmen (a steep recession in one instance and a stock market crash in the other), the Chairman deftly wielded his power and emphasized continuity with a monetary policy that was generally regarded to be successful. But the description of the multi-factor model and the FOMC minutes both indicate, in our view, that the Chairman will seek to put his own stamp on the Fed in 2007.

Bernanke made no secret of his preference for a quantitative target for inflation, although he does appear to recognize the limits of a pure model-based approach. In part of his research at Princeton, he ran a program to see what the impact on growth and inflation would be if a multi-factor model were used to generate a rule-based monetary policy between 1987 and 1998. Allowing scores of economists, strategists, and money managers to make more sense of their lives, Bernanke's study revealed, mercifully, that inflation and unemployment would have fluctuated more wildly during this period using a purely quantitative approach than they did under Greenspan's more intuitive methods. There is a certain irony that both the Fed and NYSE appear to be experimenting with "hybrid" systems. Whether Ben Bernanke's or John Thain's attempts to mix old and new are political calculations designed to assuage the fears of traditionalists while modernizing financial institutions with entrenched political constituencies is unclear and, for investors, largely irrelevant. Intentional or not, the release of the Bernanke model strikes us as a political masterstroke.

This should not only assure the markets that changes in monetary policy, although real, will be gradual but also should ease political tensions within the Fed itself. We believe the Fed is likely to stay on hold for the foreseeable future, with an easing by May. In the short-term, it wouldn't actually surprise us if talk of further Fed tightening resurfaced as the decline in oil prices, the stock market rally, and the continued strength in employment raise the odds of a stronger-than-expected holiday shopping season. Such fears are unlikely to evidence themselves until well after Christmas and so we remain bullish on high-beta stocks in the short-term. Ultimately, we believe the slowdown in housing will take a percentage point off of GDP growth in 2007 and allow the Fed to ease by May.

# *What's a Strategas?*

*Originally Published—December 8, 2006*

Of all the frequently asked questions we get on the road—what inning are we in in the private equity game, how can you be bullish when profit margins are at all-time highs, and what are your thoughts on the twin deficits?—the one I've received the most since we started our little company has to do with the derivation of our company name and logo. Most people are kind in their questioning, but more than a few have been less than shy in their bewilderment. A master of nuance, Joe Kernen of CNBC said on the air, "Jason, you've been dreaming of starting your own company your whole life and this is what you came up with?" Similarly, a friend and paying client in Texas asked me bluntly: "what the $%*& is a strategas?" I found the phrasing of the question so viscerally funny that I was able to experience, for the first time since I was about 7, the unique sensation of having Dr. Pepper come out of my nose. The question also reminded me of my Georgetown days when, in the height of our basketball team's dominance, opposing fans would carry signs that read "What's a Hoya?" or its more ribald and amusing derivative "Your Mother's a Hoya." (The "Patrick Ewing Can't Read This" signs went over the line.) And so, without further ado, I'd like to explain once and for all how we came up with our rather unique name.

It is a little known fact that the word strategy is derived from the Greek word "strategos" which means "general." In Athenian Democracy, the strategoi stood between the elected officials and its military leaders to provide counsel in balancing the needs of protecting individual liberties while, at the same time, providing for the overall security of the state. Satisfied that we had found a name that had real meaning and the requisite pretension of antiquity, we had decided, perhaps naively that "strategos" was as good as we were going to get. In the 11th hour, however, our lawyers informed us that name the firm "strategos" could invite trademark litigation. Having invested some time in the decision and becoming attached to the logo of the warrior we now affectionately call Gus, we asked our lawyers to find a vowel that would complete the word "strateg_s" without inviting legal action. They came up with "strategas" which, at that point was close enough for us and actually looked kind of cool when using Greek lettering. I must say that there is a certain irony and sadness in the fact that, in the post-industrial and litigious society in which we live, we essentially had to choose a name that was so devoid of meaning to actually steer clear of a lawsuit. In any event, the name has been a source of amusement among our clients and friends. And, as the saying goes, "we don't care what you call us, as long as you call us."

# BEST ESSAYS OF 2007

## *Information Arbitrage R.I.P. & the Need for the Long View*

*Originally Published—March 2, 2007*

The guys in our shop read with great anticipation Warren Buffett's annual letter to shareholders yesterday, which is justifiably considered to be required reading for anyone that has a genuine interest in long-term value. There was a great irony in this I thought given the fact that the letter was released amid the near breathless coverage in the media of what at least thus far has been a relatively shallow, although painful no doubt, correction in the markets this week. It doesn't take a master of observation for anyone who's ever worked for a relatively large institution that intellectually honest people like Buffett are either forced to conform or are forced to "pursue other interests." There is little doubt in my mind that Buffett would never have had a long career in a traditional corporate mutual fund complex. Aside from Bill Miller and a handful other superstar managers, a few years of underperformance would cause the vast majority of money managers to start worrying about the next tuition payment. And yet, despite strong evidence that those who treat equities as long duration assets can outperform the crowd, a focus on short-term information (i.e. noise) and performance persists. Compounding this problem is the fact that fund of funds managers often require newly minted hedge funds to generate consistently positive returns monthly. While there may be some room for discussion about whether this is even feasible on a sustainable basis, most of us could agree that the long-duration status of common stocks makes them poor candidates for *monthly* return strategies. While it might be a good way to keep your brokers happy, it sounds like a sure-fire way to underperform to us.

Having said this, and although this is almost impossible to prove categorically, the market seems to be telling us that the value of short-term information is declining for hedge funds with assets over $1 billion. (There are about 300 such funds out of a universe of 8,000.) There are two indications that the informational arbitrage game is no longer as profitable as it once was—one practical and one theoretical. From a more practical perspective it appears that the best and largest hedge funds are increasing their time horizons are seeking to expand their repertoire to include long-only strategies with long lock-up periods, increasingly activist roles, and private investments both here and abroad. This too may be some indication that a low-return, low-vol environment, rather than a dramatic liquidity event, is what ultimately rationalizes the hyper-growth in the hedge fund industry. By creating longer-duration vehicles, previously short-term oriented players seem to be acknowledging the difficulty of gaining a sustainable information edge ahead of 8,000 of their best friends. Witness SAC's recent involvement in the Freeport McMoran deal, a seemingly odd pursuit for an $8 billion fund who some believe accounts for between 2 to 3% of the *daily* trading volume on the NYSE. On a more theoretical level, the decline in the effectiveness of earnings surprise strategies also suggests that the markets are becoming ever more efficient in discounting marginal changes in information.

This brings up another question we've received with great frequency over the past few years. One of the more curious developments in the financial market over the last few years has been the slow and steady decline in the volatility of stock prices. Candidly, few of the institutional investors we've met in our travels even believe that this phenomenon has actually occurred. "Have you looked at a quote screen lately?" Whether one uses the VIX, whose mathematical cadence gives it an air of credibility, or the simple yearly trading range of the S&P 500 (a measure, incidentally, one our bond salesman derisively described as a "VIX for English majors") the decline in aggregate volatility has been undeniable. Measuring the implied volatility of index options, the VIX now stands at 15.8, up from its recent low but a far, far cry from the levels witnessed in the late-1990s.

Using the market's trading range as another measure of volatility tells a similar story—the S&P's 16.6% price band in 2006 was one of the narrowest in the Index's history, significantly lower than the 25.8% range since 1945. What makes this all the more remarkable has been the fact that this has occurred despite research from Bain & Co. that suggests that the average holding period of common stocks has fallen from 8 years in 1960 to 11 months in 2000. With brokerage firms acting more like principals rather than agents we wouldn't be surprised if the holding period were indeed even shorter these days.

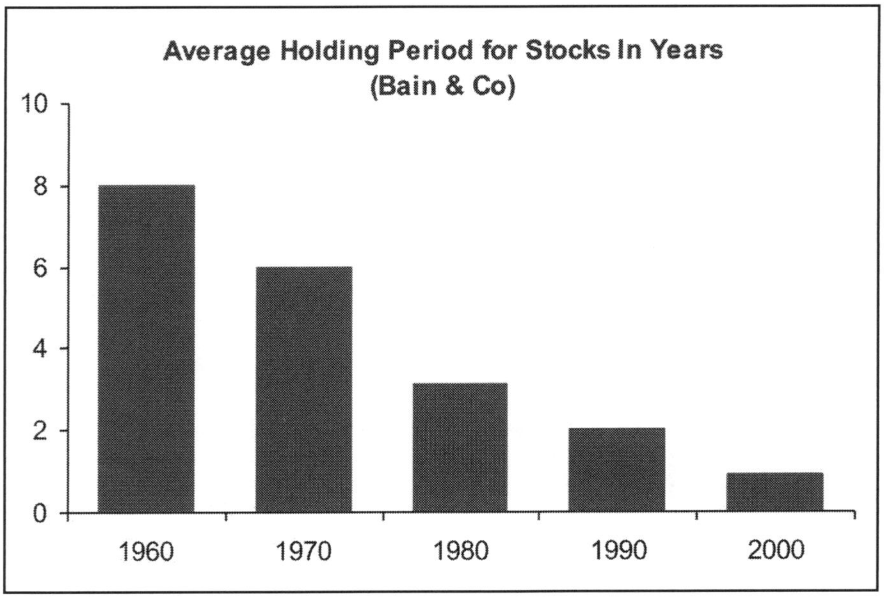


We're often asked in client meetings what we believe has accounted for these trends. The answer, of course, like most others, is "we don't know." But our best guess is that decline in volatility is due to two major changes in the world of finance. First, although it's hard for many in the long-only community to believe, the growth in the hedge fund industry has been a major tailwind for the market's more narrow trading range. With more capital than ever before playing the short side, it is not a stretch to think that security prices are more efficient today than ever before.

The second and perhaps more important change has been the democratization of information via the growth of the Internet and the resurgence of independent research shops. Although it's hard to claim that it's causal, the explosion in the number of hedge funds was contemporaneous with the emergence of the Internet, perhaps the greatest vehicle for democratizing information since the Guttenberg press. Given the explosion of information sources and the ease by which they can be accessed, I can't help but think of how quaint the discussion of market efficiency was when I was in business school. It wasn't too long ago, it seems to me, when a lot of people in the investment business felt a major sense of accomplishment when they were able to get the phone number for the quarterly earnings conference call—"I got it!", "He's got it!" Today, with a few clicks of a mouse, most of us can get the full transcripts of these calls in real time. The average retail investor has greater access to financial information at home today than the professional had five years ago.

While there will no doubt be periods when volatility spikes cyclically in the years to come, there is a chance that the growth in hedge fund assets and ever-greater access to information will lead to a secular decline in volatility. In this regard, it's important to remember that the VIX largely stayed range bound between 10 and 20 from 1990 to 1996.

How do investors take advantage of an environment in which there is greater sound and fury that ultimately signifies nothing? The key, in our estimation, is to "arbitrage time horizons" by looking for long-term value in a world oriented to short-term performance. Although it would be nice to claim that we coined the phrase, the credit goes to my friend and Wall Street legend Jim Moltz, former CEO of C.J. Lawrence and Board Member of the NYSE. **While the swelling ranks of hedge funds and the growing pressures on long-only active managers to produce short-term performance are making long-term investing difficult, we believe that prudent investors may wish to use short-term swings in stock prices to build long-term positions**. This will be even more important in an environment where big increases multiples will be difficult to achieve. Certainly, with 10-year Treasury yields near 40-year lows and profit margins near historic highs, it is very difficult, intellectually, to build a case that investors are likely to get returns in excess of earnings growth to the same degree that they did in the '80s and '90s. Some investors we know are coming up with creative solutions to separate noise from a true signal. One long-only manager we know that hired a young man out of business school to serve as the firm's own "blow-up" analyst a few years ago. Ostensibly his job is to try to use the market's short-term focus against itself, determining whether there are long-term opportunities in stocks the Street may be, at least temporarily, giving away. Our guess is that he's been busy in the last week.

There will of course be cyclical swings in volatility. The dissemination of risk among a wide variety financial players probably means that huge swings in volatility are less likely but will be more severe when they do occur. Although we didn't know it at the time, we all should have indexed our equity portfolios when the Fed Funds rate peaked at 20% in 1981. In retrospect, the Volcker-engineered decline in inflation was an enormous tailwind for earnings multiples and stock prices. It also, ironically, made it very difficult for skilled and responsible investors to consistently beat the benchmark. While we'll all have to work a little harder in this environment, the good news is that a low-return, low-volatility market should greatly benefit the skilled stock-picker, reveal real differences among active managers, and render momentum-based strategies extremely poor providers of alpha in the next few years. In this regard we all may be wise to remember Warren Buffet's claim that his "favorite holding period is forever."

# *Dividends—the Sweetest Poison Pill*

*Originally Published—March 9, 2007*

History may not repeat itself, but, as Mark Twain once quipped, it often rhymes. In a blast from the past, it is an open-secret in New York these days that Wall Street law firms are dusting off their old playbooks to help managements engage in the time-honored practice of covering their fannies. The "poison pill" is making a comeback. And why not? With the headlines filled in recent weeks with ever-larger takeovers on the first page, private equity firms flush with capital, and corporate balance sheets bloated with cash, managements should be nervous. Originally conceived of by Marty Lipton of the noted M&A firm Wachtell Lipton in the early 1980s, companies employed all manner of tactics to foil takeover artists, greatly adding to the richness of Wall Street's vocabulary, immediately introducing into the financial argot such terms as "shark repellent" and "golden handcuffs." Predictably, these strategies were ultimately abused, employed to keep ineffectual managements in place in spite of the best wishes and best interests of their public shareholders.[2]

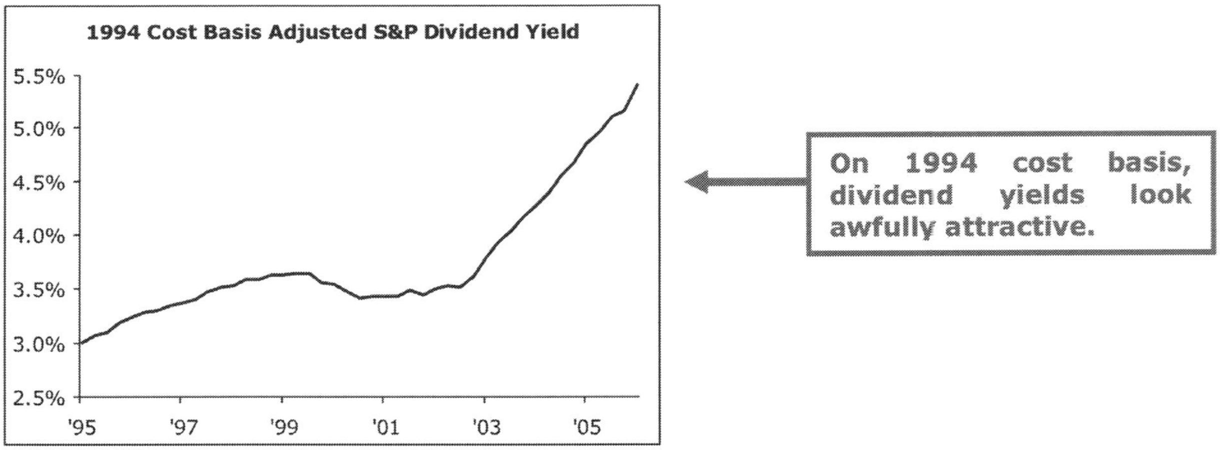


2. Although the legality of such poison pill protection was at times in question, the 1985 Moran v. Household decision upheld its place in corporate law. The irony is a 2001 study by CFO magazine found that for every company with such defenses was able to ward off a takeover, there were 20 other companies with poison pills that accepted takeover offers.

The more things change the more they stay the same. In what amounted to corporate hush money, HCA's recent leveraged recap kept the Barbarians at bay and was a sop to current shareholders, but it also arguably damaged the long-term viability of the company. One wonders why so many large cap companies bemoan the fact that their stock price has languished and then, at the same time, spend valuable time and resources on takeover defenses designed to thwart the realization of shareholder value. **In our mind, the reason why large cap stocks with heavy cash balances have languished is obvious—investors don't want to pay much of a premium on what is ostensibly a checking account.** One also wonders why dividends aren't seen as the sweetest poison pill for long-term investors—at once, a dividend wards off short-term raiders intent on stripping assets, aligns the interests of shareholders and managements and, perhaps most important, reminds executives that it isn't their company four times a year.

The good news is that, in the short term, almost anything a company decides to do with its cash, aside from just holding onto it, is good for equities and bad for corporate credit. Whether prudent or not, M&A activity, increases in dividends, share buybacks, or capex tend to make investors in equities feel good and are, almost always, deleterious to corporate spreads. While the normative case for dividends is, generally speaking, strong, experience suggests, sadly, that M&A will be the winner in corporate sweepstakes for an outlet for cash. By our lights, there are three main reasons why this is so: 1) as in 1995, a slowdown in profit growth generally leads companies to want to buy growth through acquisition; 2) there is a certain immediacy and magic bullet quality to acquisitions that shuts people up regardless of the long-term consequences for the company; and 3) it's simply more fun. In all my years on Wall Street, I have never heard of a bulge bracket firm giving a CEO a ride on a G-5 or buying him dinner at Smith & Wollensky's for announcing a dividend. This may be precisely why more long-term investors should start demanding them.

# *Learning to Love Embassy Suites*

*Originally Published—April 20, 2007*

There is probably no greater occupational hazard to being a strategist wishing to understand how the real world works than to work on Wall Street and live in Manhattan. I didn't own an automobile until I was well into my 30s and although I had an extremely middle class upbringing (my parents were both school teachers), the longer one spends on this island the harder it is to appreciate how people without expense accounts live. In short, it takes great effort not to become spoiled and clueless. Although I never stayed in a hotel more luxurious than a Holiday Inn until I started working on Wall Street, it didn't take me long to become miffed if I didn't find fresh fruit and a personal note from the hotel manager awaiting my arrival at my first class hotel. Starting one's own business is, I've learned, a pretty good reality check. Gone are the warm cashews and dry Cabernets of first class, the Carey Cars driven by guys with mirrored sunglasses, and the obsequiousness of those catering to people like me who were, in truth, merely spending other people's money. That's all different now and although I must admit that it's taken some getting accustomed to, I think I'm the better for it. I realized that this week when staying at an Embassy Suites in the South. The experience revealed a fundamental truth about business travel—free booze and free breakfast is a powerful combination at $169 a night. The chain is owned and operated by Hilton Hotels and judging by the recent performance of its stock, it appears that others have caught on to the fact that good value propositions sell. I didn't purple-light the bedspread or anything but I was reasonably sure that Paris never stayed there and the room was clean and comfortable, the service competent and unpretentious. Unfortunately, whatever positive afterglow I carried from the experience was quickly extinguished by the singular entertainment choice available to me in coach on my flight back to the Big Apple. As near as I could tell, I watched a bunch of half-naked people doing gymnastics at a luau for the better part of an hour. Only later did I learn that this was a Cirque du Soleil production and that many people found it to be entertaining. I'm clearly still learning.

# *What's It All About, Alpha?*

*Originally Published—April 27, 2007*

In the often amusing Kabuki dance that has become our regular idea luncheons at The 21 Club in New York, one thing becomes clear—when you're charging high fees to manage other people's money, your best idea can't be a company anyone else has ever heard of. "My best idea is Bosphorus Uranium. It's actually a limited partnership run by Merrill, the symbol for Boron slash seven-niner on Bloomberg." Long-only guys might actually pitch International Rectifier or Citigroup or Bed, Bath, & Beyond but hedge fund players, especially the youngest ones, feel pressure to come up with ideas that are sufficiently opaque to both impress and, sometimes, dissemble. The implicit assumption of such calls is that the stock is undercovered and therefore provides some putative edge to the investment analyst. What edge a guy two years out of business school living on the Upper West Side could have on an illiquid micro-cap stock in a country few people could locate on a map is never given. But this bias for the obscure reveals an important fundamental need for high fee asset classes to seek inefficient markets.

At our first annual conference in March, Ed Hajim, former CEO of Furman Selz and now head of his own hedge fund MLH Capital, made a very compelling case that investors needed to understand what he described as the market's "sociology of ownership." It was important, he claimed, to know who the market's dominant investor was and what could, eventually, bring about its downfall. With over 9,000 hedge funds running nearly $1.4 trillion dollars, there can be little doubt that hedge funds are today's dominant investors. While some might believe excessive leverage or regulation could lead to the decline in the influence of hedge funds, we believe it could simply be a series of big up years in the market that limits their influence. The fee structure of hedge funds provided an implicit assumption that wealthy people would put a relatively small amount of their net worth to work to shoot the lights out with an exceptional money manager. According to the CSFB/Tremont Hedge Fund Index, the average long/short hedge fund has underperformed the S&P 500 in each of the four years. A continuation of the current bull run might shake the confidence of even the *most* resolute hedge fund investor. After all, no one really ever paid 2 and 20 to beat Libor by 300 basis points.

Although we would be the first to admit that the overriding consensus could be described as "single-digit" bulls on stocks, our travels lead us to believe that the least consensus view is to expect the big return. The irony of this, of course, is that, from a probabilistic point of view, the 20°/o+ return has been the most likely outcome for stocks since 1928, far outpacing the seemingly reasonable and safe expectation for the single digit return. We continue to believe that the sheer number of market participants and the democratization of information will make it hard for investors to gain alpha through information arbitrage in traditional financial markets. This leaves two options for long-only and hedge fund players alike—arbitrage time horizons or seek new and inefficient markets that could add value.

## New Markets

Michael Lewis, of *Liar's Poker, Moneyball,* and most recently *The Blind Side* fame, has become one of the most insightful writers about the intersection of finance modeling techniques to industries, like professional sports, that had been, perhaps blissfully, ruled by conventional wisdom and heuristics that had little relation to reality. In the inaugural edition of *Portfolio* magazine, Lewis offers an interesting glimpse into the still nascent development of financial instruments designed to track the future earnings of professional athletes. Interestingly enough, a deep shadow stock market in athletes already exists—between 15 and 25 million people in the U.S. participate in fantasy sports leagues.[3]

Our Chief Economist Don Rissmiller sees some parallels between Lewis' article "The Jock Exchange" and a new book from acclaimed Yale economics professor Robert Shiller, *The New Financial Order: Risk in the 21st Century.* Both Lewis and Shiller seem to be highlighting a similar central thesis: *as people become wealthier, they are likely to seek insurance against additional risks to their livelihood. The creation of such insurance against additional risks requires the creation of quantitative ways to track various "outcomes" in people's lives through the creation of new markets.*

Shiller's book proposes "a radically new risk management infrastructure to help secure the wealth of nations: to preserve the millions of minor, and not so minor, economic gains that sustain people around the world. Just as modern systems of... insurance protect people against catastrophic risks in their lives and professions, the proposed new infrastructure would utilize financial inventions to protect people against systematic risks: from job losses due to changing technologies to threats to homes and communities due to changing economic conditions."

---

3. Lest anyone think a new sports market would be too inefficient to entice anyone to participate consider the fact that today's edition of The New York Post has nearly 50 pages of sports coverage and exactly four pages of business news.

So, in this way, the purveyor of Bosphorous Uranium may be on to something. For 2 and 20, new markets may be the only way for rank and file hedge funds to thrive, especially if there are "big up years" in equities. Hedge funds could maintain their "dominant investor" position potentially in this way, though the investments would be far afield from traditional markets. The biggest beneficiaries of this trend toward new markets may be the investment banks themselves.

# *In Defense of the Top Down Approach*

*Originally Published—June 1, 2007*

Of his remarkable face, Hall of Fame pitcher Satchel Paige said "we seen some sights, it and I." And here I am now running a business and getting older and trying to figure out what this ugly mug has seen in my years on the Street, how it's changed, why it's relevant, and how that might possibly affect the value of our work. It's not easy being a macro guy, albeit a strategist, in today's world. When I started in the industry as an institutional salesman, the men and women who were experienced enough to be running other people's money had experienced real business cycles and had, for the most part, suffered through the '73-'74 bear market, an oil shock, a Constitutional crisis, and, perhaps worst of all, the Burns years. These turbulent events introduced near-constant career risk for the professional investor and left scars that the market's salad days during the Reagan Administration were unable to completely erase. The result was a professional money management class that had a deep respect for the business cycle and who understood the importance of monetary and fiscal policy, international capital flows, and geopolitical developments. There were investment specialists, to be sure, but the sheer volatility of the economy and the relative dearth of investment analysts meant that everyone had to be a generalist and understand the economy to some extent. That's all changed now. The economy, the story goes, is less cyclical and no one's been able to make real money in macro funds in years.

Although it is undoubtedly self-serving for us to think so, there may be some sense in which the sheer size of the hedge fund industry and the depths of its bottom-up specialization virtually scream for the contrarian-minded fund manager to seek an edge in economic analysis and long-term strategic thinking rather than bottom-up information inefficiencies. While the U.S. economy is less cyclical, the interconnected nature of the global economy, after all, is undoubtedly growing. In an effort to take advantage of this trend, we put forth four suggestions for money managers to add value in an increasingly crowded investment landscape:

## 1. Focus less on "analysis execution" and more on "thought process."

The CFA Institute estimates that nearly 156,000 people will take the CFA exam this year, a nearly 23% increase over 2006. Those who pass and find their way into jobs at the world's nearly 9,000 hedge funds and 2,500 private equity shops will be given a cubicle, a computer, a list of sell-side contacts, and a subscription to a data provider. They will not be encouraged to read much of anything other than daily Street research, quarterly filings, and prospectuses. They will likely become experts on a few niche industries—specialty chemicals, soft-line retail, or whatever—and will have virtually no time to think about how their work fits into the broader scheme of their firm's investment process. This is a shame, especially since most academic studies have shown that nearly two-thirds of a stock price's movement can be traced to the relative performance of its sector to the overall market.

## 2. Put on more "macro" trades and seek more inefficient markets.

Despite the Platonic view of a hedge fund as a vehicle that seeks to generate excess returns in any way possible, there aren't too many long/short funds that are willing to put on macro trades under any circumstances. This could partly be blamed on the entrance of the consultant and fund of funds folks who force strict adherence to style, but it also might be due to some vague sense that macro bets are far riskier than long/short stock ideas. While this may be partly true, given the leverage inherent in many "macro" financial instruments, it also might have something to do with the fact that the most famous of all macro funds—Long Term Capital Management—came pretty close to torching the entire global financial system. People tend to remember that. Still, the aversion to most macro trades appears to have reached an extreme. Few of today's operators remember that some of the biggest gains for storied hedge funds like Soros and Tiger came from enormously successful macro trades. The charts on the assets under management at long/short equity funds and macro funds tend to bear this out.

## 3. Hire analysts who love the game more than the money.

There are too many young people entering the hedge fund and private equity businesses who are more interested in the quick hit to their net worth than the intellectual richness a career in the money management industry can provide. The result is, often, analysts and entire funds that are more interested in short-term performance than a long-term investment process. The irony is that that approach tends to result in poor performance and high-turnover of both portfolios and investment professionals.

## 4. Lengthen time horizons.

We have discussed this concept at length in these pages before. The sheer number of players in the investment business today, the democratization of investment information, and Reg FD have made it extremely difficult for the investment analyst to get any meaningful or sustainable edge. With the average holding period for a stock in the U.S. now at roughly 11 months (down from 8 years in 1960), the most significant arbitrage opportunities are likely to be found in time horizons rather than access to market-moving information.

The purely bottom-up analyst might be able to benefit from a broader and long-term view for another simple reason—the decline in economic focus has been even more severe in corporate America. In the old days, America's corporate titans had extensive economics departments designed to help the firm's executives navigate the shoals of an increasingly cyclical global economy. Much of that changed when the clubby atmosphere of corporate America came under attack in the 1980s. It doesn't take an overly active imagination to see Jack Welch or Al Dunlap unceremoniously dumping their economics departments at the first opportunity. The result has been, again, a tendency in all but the very best companies to follow macroeconomic trends rather than try to anticipate them. If I live to be 100 years old I will never forget speaking to the "market intelligence" group of one of the world's largest semiconductor firms in the late-1990s. I was there, ostensibly, to prove to them the value of having access to economic research. The response was, even today, breathtaking in its arrogance—"Tech spending isn't cyclical, it's secular. ASPs (average selling prices) for PCs have remained at $2,000 for the past five years. What would make that change?" It seems clear now, that the tech sector is eminently, and perhaps tragically, cyclical.

While we are undoubtedly talking our own book here, we also recognize that, as sell-side analysts, we should take our own advice by offering long-term, broad, and provocative investment ideas.

# *Lessons from Our First Year*

*Originally Published—September 7, 2007*

This has been a special week for us here at Strategas. One-year ago this past Wednesday, five of us left comfortable jobs at a firm we liked to venture out into the uncharted waters of entrepreneurship, navigating the shoals of balky technology, third world style offices, and all manner of accountants and lawyers who frequently scared us, while, at the same time, put dents in our operating account. But we are proud to announce that while the patient that is our firm isn't ready to go line-dancing, he is clearly off the table and ambulatory. Such markers in your life are bound to make you a little philosophical and so I thought I might share some of the lessons I've learned in our first year in business.

**The Importance of Partners.** It might sound overly saccharine but as I look back on the last year, it is clear that we wouldn't be anywhere near where we are today without a strong partnership structure. People can tell you how hard it's going to be to start a business but you really have no idea what you're dealing with until you are frighteningly and irreversibly on your way to entrepreneurship. This is not merely because of the sheer amount of work that goes into starting a new business but also because of the anxieties and sleepless nights inherent in any risky venture. Nicholas Bohnsack and Don Rissmiller are future stars in the investment business and I think each one of us has been happy to learn that we have complementary skills and emotional make-ups. This has been extremely useful in our approach to creating timely and useful investment research but, perhaps more important, it has been critical in the management of our business. Whatever the future may hold for us at Strategas, I will never waver from the idea that in business in general and intellectual property businesses in particular, a strong equity culture is a good way to build on people's strengths while de-emphasizing their weaknesses. As the late Wall Street legend Tubby Burnham once said of his equity, "the more I give away, the more I make."

**Fixed vs. Variable Costs.** When we told our mentor and friend Jim Moltz, the former C.E.O. of C.J. Lawrence and Board Member of the NYSE, of our plans to start our own company, he proffered a single piece of advice that we have held dear: "The only things you can predict with any precision in the brokerage business," he said, "are your costs. Watch them like a hawk and keep them as variable as you can. We tried to predict revenues but we were never even close on both the upside and the downside." To this tenet, we have held true. Just about everyone who works at Strategas is paid based on the firm's revenues and we have all been forced for the first time in a long-time to economize on corporate niceties we once took for granted. Jim is one of Wall Street's true gentlemen and he is unfailingly polite. We'll never know how foolhardy he believed our scheme to start Strategas was at the time but we will always know, regardless of Strategas' ultimate fate, that he gave us the right advice at the right time. The warm nuts and dry Cabernets of first class are long gone, Carey Limousine has stopped sending us birthday cards, and we've actually toyed with the idea of making the soda machine part of our revenue model. Becoming familiar with the frequent-stay programs of Embassy Suites hasn't been the easiest of transitions, I must admit, but since I never stayed at any hotel nicer than a Holiday Inn until I was out of college, I can't complain. It goes without saying that you tend to behave a little differently when it's your own money.

**The Virtual Economy in Practice.** As strategists and economists, there has been perhaps no greater lesson we have learned about running a business in the New Economy than the idea that technology may be the small businessman's best friend and that America's ownership society is producing scores of independent contractors that can perform many of the functions usually reserved for large firms for a fraction of the cost. It is virtually inconceivable today that we could have been as productive in terms of our research or our interactions with clients without the help of the virtual economy. As we have discussed on these pages in the past, our greatest discovery has been the company Salesforce.com (CRM, $42.38). In years past we might have had to spend thousands of dollars and hired a small department of programmers to manage our mailing list. But Salesforce.com allows us to have an extraordinarily efficient solution to this critical function for literally peanuts. Even the firm's resident old fart (that would be me, at age 39) can actually use it. This may be part of the reason the company is trading at 240x forward earnings. And so, I can actually see in practice that technology and America's entrepreneurial bent is a long-term secular bull case for both inflation and the sustainability of margins.

**No Matter Where You Work, Someone's Always Worrying.** For young people at large and established firms, I have found, there is generally a certain confidence about the business coming through the door that allows them the luxury of doing their jobs without the anxiety of the firm's potential insolvency. This allows people to feel smug and feel good about themselves but the downside of that air of the inevitability of success is that it tends to produce behaviors in people designed to benefit themselves rather than the companies for whom they work. This was especially true of my experiences at large investment banks. But when you start your own shop, you realize that no matter what the size or competence of the firm you work for, there is always someone there that is worrying about the firm's future and solvency. At small companies like ours that includes just about everybody, but none more than the partners themselves.

**True Friends.** If you want a friend on Wall Street, the saying goes, get a dog. It is, to be sure, a rather unique industry in which friendship can often be confused with money. But in my years on the Street I have found many, especially those who know the pain of losses from airline stocks and biotech companies, who possess a certain empathy and dark humor that draw people more easily together than you might think. As I look back on the past year however, I learned that it's easier to have friends when times are good and far harder to maintain those friendships when times are tough and you're worried about private school tuition. It is a testament to my own good fortune (or was it perhaps my own naïveté?) that I wasn't forced to learn this painful lesson until I was in my late 30s. The good news is that the vast majority of friends I've accumulated in my career have been extremely encouraging of our efforts to get our young firm off the ground. Certainly not everyone has been able to become a client of course but it has been satisfying enough at times to know that people you like and respect are pulling for you nonetheless. It's been far harder to deal with that tiny minority of those whom I would have classified as real friends when I had a fancy title at a big firm but whose support, or even their presence, was conspicuous by its absence when I ventured out on my own. I don't know what it is about the human condition that tempts most of us to fret more about the 2% of those who disappoint us than celebrate the other 98% who come through. I do know now however that it's both a part of life and a lot of wasted energy. It's not personal, it's just business.

Among the many justifications and rationalizations I used to leave a high-paying job at a good firm and start my own little company was that the experience of running a business would make me a better strategist and student of the financial markets. After all, I reasoned, how could I in good conscience comment on other businesses and the economy without ever having to meet a payroll myself? It was, admittedly, a little thin but it was also a necessary part of the emotional and psychological case I needed to do something that was, by all accounts, risky. And so now, here I am, one year and untold hours later, and I'm starting to believe that what I thought was the weakest justification for establishing Strategas may have, in fact, been the strongest.

# *Sociology of Ownership, Sovereign Wealth Funds, & the Coming Shortage of Public Equities*

*Originally Published—September 28, 2007*

Former Chairman of Furman Selz, serial Wall Street overachiever, client, and friend Ed Hajim has encouraged us to think frequently of the market's "sociology of ownership." The general idea is that, at any given time, the market has an "alpha investor" that can tell you a lot about the way the market is trading and, perhaps more importantly, how market dynamics are likely to change. In the schematic below, we attempt to plot the evolution of the market's dominant investor over the last 40 years. While all of the investment vehicles highlighted have enjoyed a peaceful coexistence since at least the 1950s, their relative importance at any given time has gone through dramatic changes. In the 1960s, when the average holding for a stock in the United States was a stunning 8 years, trust departments at banks were the principal buyers and sellers of stocks. The invention of the CMA in the 1970s and the bull market of the 1980s led to the growing influence and near-dominance of the mutual fund industry for much of the next two decades, and the end of the technology bubble contributed to the search for "absolute returns" and the ascendance of hedge funds. All the while, the average holding period for stocks has declined, now standing, based on a report from Bain & Company, at less than a year.

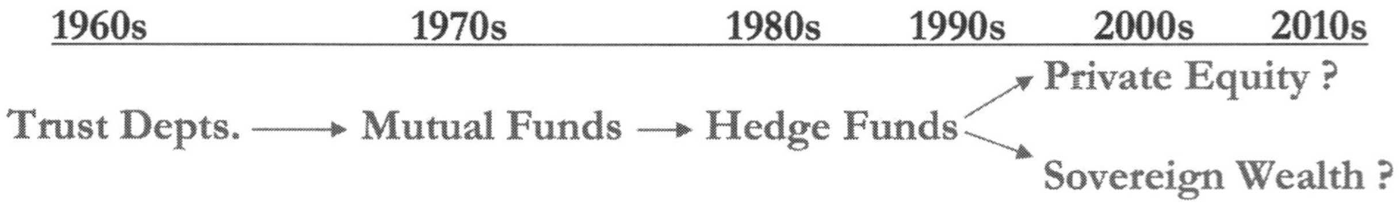


The decline in holding periods is a rather odd development for long duration assets like stocks, but after a 50% decline in the total stock market capitalization from 2000 to 2002, consultants found it to be surprisingly easy to convince fiduciaries to pay 1 and 20 (at a minimum) for LIBOR + 300 types of returns. Few could argue that hedge funds aren't now the market's dominant investors. There are now 9,000 in the U.S. sporting assets of close to $1.5 trillion before leverage. Anecdotal evidence seems to suggest that they account for more than 40% of the average daily trading volume on the NYSE and, not surprisingly, an even greater percentage of the agency business of Wall Street's major bulge bracket firms.

This is hardly a unique insight of course, but we do think it's important now, to figure out what might slow the explosive growth in the hedge fund industry and to consequently think about who might take its place. There is little question that the barriers to entry for the hedge fund industry are greater today than they were a few years ago—the Fed Funds rate is no longer 1%, growing dividend payments have made the costs of being short more expensive, and there are, little by little, calls for more government regulation. But perhaps the greatest threat to the continued dominance of hedge funds may be the simple fact that, as an asset class, they have underperformed the broader market in each of the last four years. When the S&P was down -22.1% in 2002 and the CSFB/Tremont Index of Hedge Funds returned up about 3%, it wasn't that difficult to convince fiduciaries to allocate more funds to alternative investments. But serial underperformance tends to create doubts, and it seems clear that many endowments and pension funds are starting to question the wisdom of paying high fees for performance they could get in traditional investment vehicles. Money will no doubt continue to flow into alternative investments, but it is unlikely to continue at the pace witnessed over the last few years.

Based on the Sociology of Ownership concept, the trick for investors should now be to consider who the central investor in the markets will be in the years to come. The Lord only knows of course, but we would posit two possibilities—private equity and sovereign wealth funds. Although the dislocations in the CDO and CLO markets have clearly been a lifestyle change for the private equity industry in recent months, we think it would be a mistake to count them out as potentially huge players in market dynamics in the next few years. Private equity funds are still sitting on nearly $300 billion in untapped commitments, and it would be naive to assume that the current difficulties in the credit markets might actually prompt them to start giving the money back. IRR assumptions will no doubt need to be taken down, but with the market's ROE at 17% and the Cost of Equity Capital at about 9%, we still believe there's plenty of room for leveraged players to find acceptable targets. Sovereign Wealth Funds should also be considered as another leading candidate for the market's dominant investor. In a mere 10 years, many emerging economies have gone from having scarcely two nickels to rub together to possessing enormous foreign currency reserves. Tomorrow, China will start its own Temasek-like investment corporation. Libya and other oil-rich nations are considering similar investment vehicles and some estimates suggest that the size of such funds could reach $2.5 trillion by the end of 2007 and nearly $12 trillion by 2015.

Whoever the next "alpha investor" may be, we believe the transition from hedge funds to either private equity or sovereign wealth funds to be enormously

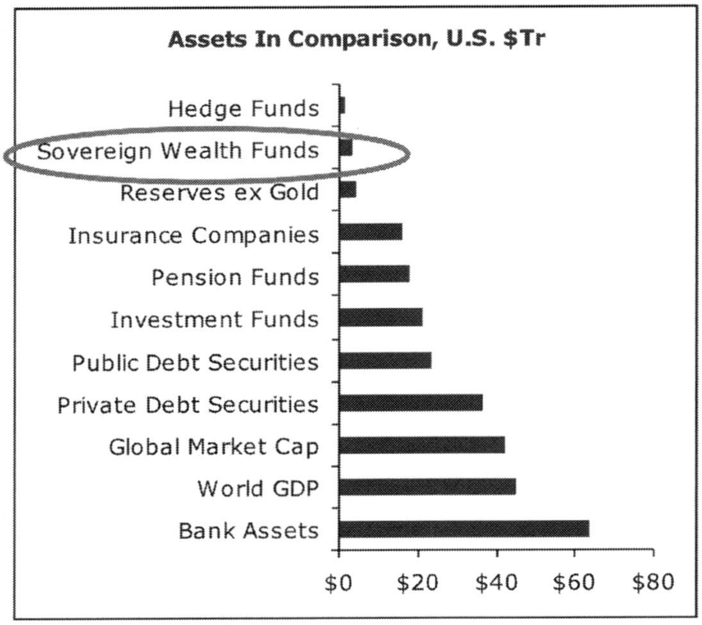


**Global Sovereign Wealth Funds**

| Country | Assets $BN | Inception Year |
|---|---|---|
| United Arab Emirates | 875 | 1976 |
| Singapore | 330 | 1981 |
| Saudi Arabia | 300 | NA |
| Norway | 300 | 1996 |
| China | 300 | 2007 |
| Singapore | 100 | 1974 |
| Kuwait | 70 | 1953 |
| Australia | 40 | 2004 |
| U.S. (Alaska) | 35 | 1976 |
| Russia | 32 | 2003 |
| Brunei | 30 | 1983 |
| South Korea | 20 | 2006 |

bullish for global equities and will likely lead to lengthening of time horizons for institutional investors. Hedge funds are, after-all, long-short vehicles. If anything, their emergence might be considered, in retrospect, a depressant on market returns due to the huge spike in short interest over the last few years. Private equity funds on the other hand are leveraged-long vehicles while newly formed sovereign wealth funds can safely be assumed to be underweight equities. Either way, the transition from hedge funds to either private equity or sovereign wealth funds should be considered a major tailwind for the world's global equity markets.

# *Broker as Agent R.I.P.*

*Originally Published—October 12, 2007*

About a month ago, there were two big parlor games taking place on Wall Street that were seen as key to the future of our current bull run. The first of course, was the future of monetary policy and the second centered on the off-quarter earnings of the brokers. On both fronts, it appears that the markets dodged a bullet, at least for now. Defying what seemed like incredible odds, the investment banks posted, by and large, better-than-expected earnings and, in the process, secured their position among business history's most incredible money-making juggernauts. But lost in the drama of those earnings releases, it seems to me, was a more fundamental question about the role of the broker in a post Glass-Steagall world. It's hard for the casual observer not to wonder how bulge bracket firms didn't suffer bigger hits as some of their clients suffered what was ultimately a death sentence. And I often wonder whether it is my own romantic vision of the old partner-driven Wall Street firm or a more cynical vision of the modern world that makes me question the increasingly dual role of brokers as both agents and principals. One doesn't need to be a misanthrope to wonder how some major Wall Street firms, with a rapidly growing dependence upon principal transactions, seem to defy all odds and produce consistently positive returns regardless of market conditions. Even the greenest rookie on the Street knows that no one bats a 1.000. And so, it seems natural to question whether the Bulge Bracket firms have created what is ostensibly one of the easiest and perhaps most profitable open-book exams in business history. Some of these firms are starting to remind me of those delicatessens on Avenue U in Brooklyn from my youth where the sandwiches were made for the regular patrons out front but the real money was made from the casino in the storeßroom. This may be a terrific development for shareholders but may not be so wonderful for clients.

**Business Segment Pct. Contribution to Net Revenues***

| | Merrill Lynch (MER) | Goldman Sachs (GS) | Morgan Stanley (MS) |
|---|---|---|---|
| Asset Management | 28.4% | 19.2% | 21.2% |
| Commissions | 25.3% | 12% | 14.3% |
| **Principal Transactions** | **16.9%** | **54%** | **35.6%** |
| Investment Banking | 16.9% | 14.8% | 16.4% |
| Other | 12.4% | NA | 12.5% |
| | 100.0% | 100.0% | 100.0% |

*Latest Reported Fiscal Year

In the old days, when Salomon Brothers was the leader in proprietary trading, their earnings were predictably volatile and sometimes, if you can believe it, led to losses. As a result, the firm traded at an understandable discount to its peers. Money, of course, can prove to be a strong incentive to already motivated and intelligent people to produce incredible results. But these firms are made up of human beings, albeit well-educated once, rather than some "pride of supermen" are they not?[4] In any event, it seems clear that many large Wall Street firms are training their rookies on clients and reserving their veterans for their own higher ROI proprietary businesses. I have heard on more than one occasion from large traditional long-only buy-side shops that their sales coverage at the major brokerage firms, if they can be identified at all these days, possess less and less experience and expertise. As a proprietor of a small independent research shop who's finding it hard to find a family apartment for less than $1,400 a square foot in Manhattan (that's not a misprint), there also may be, admittedly, a touch of envy in my question. But as someone who loves the brokerage business and its history and believes that it serves an important function in society, I question whether this unholy alliance is good for our industry, risking scandal and potentially even greater oversight. As they say in the Good Book, "No man can serve two masters: for either he will hate the one, and love the other: or else he will hold to the one, and despise the other." (Matthew 6:24) Consider the source of course—we just started our own independent research firm.

4. Sandy Koufax, Hall of Fame pitcher for the Dodgers, once commented on an exceptional performance against the Yankees in the World Series "I felt that I had to show myself and my team, and the Yankees, too, that they were just a team of baseball players, not a pride of supermen."

# *Gradually, Then Suddenly*[5]

*Originally Published—April 26, 2016*

My wingtips hit the cold wet pavement in front of my apartment and I entered the car my hosts had sent me. It was 6:15—am—and the warm winter rain was refreshing for a guy still feeling the all-too-familiar after-effects of a rich Chianti and a marbled ribeye from the night before. The driver was a short guy of about 25 some odd and was all New York—the kind of guy you might strike up a conversation with while you were in line to grab a hot dog at the Stadium. I was looking forward to a quiet 20 minute trip over to Englewood Cliffs while I waited for the Aleve to kick in. He had other ideas and I was fortunate—it was probably the most instructive conversation I've had in weeks.

"You follow the markets over there for CNBC?" he asked.

"I try. They have me on once in a while."

"So whaddya think? Are they going to cut rates today?"

"I don't think they have much of a choice. The economy's slowing and the markets are a mess. But I don't know, when things are this volatile it's hard to have a lot of answers...It's been a tough month."

"I hearya. I hearya. Half the bigshots in this car spend their time whining to me or begging the banks for money these days."

"How's your business?" I asked.

"I work nights so I'm fine. The law firms are still cookin' and the older guys at the banks are busy. But the young bankers gotta wait 'til 9 o'clock now to use a car service."

5. This was the response of one of the characters in Hemingway's The Sun Also Rises when asked about how he went bankrupt.

"And the others?"

"This is New York—there are no others...Whaddya think about Merrill Lynch here?"

"The stock?"

"Yeah, would you buy it now?"

"I'm a big picture guy so I don't really know. They have a real pro at the top now but it's going to take a long time to clean the trouble they've gotten themselves into." I noticed how beautiful the George Washington Bridge is before the sun comes up.

"I just bought a few hundred shares myself last week." He was proud of himself.

"Wow. You've got more courage than a lot of guys in my business."

"It's a great company and the stock's down a lot. What's gonna happen? Are they goin' outta business? I don't think so. Plus I gotta make more money somehow. What am I gonna do, buy a house—forget about it."

"Yeah, guess you're right. Stocks may be cheaper than anything else you can buy these days. But house prices haven't really dropped much around here."

"Just wait," he said. "My brother's got a good job and he bought a house for 500 in Montvale a few years ago. It's funny though. He didn't put a dime down and actually got money back to fix the place up."

"It's a brave new world boy. I don't think he'd be able to do that now."

"No way. And he knows it. He's making the payments but he's scaling back on everything else. He watches CNBC. He knows and he's worried."

"What about you?" I asked.

"I don't own a house and I'm single so I'm happy. I'm good. But it's, like, weird. I just got a letter from my credit card company telling me they took my credit limit down from $8,000 to $6,000. I can't figure it out. I'm never late with the payments. What's up with that?"

"I don't know...Maybe they're really more worried about your brother than they are about you."

"That's funny," he said, laughing. "That's what my mother said."

# *East of Eden*

*Originally Published—April 11, 2016*

There exists in midtown Manhattan a little street that could tell you more about what's happening in the world of finance in an hour than you could find out at the corner of Broad and Wall in a whole day. In the context of this great metropolis, there is nothing particularly special about 54th Street between Madison and 5th. There's a deli on the corner that sells just about everything known to man and where people buy their lunch by the pound. There's a shoe store across the street and a beautiful neoclassical building down the block that houses perhaps the best and most expensive men's clothing store in the City. But what makes this boulevard important as far as Wall Street is concerned are two restaurants that sit across the street from each other, San Pietro, an elite Italian bistro on the south side of the street and Rothmann's, a steakhouse, on the north side. While their prices aren't all that different, that is to say they cater to those who don't pay their bills with their own money, the 75 feet of asphalt that separates them might as well be the difference between Athens and Marathon. San Pietro caters to the market's chess masters, Rothmann's its well-polished pawns.

I have spent considerable time in both establishments but I am a visitor in one and a member of the family in the other. I make my pilgrimage to San Pietro once a month to see the Masters of the Universe the same way others might visit a zoo. I have tried vainly to become a "regular" on two occasions using my dining companion, a strategist of considerable fame, on the first, and my Neapolitan roots with the restaurant's host on the second. Both overtures were greeted with a wan smile that said "nice try, *uaglio*, but you're about 20 years and nine figures short." And so, like just about every other place in the City, I have been relegated to the role of visitor and go with my friend Charlie, who has carved out what seems to be lifetime employment as the journalist who knows more about what's under the fingernails of the financial industry than any other. And he spots it instantly, even here, a place I view as hallowed ground for the titans of modern finance. "YOU SEE MACK AND FINK OVER THERE?" he pleads excitedly. "THEY'RE PROBABLY TALKING ABOUT HOW TO SPLIT UP THE WORLD BETWEEN THEM!" And then he checks his Blackberry nervously, and spots other stars. "THAT'S GREENHILL. THERE'S LANGONE. AND PERELLA!!" and he's whispering but he's really shouting. "THE GUY WHO RUNS FM GLOBAL, WHAT'S HIS NAME?" and he checks his Blackberry again and we resume our typically desultory conversations about the latest dramas in a business that has become somewhat of a spectacle of itself. Lunch with Charlie is fun, but it's exhausting.

While San Pietro is a canteen of sorts for the City's financial elite, the rest of us feel more comfortable across the street, at Rothmann's, where brokers and traders drink and talk about the things that most men in their 30s and 40s in this business talk about—golf, the markets, office politics, and women. And I feel so comfortable in this place I count its maître d', Pat, as a friend who is the type of guy who would, in a pinch, let you sleep in the store room if your wife threw you out. Rothmann's is by no means cheap—a Martini's still going to cost you $14—but it's hard to feel insecure there. A group of us have been assembling at the bar there every Thursday for years. We are a dog's breakfast of Wall Street personalities. There's Jimmy who uses "the box" and dark pools and IM the way guys of a different era used to use a pick and shovel. He likes the business well enough but prefers to talk more about sports and "broads." If he beats the VWAP and takes clients out a few times a week his manager is happy and can sleep the sleep of the just. "In the midst of all this," he says sardonically, "our cents-per-share has gone up to 4.6. I'm half expecting the sun to set in the East and the birds to fly north for the winter." And then there's Billy, an irrepressibly likeable and fun guy with a head as big as a stop sign who couldn't tell you where the S&P is trading at on any given day if you put a gun to his head. He's hit the jackpot with this job as an institutional salesman and, at 43, can afford to count among his dependents two wives, three vacation properties, and two bartenders. Then there's Brian who works at a hedge fund and looks like he's from central casting as an Ivy League fraternity brother from the '50s. He senses the great ironies in this business and is one of the funniest guys you've ever met.

Billy's trying to get one of the big long/short guys to do more business and he invites one of the new quants on their desk, Omar, to join us. He's very young, or at least appears so, and graduated 1st in his class from a college in India where they only accept 1 in 10,000 with a degree in chemical engineering. They say he can make an Excel spreadsheet sing. Not knowing a lot about baseball or the Masters, he is quiet. But the conversation inevitably lurches toward the collapse of Bear and he spits out, in an amusing East Asian accent, "what the f—is VAR anyway when you're leveraged 33:1?" And we all laugh at the random bitterness emanating from this elegant young man. Omar has been betrayed by youth and an over-confidence in the power of math when it comes to the prices of securities. He's never heard of PennCentral or Continental Illinois or Drexel and he doesn't care to for that matter. He came here to make money and the market's fat tails are screwing that up. The laughter is followed by silence as we are again forced to face the sad fact that we know guys just like us who have lost their fortunes and are about to lose their jobs. As I look around the room, I wonder whether a lot of us have traded our adult lives for free rounds of golf, unlimited use of the company's car service, and the shellfish tower at Smith & Wollensky's. I look out the window at San Pietro and realize that while the guys across the street are the virtuosos, the Mozarts, of the modern financial system, we at Rothmann's are merely players, the Salieris.

The tenor of our conversations has changed a lot in the last few months and no one is quite as sure of themselves, or of their futures, as they once were. "Hey, Jase, you think you could interview my cousin for a job this summer? I've been telling him to get into research," he says wistfully looking into the bottom of a rocks glass. "I wouldn't wish the trading life on anybody these days. I told him it's all about providing value." If you're under 50, it's strangely unsettling to hear a guy who went to Duke talk about his chosen profession the way guys on the line talked about autos and steel a generation ago. This is the nuance the financial media has missed in its reportage of the market's current conflagration. I can't help but think about my first stop in this crazy business, in the purchase and sales department at Morgan Stanley in Brooklyn, sitting next to an old guy who would use his lunch hour every day to collect aluminum cans for the deposit. The media isn't talking about him or what Bear's collapse might mean to this city and its principle industry. It is too intent on making sure power and wealth is brought low. To many in the fourth estate who should know better, Wall Street is solely made up of overpaid soulless overachievers who make things too expensive for "average" people—like psychiatrists and newspaper editors. This is, indeed, partially true but a greater and more important truth is being lost—that the financial services industry is to New York what autos once was to Detroit or Hollywood is to LA. The business has far more than its share of billionaires, but it has far many more people who take the subway to work and worry about paying their mortgage. My colleague who collected cans "worked on Wall Street," in a sense, but he was part of this industry's machinery and he isn't what the press has in mind when it talks about "retribution."

It now feels as if a significant portion of this city is in a foot race between reaching their "number" and the discovery of their own fair value. What is the price of mediocrity when it has been overpriced for so long? Does it matter that you were a decent student and a great lacrosse player at Georgetown when budgets need to get cut? Will your bosses care? Your clients on the buyside? Co-ops will get cheaper as will Pilates classes, 450cc drivers, and perhaps even private schools. The Mozarts will always get paid, but the rest of us, the Salieris, are going to have to scrap.

# *Trading as a Source of Alpha & the Changing Role of the Buy-Side Trader*

*Originally Published—June 20, 2008*

A decent bar bet at, let's say, Rothmann's in New York, or any other watering hole that our industry's inveterate gamblers, prodigious drinkers, and skirt-chasers are likely to congregate, might be to ask the unwitting what the average annual percentage range the S&P 500 Index has traded in over the past 50 years or so. Maybe one in fifty might guess that the actual average annual peak to trough change in the S&P 500 has been 26% since 1945. The range is what Classics majors might refer to as volatility, and is unlikely to impress anyone who still believes in the certainty of math. Still, the size of the market's range is a decent proxy for the magnitude of tradable rallies and declines available to those who ply their trade in the financial markets. Remarkable for those witnessing the sound and fury on CNBC every day, the range has collapsed in the past four years, averaging only 14% from 2004 through 2007. While this appears at first blush to be bad news for momentum types, there is a simple yet compelling reason to believe that the market's volatility will revert to the mean, increasing markedly over the next few years—nominal GDP growth is likely to remain well-below its long-term average. As the linear regression line on the chart below indicates, there is a strong negative relationship between nominal GDP growth and the market's volatility—the weaker economic growth gets, the greater the market's volatility becomes.

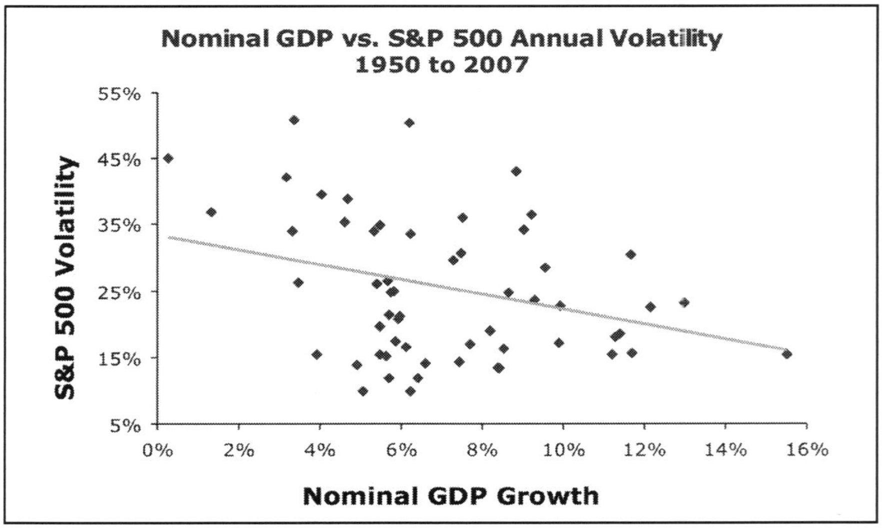

While we continue to believe that the true arbitrage opportunities in the market lie not in access to information but in the ability to lengthen time horizons, we also recognize that there are times in which very-short time horizons might be able to add alpha. We believe we are entering such a period now. The current cocktail of heavy public and private debt loads and a hobbled financial system lead us to believe that nominal growth is likely to be weak for some time. While this will almost necessarily lead to lower average returns, it also means that the truly active manager has a much greater chance of adding value. **Recession and recession-like environments tend to widen the differences between winners and losers across all industries, provide fertile ground for winner-take-all markets, and often introduce exogenous shocks in public policy that benefit the manager willing to trade around long-term, core holdings.** Such environments also make buy and hold strategies extremely unpleasant for those who don't share the job security of Warren Buffett or Wilbur Ross. Mistakes are always costly, of course, but never more so than in periods of weak nominal GDP growth. Last year, for example, not owning the S&P 500's worst 50 stocks would have contributed nearly 1,000 basis points in relative performance. Of course, good trading skills require good buy-side traders and, as we will see in the next section, the difficulty and importance of that role has increased in recent years.

**Distribution of Market Volatility Under Various Nominal Growth Scenarios**

| Nominal GDP Growth | S&P 500 Annual Volatility |
|---|---|
| < 4% | 35.8% |
| 4% > 8% | 23.8% |
| > 8% | 24.4% |

Data 1950-2007
Annual Volatility = S&P 500 Annual High minus Low as % of Low

## The Changing Role of the Buy-side Trader

It was a small news item buried in the C section of *The Wall Street Journal* on the cusp of summer. Lost in what now seems to be the quaint myriad of stock prices and market statistics was a piece entitled "Everybody Into the Dark Pool" which reported that the New York Stock Exchange and the NASDAQ were going to offer clients access to the "dark pool" networks that have been their major competitors over the last few years. For those of a certain age and who remember Dick Grasso's zeal to maintain an 80% market share in the Big Board's listed securities, this small article was roughly the equivalent of reading that the Steinbrenner family had taken a controlling interest in the Red Sox or that Hillary Clinton had decided to become a Republican. The size and placement of the piece seemed at odds with its potential importance, leading me to reflect on the changes taking place on the Street and the role of both buy and sell-side traders alike.

Running our own shop has given us a rudimentary education in the subject of trading and, perhaps more important, given us a greater opportunity to get to know traders on both sides of the Street. Despite the still-extant stereotypes (Duncan Niederauer's comment that there were too many "Vinnies on the floor" wasn't exactly a shining moment for the NYSE's new management), it's clear that liquidity is harder to source today than perhaps it's ever been, rendering the role of trading both more difficult and more important at the same time. Of course, the transition from what was essentially the role of a clerk to that of an investment professional has been unfolding for the better part of two decades, but it's gotten a big push in recent years as investment banks became less interested in being agents and more interested in becoming principals. The unwillingness of bulge bracket firms to commit capital for their customers and the steady decline of one of the industry's more traditional and respected roles—block trading—has changed the very nature of trading in common stocks—arguably not for the better for both the institutional money management community and the investment banks alike. While it is well known to one and all that block trading was always a loss leader for the Street, the old-timers looked at the practice in much the same way a criminal might look at jail-time—a cost of doing business. Today the practice has all but disappeared for the average buy-side institution, as brokerage firms have become far more interested in trading their own pads than accommodating their clients.

Decimalization has also played a role. The concept of "eighths" seems hopelessly anachronistic now but the Big Board's decision to abandon fractions in favor of penny increments in 2001 was a game-changer for the specialist system. Designed to help the average investor, it's hard to argue with decimalization if you believe in free markets. But like most good-intentioned reforms, it carried with it unintended consequences—most notably the decline in the displayed depth in the markets for all stocks. In 2001, block trades of 10,000 shares or more represented more than 60% of the NYSE total trading volume. Today such trades represent only 18%. The average trade size has declined steadily over the past seven years as the Floor starved. Enter in recent years the emergence of nearly 40 dark pools, private trading systems that allow orders to be matched more frequently without first having to route them to an exchange. For those trading small and mid-cap stocks these pools have afforded the buy-side a certain level of anonymity never before thought possible. But one wonders whether secrecy and lower nominal transactions costs are being completely offset by the growing difficulty of finding liquidity and price discovery, the cornerstones of efficient markets and transparency. It appears to be a trade-off many institutional investors are willing to make and this is good news for the role of the buy-side trader. With liquidity harder to source and the likelihood of single-digit returns over the next several years high, the best buy-side shops will likely view their traders as an integral part of the investment decision-making process and it may even mean the relative power of the competent sales trader will grow more important for those still interested in the institutional equities business.

*Note: Three buy-side traders, all friends and clients alike, contributed to this piece and I wish to thank them. Two wished to remain anonymous, a lot like their style of trading, while the third, let's call him "Bob," shamelessly begged me to have his name included. I decided against it for his own good.*

# *Dolce Far Niente?*

*Originally Published—August 15, 2008*

I am not afraid to admit that I have always enjoyed Andrea Bocelli's music. But I must shamefully confide that his angelic voice and movie-star good looks always made me somewhat skeptical about the seriousness of his infirmity. My doubts were only heightened when I saw him riding his own bicycle with his stunningly beautiful 26–year old girlfriend on the Tuscan coast last week. She was riding alongside him and would occasionally guide him this way or that by putting her hand on his shoulder. My wife, along with, apparently, the vast majority of her gender, absolutely lose their marbles when this guy is around and so I was somewhat relieved to hear that I wasn't the only one to wonder whether old Andrea was the perpetrator of some elaborate scam upon the gullible and unsuspecting patrons of popular culture. Once I had heard that a comedienne on daytime television claimed that he had been coming on to her on his recent visit to *The View*, I knew that my cynicism was unfounded—let's face it, only a blind man would flirt with Joy Behar.

In any event, my family and I have been visiting the same beach town in Italy for the last few years and have become familiar with its customs and a few of its permanent residents. It has become a place my family and I go to forget about our petty problems and become reacquainted with one another for a couple of weeks a year. Although the weather, the food, the people, and the sheer beauty of the land have made this coast a favorite destination of Northern peoples seeking warmth for centuries, "our" town catered mainly to politicians from Rome and businessmen from Milan until the early 1980s. Modern transportation and information flows, mass affluence, and globalization attracted the English and Germans and more recently Americans to a part of the world so stunning that Dante and Byron felt compelled to speak of its natural beauty. The shops and restaurants have become increasingly fancy although its people have remained, thankfully, unpretentious and warm, those most appealing of Italian traits. We made our pilgrimage in late July and August and, given the recent events in the Caucasus, it seems somewhat ironic that we arrived this year to find that the Russians were the newest group to "discover" this beautiful spot on the Tyrrhenian. I'm embarrassed to admit that I felt a tinge of nostalgia when I saw that my favorite restaurant in town had added a Russian translation to its menu this year. In a flash, I realized that this was simply another act in the current wealth transfer drama.

This has created no shortage of indigestion among the town's native hosts or the few American regulars who remain, made all the more unpalatable by what appears to be a common Russian practice of sending what was likely perfectly good wine back to the cellar (I saw this maneuver no less than 4 times in 10 days) or seeing middle-aged people exhibit behaviors I last saw on Spring Break in Fort Lauderdale in 1987.

"Caro, Giasone, we don't like it either," a local maître d' and friend said, "but they have the money now. The Americans simply aren't coming anymore. We'll all be working for them soon, you'll see."

It is infantile although human to mourn such transformations, especially in those few parts of the world that deserve some level of romanticization. It is a rare person or people who can confront such changes and not feel some sense of self-pity for who they once were, who they wanted to be, or how others now see them. Italians have become relatively accustomed to this phenomenon over the better part of the last two millennia. Americans, myself included, have not.

# *What I Saw at The Revolution*[6]

*Originally Published—September 26, 2008*

## Let the Scapegoating Begin

It has been estimated that hedge funds account for more than 50% of institutional equity commissions, and so it isn't every day that you'll see the head of a brokerage firm take aim against short-sellers (read hedge funds) for his firm's precarious financial position. And yet so great was the stress on Morgan Stanley and Goldman Sachs, that John Mack took the rather unusual step of pushing for, and receiving, a ban on short sales of more than 800 financial stocks, button-holing any policymaker in Washington that could make a difference. Few of our hedge fund clients have viewed the move with equanimity and many have expressed emotions ranging from simple rage to complete apoplexy. Some have discussed a class action lawsuit against the S.E.C., while others are merely exiting their exposure to financial stocks. As analysts, we try hard, succeeding often but not always, to keep our normative judgments out of our forecasts of what we believe will happen as opposed to what we want to happen. As a bull by nature, I have not enjoyed discussing our double-dip scenario over the last year. And to our hedge fund clients today we simply say that, as we have seen, the federal government has grand powers to do as it wishes in what it believes to be exigent circumstances. If President Lincoln could suspend habeas corpus during the Civil War, the S.E.C. can ban short sales of financial stocks during a financial crisis. **We would suspect that the ban will be extended well beyond October 2nd, perhaps through the election, and that an uptick rule (which has thus far been opposed by both Secretary Paulson and Commissioner Cox) could be reinstated before this is all over. Fair or not, "speculators" have few friends in Washington now and it would not surprise us if politicians on both sides of the aisle took square aim against the hedge fund community during the inevitable "pound of flesh" phase of the political process.** This feeling is being driven by rumors of those who bought Credit Default Swaps of vulnerable financial institutions and then sold shares of those companies short, a strategy somewhat akin to buying insurance on your neighbor and then deciding to run him over with your car. It may not be illegal but it could easily be described as unethical. While this is a distinction often ignored by lawyers, it is precisely the type of practice that will be the basis for grand political theatre and scapegoating long after the deal to buy troubled assets is over. All of

6. Title of Peggy Noonan's classic on her years in the Reagan White House.

this means that the cost of doing business for leveraged investors has, like it or not, just taken a step-function higher. Dick Fuld may have been the first witness for the prosecution a week ago but the situation in Washington is fluid. Watch your back.

## Broker as Agent Reborn/The Rise of the Partnership

I love this business and I always have. This, combined with a weakness in my character that often leads me to be nostalgic for times I never experienced, has long made me forlorn for the old days of Wall Street, when the broker was an agent, trying to do his best for the customer and, it was hoped, make a few bucks for himself. In the early 1970s, when the Financials were only 6% of the S&P 500, DLJ's decision to become the first Wall Street firm to become public was seen as somewhat heretical. Until that time, investment firms had always been run as private partnerships where the reputations and fortunes of the partners were put on the line every day. It seems quaint now, but many old-timers wondered whether their firms could really serve two masters—a contemporaneous responsibility to outside shareholders and the solemn public trust of the nation's capital formation. By and by, those concerns fell by the wayside, especially with the introduction of negotiated commissions in 1975 and the growing popularity of "modern" financial products, like structured finance and derivatives.

After the carnage that followed May Day, all the great old firms became public companies and, in the process, gave themselves opportunities to use other people's money to produce asymmetrical payoffs through perverse incentives. Little by little, the concept of the grand old Wall Street partnership died too and the notion of public responsibility was replaced with greed, while dollars and cents were placed where a heart and soul should be. Research suffered, becoming bought and paid for by the investment banking departments, the use of leverage skyrocketed, aided in large part by more muted business cycles and "the great moderation," while agency fees were replaced with principal transactions. For a long time, it was hard for the casual observer not to wonder how bulge bracket firms didn't endure bigger hits as some of their clients suffered what was ultimately a death sentence. One didn't need to be a cynic to wonder how some major Wall Street firms, with a rapidly growing dependence upon principal transactions, seemed to defy all odds and produce consistently positive returns regardless of market conditions. In the old days, Salomon's proprietary trading resulted in wide swings in their quarterly earnings. With the benefit of hindsight, far too few investors wondered how the brokers could bat a 1.000. Despite all the talk of financial innovation, most of what Wall Street has invented in the past 20 years has been revealed to be little more than old fashioned leverage and a sham.

**Business Segment Pct. Contribution to Net Revenues**

| | Goldman Sachs<br>(GS) | Morgan Stanley<br>(MS) |
|---|---|---|
| Asset Management | 19.2% | 21.2% |
| Commissions | 12.0% | 14.3% |
| **Principal Transactions** | **54.0%** | **35.6%** |
| Investment Banking | 14.8% | 16.4% |
| Other | NA | 12.5% |
| | 100% | 100% |

In light of recent events, I really wonder whether, in a few years, when the books are written and some perspective is gained through the passage of time, financial historians will ask whether one of the central ironies of the soap opera that has gripped Wall Street for the past year is that lightly regulated hedge funds posed far less systemic risk than their publicly-traded and more highly regulated sell-side counterparties. It's true that hedge funds take 20% of the profits, but is that any more outrageous than the top management ranks of the big banks who routinely distribute 50% of the revenues—with no high water mark? Based on my own limited experience I have come to learn that the partnership structure may be perhaps the single best risk management system ever invented and I wonder whether hedge funds have come through this crisis better than most because the managers themselves have a lot more of their own capital on the line at any given time. It is hard to bet against innovation on Wall Street but the events of the past several weeks that suggest that Wall Street firms are going to have to make a choice between being true agents servicing customers without conflict, or simply principals, who, without pretense, attempt to provide superior returns through speculation.

## A Manhattan Tale

As the readers of these pages may remember from earlier missives, I have, in the midst of starting a new company and dealing with the greatest financial crisis in a century, been in the market for a new apartment in Manhattan. SHE WHO MUST BE OBEYED had been harping on me about this for a year and I finally relented about six months ago, the only concession I was able to wrest being that we sold our apartment first before entered the market for a new one. It took us a while, but accepting a bid 10% below our asking price allowed us to sign a contract on our place in August to a nice family from Switzerland who had just come into some money. About a week later I learned that my wife was pregnant and that we'll be expecting our second child in February. The vagaries of the

New York City co-op market means that our buyers will need to pass the board and that we won't close until early January, a little time but perhaps not enough if we wish to avoid re-enacting our own version of the Nativity in the middle of a Northeastern winter. Perhaps I'm being stubborn, but I have steadfastly refused to pay up for Manhattan real estate in a period where half my friends on the Street have lost their jobs and the other half are fearful of the same fate. Remarkably, the potential stress on home prices in this town in the wake of the financial crisis seems to have been totally lost on many sellers and virtually all real estate agents, that most helpful and ethical species of financial professional. I didn't know whether to laugh or cry after this e-mail exchange with a broker on Wednesday:

> *"Large apartments are still selling for close to asking and no one is having any problems getting a mortgage. It is the young studio and 1 bedroom buyer that has problems," said she.*
>
> *"Yeah I guess, but a lot of high-end jobs have already left the City and it's hard to see Manhattan real estate prices do anything but go down for the next few years, don't you think? I have a long-term view so I don't mind stepping in but I'm not going to pay up." said I.*
>
> *"I listened to Jim Cramer, who is on television every night, and he said that he thinks the market will bottom in June 2009. He said so in New York Magazine."*

This may be surprising, but I didn't find this to be overly confidence-inspiring conversation. It's looking more and more as if I'll be entering the rental market.

# BEST ESSAYS OF 2009

## *Bear Market in Intellectual Orthodoxy -or- Things I Learned in Business School I'd Rather Forget*

*Originally Published—April 26, 2009*

In what seems like ancient history to many of our associates at Strategas (At 40, I am, remarkably, the eminence grise of this place), I decided to leave a good paying job at a great firm to go to business school in the middle of a bull market, convinced that I didn't have the academic background necessary to compete in a world of ever-accelerating financial modernization. Before my very first class on my first day of business school, one of the students in my "cohort" stood up in front of our class in Corporate Finance, introduced himself, and then attempted to sell us all lanyards for our I.D. cards for the "low, low price of $3." A little later that day, I went to a recruiting presentation for Lehman Brothers. As luck would have it, the speaker was none other than the Chairman, Dick Fuld. "Not all of you are cut out for this business. Our interview process will ferret you out," he thundered, the vein on the side of his temple almost bursting under the strain of his obvious intense passion for the business and his firm. An old high school girlfriend worked in the recruiting office at Lehman (she was attractive and sweet), and I was able to catch up with her after Mr. Fuld's performance.

"Jeanine, I'm not sure I would lead with Dick as a recruiting technique. Half the guys in the room are going home to change their boxer shorts now" I chided.

"I know. Alec and I try to dissuade him from coming but he insists on being involved with recruiting the "next generation."

And so, while it feels like an eternity ago, it seems as if my first day of business school was punctuated by the performances of two salesmen, one a rookie, the other a veteran, but both obnoxious harbingers of the period of excess that was to ensue. I have thought a lot about business school in the last year and half, when, one by one, many of the basic academic financial orthodoxies I learned there have been almost completely discredited. They include the ideas that:

## 1. Debt is always cheaper than equity.

There is obviously some logic to this, especially in periods of stable interest rates and growing earnings. Add inflation and tax considerations into the mix, and the decision to use debt as a form of capital is even easier, as prices rise and debts can be paid with even cheaper dollars while interest expense becomes tax deductible. Like a lot modern economic theories that rely more on mathematics than common sense, this financing technique works extremely well until it stops working, at which time it fails spectacularly. In periods of deflation and weaker economic growth, the fixed nature of interest payments becomes a very difficult burden to bear. A greater reliance on the great moderation of economic cyclicality and an arrogance that cash flows could be consistently and accurately predicted allowed many Masters of the Universe to feel comfortable with leverage ratios of 30 to 1.

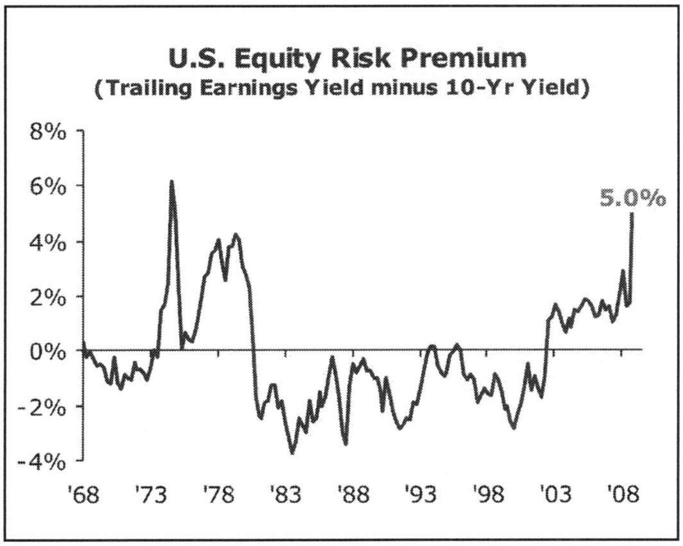


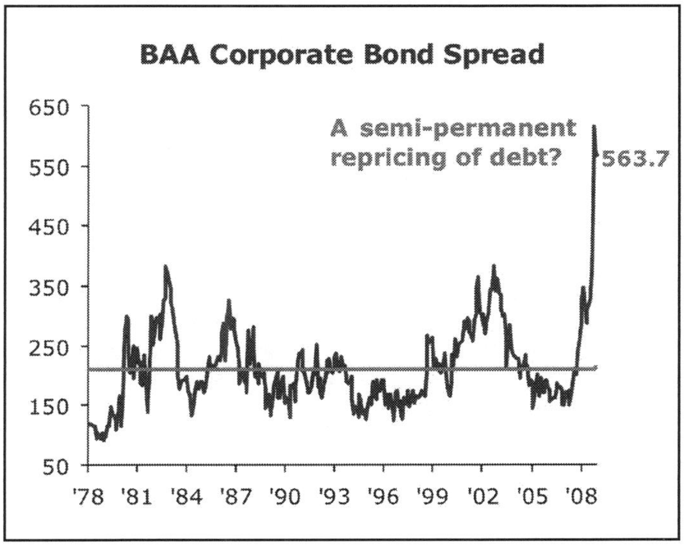

## 2. Financial Markets Are Generally Efficient.

This old chestnut came to us courtesy of Eugene Fama of the University of Chicago and generally asserts that financial markets are informationally efficient, reflecting all known information. To be fair, my professors at business school always offered up intellectual trap-doors of the weak, semi-strong, and strong forms of the Efficient Market Theory to allow all of us to hold onto an academically popular orthodoxy despite an almost overwhelming amount of evidence to the contrary. If you put enough monkeys in front of a typewriter, one of them will come up with *War and Peace*. George Soros and Julian Robertson were really just two examples of extraordinarily lucky coin-flippers. Right—whatever. While few would quibble with the idea that the sheer amount of information available to investors today makes true information arbitrage ever-more difficult to achieve, the re-emergence of government policy on business and financial market decisions will provide fresh opportunities for investors willing to do their homework.

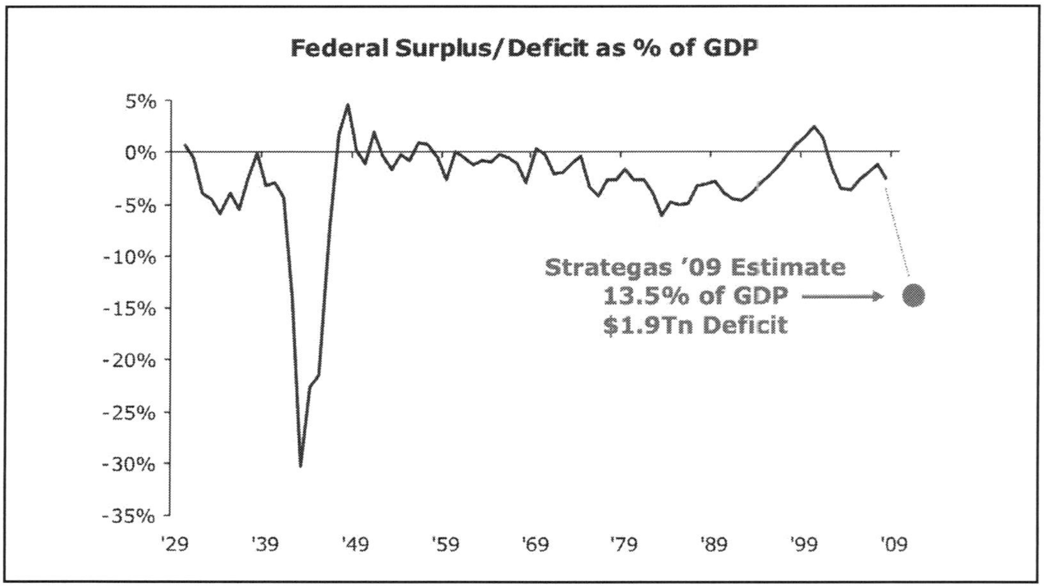


## 3. Modern Portfolio Theory (MPT)

Pioneered by Harry Markowitz in his paper, "Portfolio Selection," published in 1952 by the Journal of Finance, MPT holds that it is possible to construct an "efficient frontier" of optimal portfolios that allow investors to use diverse asset to provide stable returns given a certain level of risk. Again, this can work pretty well in periods of stability, but fails miserably in times of intense stress. In some ways that makes the theory more dangerous than no theory at all, a little bit like how

David Einhorn described the concept of VaR as an airbag that works perfectly until you have a car accident. The problem with MPT, it now seems obvious, is that it ignores the impact of liquidity on correlations between asset classes. When you can't sell what you want, the old saying goes, you sell what you can. This was especially true last year, when the correlations of most asset classes all converged on one. In the future, we will likely learn that gardeners on University campuses were probably most affected by the failure of this once popular theory.

**Rolling 12-Month Correlations to S&P 500**

| | S&P Small-Cap | S&P Mid-Cap | MSCI EAFE | MSCI Emerging Markets | Crude Oil |
|---|---|---|---|---|---|
| 12/31/2003 | 85.3% | 86.3% | 87.6% | 74.2% | -21.5% |
| 12/31/2004 | 83.3% | 93.8% | 72.1% | 61.9% | -55.5% |
| 12/31/2005 | 92.6% | 95.9% | 71.0% | 77.1% | 3.3% |
| 12/31/2006 | 74.6% | 81.2% | 80.7% | 83.8% | -2.6% |
| 12/31/2007 | 89.3% | 89.6% | 87.7% | 51.4% | -8.0% |
| **Oct-08** | **96.1%** | **98.0%** | **93.6%** | **85.8%** | **67.3%** |
| **Nov-08** | **96.0%** | **98.1%** | **92.5%** | **83.5%** | **68.4%** |
| **Dec-08** | **95.7%** | **97.9%** | **92.8%** | **83.9%** | **56.1%** |

## 4. Home Prices Always Appreciate

They ain't making any more of it, every real estate speculator proclaims to anyone within earshot. This one is a little harder to pin on the academic community but was put forth by so many market prognosticators (ourselves included) that it entered the realm of conventional wisdom, just shy of the imprimatur of academic theory. It was also empirically true for nearly 70 years. Certainly, we aren't making more land, but we greatly increased, through financial wizardry and social engineering, the number of those willing to extend home loans to people that couldn't possibly afford them. The price of any leveraged asset is ultimately directly proportional to the availability of credit used to finance it. The structured finance industry isn't dead but it's close and will never be the same. It will likely take another three generations of bankers and politicians to devise "new" methods of financing that would allow us to recreate the mass delusion that real estate prices can't decline. While we may be close to a bottom in housing in terms of units, stable price appreciation, sadly, seems a long way off.

And so, I leave you with an imponderable as we enter the long weekend—who can we turn to when the academic basis for our industry has been totally turned completely upside down? There are no easy answers for this but I suspect that they lie not in fancy academic journals and textbooks but in the more fundamental concepts of fiduciary responsibility, knowing one's customer, and common sense.

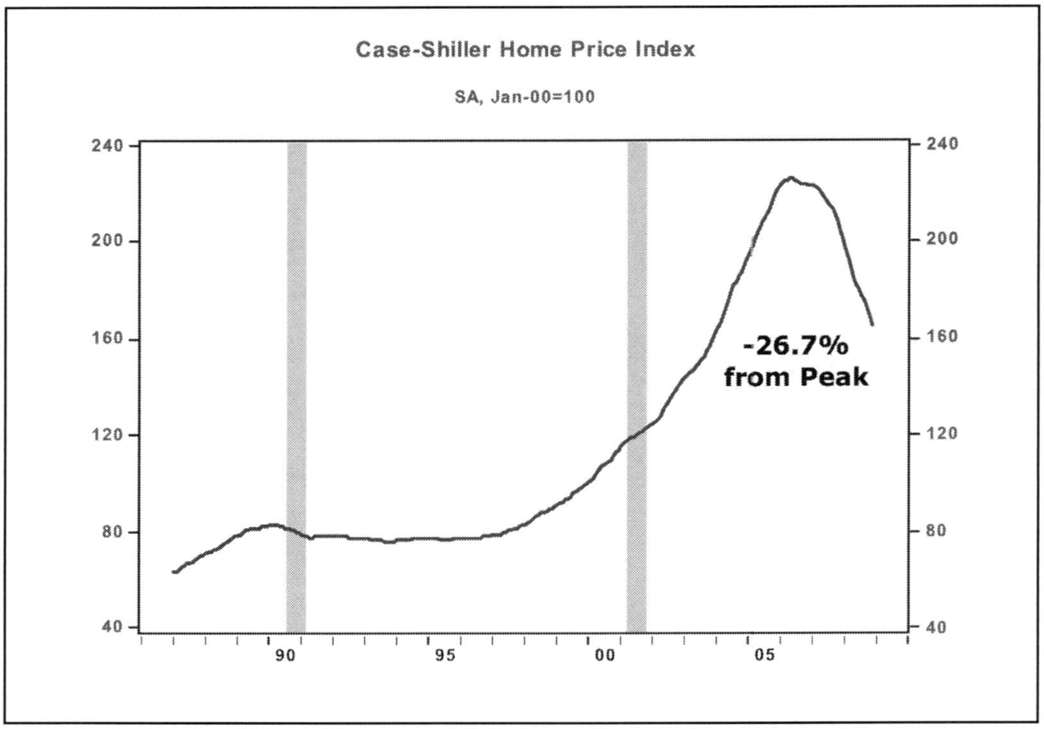

# *To Live and Die in Manhattan*

*Originally Published—April 24, 2009*

"Money isn't everything," said my Manhattan real estate broker with absolutely no sense of irony in the on-going drama surrounding my attempts to find shelter on an island that has become the epicenter of the global financial crisis. This was only the latest in a series of laugh versus cry moments in a quest that started almost two years ago. To review for my friends and clients who may have forgotten or haven't yet been completely bored by the subject, I have, in the midst of starting a new company, dealing with the greatest financial crisis in a century, and having a second child, been in the market for a new apartment in Manhattan. SHE WHO MUST BE OBEYED had been harping on me about the subject for what seemed to be an eternity and, at the start of 2008, I finally relented, wresting only one concession—that we sell our apartment first before deciding to buy a new one. It wasn't easy but we accepted a bid 10% below our asking price last August, a not inconsiderable achievement I thought at the time. In retrospect it would have been exquisite timing if it hadn't been for my co-op board (an almost perfect example of the concept of adverse selection) who decided to reject the all cash bid for our home the same week Lehman Brothers failed, adding a somewhat more personal and surrealistic[7] quality of the financial crisis. To this day we haven't been able to figure out why our Board rejected the buyer. Perhaps it was because they had 3x the purchase price of the apartment in a risky asset allocation of 2/3 municipal bonds and 1/3 cash, or that they hailed from that most aggressive and bellicose of foreign lands—Switzerland.

The good news is that the Board finally accepted a new buyer just this past week. The bad news is that it was for a price 13% below what we were able to receive a scant six months ago. Of course, once we passed this hurdle, real estate brokers, that most helpful and ethical species of financial professional, informed us that the "market has picked up considerably" and that we would have to move quickly if we didn't want to be "homeless." The absence of shame in the profession is quite remarkable but I've decided that this is what one must endure if one wants to live on this island, even after the end of the great boom in structured finance. Despite protestations to do the contrary, I think I may actually take my time and search for all those bargains people keep talking about. I was, incidentally, able to secure a

7. A favorite of Hollywood's varied geniuses, I have eschewed the use of the word surreal for several years but have recently reintroduced it into my lexicon given the events in the financial markets of the past year when it actually seems appropriate. My new nails- on-a-chalkboard word is "narrative." Basically, any word Ben Affleck uses in a sentence to convince me that he can actually read and write I'm out.

commitment for a jumbo mortgage, although not for my preferred 30-year fixed term. In another example of the fact that old habits die hard, Citi was able to give me a 10/1 LIBOR Interest Only mortgage for a fair rate. The Lord only knows to whom I'll have to be writing my checks in the next few years.

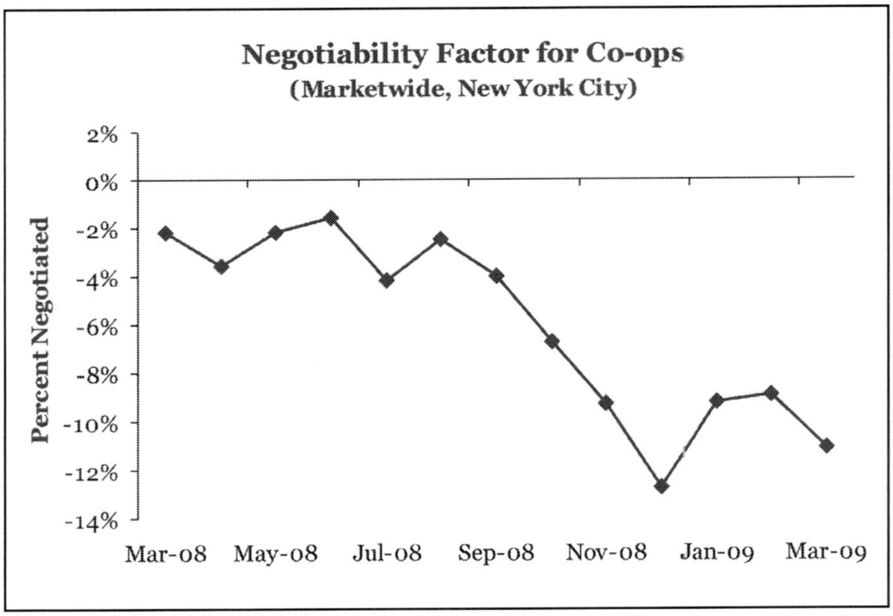


## Fanfare for the Common Man

For the first time since Lehman failed in September, I was able to actually get away for a vacation to a warm climate last week. There's nothing like a little Vitamin D and some sand between your toes to gain some perspective on things. A little time off also provided me with the mixed blessing of becoming reacquainted with popular culture for the first time in what has seemed to be this endless financial crisis. In truth, I am convinced that subjecting our guests in Guantanamo to a continuous loop of *The View*, *Dancing with the Stars*, and *American Idol* would be far more effective than waterboarding in obtaining intelligence. I, for one, would tell you my deepest secrets in 10 minutes if subjected to such treatment. But the blessing in seeing daytime television last week was that I realized we may be, little by little, eschewing the siren songs of fame, fortune, and celebrity and focusing more on the traditional values of hard work, discretion, and humility that define class. In short, our heroes are changing. The emergence of US Air Pilot Sully Sullenberger, Sea Captain Richard Phillips, and singer Susan Boyle might suggest that we have, with the decline in our collective net worth, started to value the quiet humanity of regular people. Misshapen and imperfect like the rest of us, these seem to be normal people who didn't particularly seek out the limelight or great fortune who are perhaps, just perhaps, providing an example for the rest of us to be content with what we have and the simple gifts Providence has bestowed upon each one of us.

# *The Greatest Games—Golf & Investing*

*Originally Published—July 2, 2009*

Being of Italian descent and a huge fan of Sinatra, I've always dreamed of having the lifestyle and traditional vices of the Rat Pack. And while I must admit that wine and song are very much a part of the program, the fact that I am married and have two kids makes the women part O.B., buddy. Of course, my widening girth and receding hairline probably render such vices behind white stakes anyway, so who am I kidding? But a man's got to have at least one healthful diversion apart from work and family, and like many guys on Wall Street that have some interest in sports, golf has become an integral part of my leisure time. Candidly, I play less than I want to and worse than I should, but it's become the one thing I can count on to take my mind off of life's problems and the fact that the vagaries of the market over the past few years might force me, finally, to learn a trade, like, perhaps, plumbing. The nice thing is that the more and more I play, the more I see similarities with the other great game in my life—the financial markets. For those of you who don't play golf, I apologize in advance for this essay because I know that the sport, like being surrounded by a bunch of Georgetown graduates, can be enormously amusing to the participants, but stupefyingly boring for others. But if you love the game as much as I do, you might agree that golf and investing are not all that different:

## 1. It's hard to have everything going for you at the same time.

It would be a cliché if it weren't so true, but the eternal mystery of golf is that, like investing, it's hard to have all parts of your game going well at the same time. Only occasionally will you be equally as proficient off the tee and on the green. This is no different than the Herculean task of capturing the market's fundamental, technical, and psychological rhythms simultaneously. More often than not, success comes not from perfection but from a series of small successes that allows you to grind out solid performance.

## 2. Each investment decision and golf shot is independent of the next and performance can be fleeting.

This is the main reason why one of my friends insists that "there are no gimmes, and no tears" in a real game of golf. "If it's a gimme," he says, "knock it in." You may have just knocked a 7-iron to three feet, but in a real game, you've got to make the putt. In the markets, we all know that it doesn't matter if you once *had* a profit in a stock. It's where you sold it that counts. All golfers have known the pain of having one bad hole ruin an otherwise good round. It's not all that different in investing these days where outperformance has increasingly become a function not of picking the right stocks, but avoiding the bad ones. In either case, execution is everything.

## 3. Both games are humbling and can seem like they're unfair.

I've lost more matches than I care to remember to guys that had a loopy swing, bad address, and a bad grip. Since I merely have a bad grip and a bad swing, I have often found this unfair. More often than not, these guys grooved their bad habits and developed a way to win, often pocketing a car payment in the process. My buddy and I got smoked in a member/guest last weekend by a guy who looked like Craig Stadler's unhealthy brother. In investing, the real pros know that there is no difference between being smart and making money. It doesn't matter where you went to school or how nuanced your thesis may have been, performance ultimately equals smarts in the investment business. Because no style points are awarded in either activity, investing and golf may both be the fairest games of all.

## 4. Ultimately, the highs and the lows keep you coming back.

My friends who don't play golf or don't work on Wall Street sometimes ask me why I would torture myself with preoccupations that can never be mastered. But to me this is precisely why there is a certain romance involved in both activities. The fact that both games are difficult is the reason so many of us are attracted to them and success can be so sweet. Ultimately neither game may be that healthful for your psyche, but as we all know, there are worse vices.

# *Don't Be Koi—Seeking Insight from a Summer Rental*

*Originally Published—August 21, 2009*

As readers of these pages know, my family and I generally visit the same beach town in Italy at this time of year to get "off the grid" as they say, attempting to forget about our petty problems and become reacquainted with one another for a couple of weeks a year. But the combination of kidney-stone passing real estate transactions and the newest addition to our household, a six-month-old by the name of Marie, led us to forgo *Il Bel Paese* this year and seek a shore vacation closer to home. Because I don't generally consider structured finance or M&A gossip appropriate beach conversation, I have never been a big Hamptons guy and we decided to rent what we remembered to be a little house in the modest Borough of Manasquan, about 70 miles away from Manhattan.

Meaning "stream of the island of squaws" (seriously), Manasquan was incorporated in 1877 and became a beach destination for boaters and families escaping the City heat by the 1920s. It is a nice and curious little burg where it's not uncommon to see a beautiful family beach house next to a fishing cottage that might house 10 people in their 20s with a penchant for tattoos and front-lawn beer pong. The dress is casual and there are, mercifully, few incentives or opportunities to display one's social or professional status. Not having visited the town for five years, I got a kick out of the refrigerator magnet we were given by our real estate agent on our first day for Wally's, a cab service that claims, with absolutely no sense of the absurd, to be "the Goldman Sachs of transportation." I'm not sure how Wally could confidently make such a claim and I am reasonably certain Lloyd Blankfein's shadow has never graced the town's most famous and raucous watering hole, The Osprey, a cover-band mecca for scantily-clad tramp-stampers and guys who have spent long winter hours in the gym working on their pectorals.

Upon our arrival we were surprised to see the simple bare-bones house we rented in the midst of the real estate boom in 2005 completely transformed, sporting another floor, a swimming pool (the house is ON the Atlantic Ocean), a hot tub, a rec room replete with pool table and wet bar, a koi pond[8], and countless other paeans to consumerism and indulgence that became commonplace in the early part of this decade. We're not complaining of course. The house is a lot of fun,

8. A pond for big goldfish, allegedly of Japanese origin, whose ability to serve as "symbols of love and friendship" allow pet stores to routinely charge $450 for them.

the location is ideal, and the weather has been terrific. Eating the wrong foods and engaging in mindless family activities like naming each one of our koi after characters from Snow White has allowed my son to have the time of his life, his transformation from City kid to beach bum becoming complete with a killer tan and what appears to be a precocious facility with a boogie board. Getting into the act, and much to the dismay of SHE WHO MUST BE OBEYED, my son (a.k.a. Mr. Mayhem) and I even decided to sport our own temporary tatts—a red Jolly Roger for him and a black and blue anchor for me.

Unfortunately, the house we knew and loved has also since been stuffed with all manner of cutesy antiques that make it feel as if Magnum P.I. had hired Beefsteak Charlie to do his interior decorating. In fact, the owners have added just about everything one could want while removing everything anyone might actually need. The antique barber shop chair, vintage ice cream churn, and cash register from the turn of century are all mildly interesting but don't, oddly, make up for the fact that our home's owners decided to put their pillows, ice trays, salt and pepper shakers, and every other staple under lock and key this year (thanks for the heads' up).

The good news is that, despite all of these expensive improvements, we were able to rent this sandy cathedral to easy credit for 10% less than we were 4 years ago. The bad news is that we have proved to be woefully inadequate stewards of the koi...Doc was the first to go, Dopey and Grumpy quickly joining him in that great koi pond in the sky. Wracked by sadness and guilt and unable to get in touch with the home's owners, my wife excitedly pleaded for help from the real estate agent and the local pet store. Fishing another one of our adopted dwarfs out of the pond in what was obviously a rare house call, the shop owner put my wife's conscience at ease by explaining that the koi were most likely the victims of sustained overfeeding. And I wondered, with only Sleepy and Bashful able to survive the blight the Trennert family had rained upon them, whether this little community under the front porch didn't offer a broader lesson for American consumers.

# *DMV: A Glimpse into Our Future*

*Originally Published—November 13, 2009*

**From:** **Insurance Broker** **Sent: Thurs. 11/5/2009 4:21pm**
**To:** **Jason Trennert**
**Subject:** **DO NOT DRIVE!!!!!!YOUR LICENSE HAS BEEN SUSPENDED********

Hi Jason,

I just called your office and they said you're on a plane coming in tonight.

Chubb just emailed us after they pulled your Motor Vehicle Report that your NY LICENSE IS SUSPENDED. PLEASE DO NOT DRIVE AS YOU COULD BE ARRESTED FOR DRIVING WITH A SUSPENDED LICENSE! It appears that you failed to answer a summons order [xxxxxxxx] in Nassau County for a Traffic and Parking violation on 9/13/1998.

Tomorrow please call NY DMV @ 518-486-9786 (press option 2, option 1, option 1, option 8 and option 5). The hours are 8AM - 4PM but, please do this first thing in the AM. NY DMV would only reveal to me that you should be able to clear it up on the phone but that the NY LICENSE takes 24 hours to be updated and with the weekend you may not be able to drive until Monday.

PLEASE RESPOND TO ME SO I KNOW YOU GOT THIS EMAIL. I'M IN TOMORROW AND WILL TOUCH BASE.

Thanks,

This little chestnut greeted me almost immediately upon my landing at JFK after a 14-hour flight back from the Middle East last Thursday, standing as a testament to former Italian Prime Minister Bettino Craxi's famous observation that nothing good ever happens when you leave the country. Tired and disoriented, I didn't know whether to laugh or cry. My mood didn't improve this week when I attempted to navigate the New York Department of Motor Vehicle's Kafka-esque phone system to resolve the matter. Two hours of random number-punching actually allowed me to speak to a human being, and a relatively nice one at that, who patiently explained to me that under normal circumstances I would be able simply to pay a fine over the phone for my transgression (speeding, predictably) and move on with my life. Unfortunately, the **11 years** that had transpired since the ticket was issued meant that I would have to make a personal appearance, joy of joys, at the Department of Motor Vehicles in Hempstead on Long Island.

"Isn't there a statute of limitations or something on traffic tickets?" I pleaded. "I mean that was four cars and 40 pounds ago. I've gotten plenty of tickets since then *(Why did I just say that?)* and nothing ever came up."

"I hear ya, Mr. Trennert. But what can I say, the County needs the money. We're going through all the old files now."

This smoking gun that provided a momentary triumph to my cynicism quickly gave way to resignation as I realized that although it might seem unfair, there wasn't a damn thing I could do about it. I was going to have to pay the Man if I wanted to avoid last weekend's humiliation of having my wife chauffer us to all the most mundane aspects of our personal lives. (The parents at my son's basketball game started whispering when they saw SHE WHO MUST BE OBEYED at the helm of the family truckster.)

My morning in County Court put on full display a virtual cottage industry of state workers employed to separate ordinary citizens from their money. Hundreds of us waited in line under dim fluorescent lighting to "get processed" by a phalanx of bureaucrats.

"Whaddya you here for?" asked the carpenter in line in front of me.

"74 in a 55...You?"

"Cop said I didn't properly stop for a school bus. Eight points on my license so I'm fightin' it. It's all about money," he said wistfully. "They're stoppin' everyone for everything now."

And so I wasn't at all surprised to read in the car service on my way back from court a story in *The Wall Street Journal* highlighting a virtual dog's breakfast of new fees and taxes being employed to deal with greatest state revenue declines on record—Missouri has started taxing Yoga and Pilates classes, Maine increased taxes on candy, haircuts, and lawn care, and Illinois was thrown into complete chaos when a sales tax change forced lawmakers to determine what precisely distinguishes candy from food. According to a new Pew Center study, nine states, including Arizona, Florida, Illinois, Michigan, Nevada, New Jersey, Oregon, Rhode Island, and Wisconsin, are facing a similar fate as California, replete with burgeoning budget deficits and IOUs. One wonders when the natives will get restless and demand better fiscal management from their elected officials. Until then, the DMV might offer the best insight into what awaits all of us.

## *The Gathering Storm of Populism and Protectionism*

*Originally Published—January 29, 2010*

Perhaps they were just putting on a brave face, but the initial interpretation of Brown's victory in Massachusetts a week ago revealed a surprising tin ear for inside-the-beltway panjandrums that were able to secure the Presidency and, at least for a spell, a 60 vote super majority in the Senate. For whatever reason, it reminded me of my vain attempts to woo the fairer sex in my high school and college days—a pathetic combination of misplaced self-confidence, delusion, and a complete inability to discern signals a blind man could see in a minute. Fortunately, I had a wingman in those days, Paul Mastrorocco, who was nothing if not honest and willing to set me straight. Somewhat painfully I remember him warning me not to read too much into the kindness of a certain Jeanine Buonaparte. "Jay," he intoned, "two things. One, She just asked you for a #2 Ticonderoga pencil and B, she goes out with Chris Giovinco, an all-state full-back who is the undisputed swirlie king of Hauppauge High."

The President and Congressional leadership, it became evident, didn't have a wingman in the aftermath of the upset last week. While worries about China's willingness to maintain easy money kicked off the decline in stock prices, it was, in our view, the political elite's unwillingness to look within for what went wrong, and its insistence instead on hurriedly casting about for a populist issue that could tap into the electorate's palpable anger that turned what might have been a minor sell-off into something more serious. The good news is that it appears, at least for now, that cooler heads are likely to prevail. Despite the Congressional burlesque of the AIG hearings, the President appeared somewhat more conciliatory in his State of the Union speech while Congress voted, rationally, to reconfirm Chairman Bernanke. While we believe that a combination of stronger GDP and earnings growth may wind up making last week's political drama a buying opportunity, we worry that the silly season of midterm election year politics has just begun and that a whole host of populist issues could emerge that could once again vex the financial markets.

Nowhere is this potential greater, in our view, than when it comes to the subject of free trade. It was a small item buried in the never-ending cascade of Reuters news items hitting the tape at any given time, but for some reason this headline caught our eye on Wednesday of all days:

**US SLAPS DUTIES ON ELECTRIC BLANKETS FROM CHINA**

The Commerce Department's decision to slap anti-dumping duties from 90 to nearly 175 percent on a mere $30 million worth of electric blankets from China is, admittedly, hardly the stuff of which trade wars are made. But given the growing sense of economic angst in the country, and the potential for political grandstanding in an election year, we are watching closely for any indication that protectionism is on the rise. Growing protectionist sentiments are yet another element on our checklist of developments that could signal that there will be a cost of our fiscal and monetary munificence. While perhaps somewhat less important than higher long term interest rates or higher taxes, they would be no less dangerous if taken to a populist extreme. As strong believers in free trade, we share German film director's Wim Wenders belief that "you cannot protect something by building a fence around it and thinking that this will help it survive." But given the grave challenges and attendant economic anxieties engendered by the financial crisis and the recession, it is somewhat surprising that there hasn't been more debate in the public square about the potential costs of our current free trade system. While this may be attributable to the fact that the benefits of globalization are a protected intellectual orthodoxy of both the intelligentsia and the political elite, one doesn't need to be overly-cynical to believe that the time is ripe for politicians on both sides of the political aisle to heed the siren song of protectionism, especially when any fair-minded person would have to admit that China's decision to peg its currency to the dollar may, in the final analysis, be seen as the root cause for so many of the world's economic imbalances. Said perhaps more simply and controversially, this may be a time when protectionist sentiments could gain political traction because they have some merit. Stay tuned.

# *Bar Bets for Restless Financial Professionals*

*Originally Published—February 26, 2010*

Spending my entire adult professional life on sales and trading desks surrounded by other information junkies and thrill-seekers has taught me that a slow tape often tends to lead to other less-than-healthful diversions, not the least of which is the inveterate gambling on all manner of things, financial and non-financial alike. I've witnessed imported car payments lost on bets ranging from being able to eat a packet of Saltines in one minute (impossible) to consuming, in the space of 24 hours, the entire contents of a vending machine off the fixed income floor at Merrill (possible, but only with a blender). I've seen grown men forced to wear women's clothes after incorrectly wagering on the most popular nut in a holiday assortment (always bet on cashews), and I once saw a junior salesman bet a senior trader that he wasn't 5' 11" as he claimed. The trader, not surprisingly, was intimately familiar with his own height and pocketed 50 bucks in the process. I thought about all this with an O'Doul's in my hand at Rothmann's the other night (for some inexplicable reason I decided to give up drinking for Lent—painful), and thought it might be fun and worthwhile to recount the most popular market bets my buddies and I have made with each other during the market's recent directionless volatility. While the amounts at risk vary, all bets were made at even money. The odds accompanying each wager are based on Strategas' handicapping of the events in question.

## OUR BEST BAR BETS

1. The Euro will not exist in its current form 5 years from now. ***Odds 2-1***
2. A corporate credit will trade through Treasuries. ***Odds 2-1***
3. The S&P 500 will trade to 1300 before it sees 900 again. ***Odds 1-2***
4. S&P 500 EPS will not exceed peak levels this cycle. ***Odds 2-1***
5. The annual U.S. savings rate will not eclipse 8% this decade. ***Even odds.***
6. The unemployment rate will not break below 5% this decade. ***Even odds.***

## 1. The Euro will not exist in its current form 5 years from now. Odds 2-1.

In sooth, it was always a grand experiment to seek monetary union without political union despite the altruistic desire of the Continent's political elites, after a century of war and strife, to seek a more stable and peaceful coexistence with their neighbors. While some have tried to claim that Europe's currency union wasn't, in fact, all that different than America's own experiment with single currency in the 19th century, the cultural and social divides between, let's say, Germany, and Greece, will forever and always be greater than the differences were between Maine and Delaware 150 years ago. Of course, the political elites on the Continent appear to be stronger than they have ever been here in the lower 48, and so the grand experiment may continue. Germany has geared its economy toward exports to other Euro members and may, as a result, have a vested interest in seeing the Union stick together. **Still, one wonders how long the average guy in Berlin really wants to pay for the profligacy of those in Madrid, Rome, or Athens.**

## 2. A corporate credit will trade through Treasuries. Odds 2-1.

This is, admittedly, a little bit of a stretch. For global investors, U.S. Treasuries are likely to remain, to borrow a cliché, the best house in a bad neighborhood. But, stipulating the unique position America is in with regard to its ability to fund itself, Washington's persistent lack of seriousness about the nation's fiscal circumstances is likely to cause many to conclude that Exxon, for example, is a far better credit risk than Uncle Sam. Such a circumstance is not without precedent—**corporate credits have routinely traded through government paper in places like Argentina and both Harvard and Stanford have both issued debt cheaper than U.S. Treasuries this year.**

## 3.The S&P 500 will trade to 1300 before it sees 900 again. Odds 1-2.

While our meetings with clients in recent weeks suggest that the most consensus bet may be to be cautiously optimistic on the market, the least consensus view is the expectation for a significant rally. The reasons for this lie with the panoply of secular headwinds likely to buffet the U.S. economy in the coming years and the circus that has become our nation's capital. **Still, we believe the path of least resistance for stocks is higher.** While we're below consensus, we believe the S&P will earn $74 this year, which at a 17x multiple, would lamp fair value for the Index at around 1260. This combined with the yawning gap between cash flow and capex and the still-unused fiscal stimulus leads us to believe the market is likely to be surprised by both the strength in the economy and in earnings in 2010. Strategas' technical analyst, Chris Verrone, also points out that sentiment remains broadly supportive, as upward sloping 200-day moving averages are providing a reliable support base, and new 52-week highs have begun to reaccelerate.

## 4. S&P 500 EPS will not exceed peak levels this cycle. Odds 2-1.

Believe it or not, bottom-up consensus estimates for 2011 S&P operating earnings are currently at $95.66—meaningfully higher than the prior peak in earnings of $91.47 through the second quarter of 2007. Far be it from us to question the accuracy of our brothers in arms on the sell-side, **but we believe it's unlikely aggregate earnings will exceed the levels reached at the height of the economy's love affair with financial engineering any time soon.** Predictably, this has almost everything to do with the contribution of the financial sector to earnings then and now. At the peak, Financials accounted for almost one-third of S&P earnings. Barring a Lazarus-like resurrection of a sector which, through leverage, enhances the earnings of all other sectors, it is difficult to see another industry that could make up the difference over the next few years.

## 5. The annual U.S. savings rate will not eclipse 8% this decade. Even odds.

Given the drama in the credit markets and in the economy over the last few years, it might seem reasonable to expect the personal savings rate to continue to rise as a form of insurance against future financial dislocations. There has certainly been an inverse correlation between the saving rate and consumer net worth as a share of disposable income, for instance. However, we believe that the consumer saving story is likely to play out over a very long time frame.

While a significant increase in personal savings would be a welcome development for a nation that is likely to have increasing difficulty funding its public debt, the likelihood of a subpar expansion and structurally high unemployment probably suggests that consumers will be unable to save too much after essential spending. Additionally, politicians will likely have a continuing incentive to support a spending culture (cash for clunkers, cash for appliances, etc.) with an economy that's still 71% consumer-based. Even in the 1930s, with the pain of the Depression, the personal saving rate was relatively range-bound. Consumers may have wanted to save more, but in many cases with a double-digit unemployment rate they were not able to. It was only in the 1940's, with the income from WWII and rationing, that the saving rate rose dramatically.

It is a fact that Saving has to balance with Investment (it's an accounting identity in the construction of the National Accounts), but with personal saving still under pressure, our bet is that the U.S. will again look for foreign saving to fund the recovering activity in the domestic economy, rather than adopt a true culture of austerity.

**CONSUMERS MAY HAVE WANTED TO SAVE MORE IN THE 1930s, BUT IT TOOK UNTIL THE 1940s BEFORE THEY COULD.**

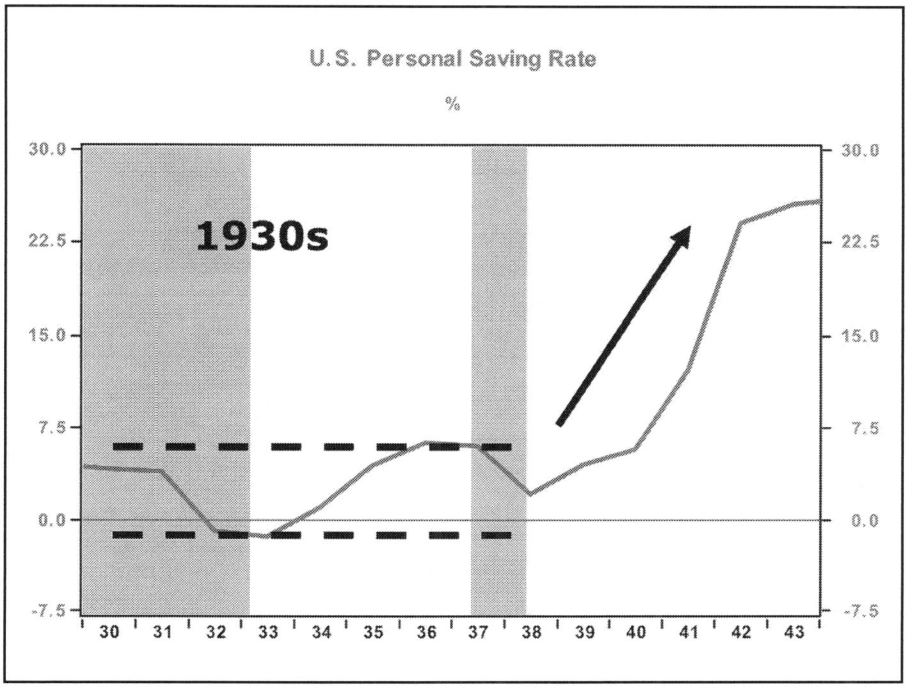


## 6. The unemployment rate will not break below 5% this decade. Even odds.

As everyone knows, and every politician is quick to remind us, small businesses are the backbone of the U.S. economy and employment growth. Generally speaking, there has been a strong relationship between capital formation and real estate, as many entrepreneurs use the equity in their homes as collateral when seeking small business loans. Our Chief Economist, Don Rissmiller, has used a long-term ratio of homes to households to estimate that there are, sadly, still likely 5 million too many homes in the U.S. This suggests that it will be a long time before a strengthening housing market can be relied upon to be the basis for robust job growth—either directly though housing-related employment, or indirectly through home equity loans that are used to finance small businesses.

We believe that the trend growth rate in the economy is likely to be more like 2% versus the 3.5% "speed limit" that has prevailed over the past several decades, which brings up the question of what this type of recovery/expansion means for both consumers and companies. We would generally expect a slower trend growth rate in the economy to be associated with a higher structural unemployment rate (i.e., a higher NAIRU—say, 7%+ versus the 5-6% estimates that have prevailed for the past several decades).

**HOUSING'S CONNECTION TO SMALL BUSINESS MEANS ROBUST JOB GAINS LIKELY ELUSIVE IN THE EXPANSION.**

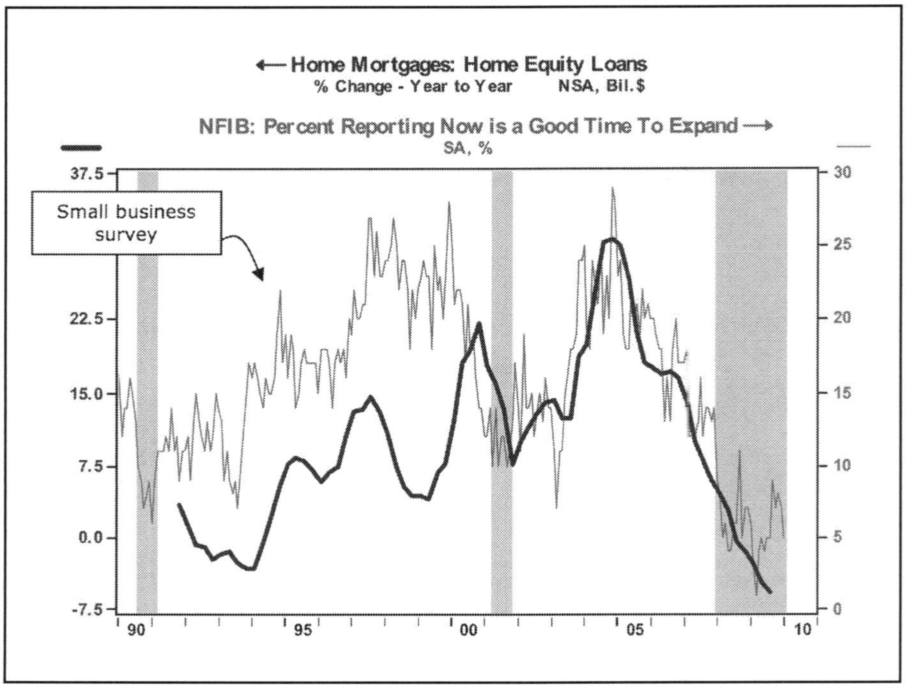


Ultimately, all of these bets are more likely than me making it to Easter Sunday without a Jack Daniel's or a Chianti passing my lips.

# *The Sovereign Debt Crisis: Handicapping the End-Game*

*Originally Published—May 28, 2010*

John Kenneth Galbraith famously quipped that there are two types of financial prognosticators—those that don't know and those that don't know they don't know. And so it's been for the last three weeks, during which we've been repeatedly told that deflation is inevitable and that our much vaunted "bill" for massive fiscal and monetary stimulus was coming due right now. We've also had to endure perhaps the worst of all potential put-downs for the financial professional—the claim that we are "consensus." It is a perhaps a testament to my age that I find this actually hurtful, but of course, as Hyman Roth put it, this is the life we have chosen. Perhaps it's a foolish consistency on our part, but after a particularly bad month for global equities, we still believe that large cap growth stocks may be the best value among the various asset classes competing for increasingly restive global capital flows. But in truth, we would place ourselves solidly in the first camp of Galbraith's two species of financial prognosticators—we don't know. What we do know is that debt as a percentage of GDP can't continue to rise indefinitely without interest costs consuming the entire budget. We also know that piling debt upon debt, especially short-term debt in the case of the U.S., will, barring some deus ex machina ending, lead to massive financial dislocations. The enormity of the global sovereign debt crisis has led investors, economists, and strategists to discount a wider array of potential outcomes for the long-run than at any time in the past 30 years. We thought it might be useful to highlight these potential endgames, place our own current odds on their likelihood, and provide our clients with actionable investment ideas to play them.

1. **Austerity/Policy Error Induced Deflation**
2. **Currency Devaluation Induced Inflation**
3. **Luck**—Innovation Generated Productivity Gains
4. **Expanding the Tax Base**—a) War b) Immigration
5. **The Chris Christie Option**—Pro-growth Tax policies AND Cuts in Govt Spending

## Austerity/Policy Error Induced Deflation

Our travels to visit clients over the last few weeks tell us that this is probably the most consensus view as the potential denouement of the current sovereign debt crisis. It certainly has a solid academic backing given the recent Reinhart-Rogoff tome on the subject. Given the recently passed austerity measures in both Greece and Spain, the odds of such an endgame are high. But our feelings about human nature lead us to believe that, when push comes to shove, U.S. policymakers will likely be unwilling to take the chance of flirting with a severe recession and will ultimately counterbalance tight fiscal policies with increasingly accommodative monetary policies. Of course, the ECB's attitude towards quantitative easing and the U.S. Congress' propensity to create a financial regulation bill meant more to punish than to reform are wildcards in this process. The potential for a policy-error is not insignificant.

## Currency Devaluation Induced Inflation

"The first panacea for a mismanaged nation is inflation of the currency; the second is war. Both bring a temporary prosperity; both bring a permanent ruin. But both are the refuge of political and economic opportunists," so said Ernest Hemingway almost a century ago. Old Papa was no economist but he was a great observer of humanity. Of course, the more things change the more they stay the same. While a competitive round of devaluations seems unlikely today, we do find it interesting that gold has been rising in all currencies, perhaps some indication that while the Dollar is seen as the most formidable gazelle in an ever-weakening herd, investors have increasingly little confidence in fiat currencies in general. We place the highest odds on this option simply because it is the most politically expedient for elected officials who have little willingness to make difficult choices. An increasingly inter-connected global economy probably means that the nature of inflation will be far less homogenous than it was during the wage/spiral of the 1970s. Still, we would have a bias toward commodities and commodity-related equities, especially those commodities which are in short supply in China.

## Luck—Innovation Generated Productivity Gains

Also known as the "cold fusion solution," another potential way out of the fiscal mess in which policymakers find themselves would simply be luck—a technological innovation—an easily implemented source of alternative energy or medical advances—that would greatly increase productivity and, by extension, the trend rate of economic growth. Then, it would be easier to "grow out of the problem." While it would be easy to underestimate the potential for such a development in dealing with our long-term problems, the power and beauty of the United

States, at least thus far, has been its ability to provide an hospitable environment for risk capital and to innovate. I have personally heard members of the current Administration use this as a justification for deficit spending. While it is true that the U.S. has always found a way out, it seems unwise to use this as a justification for profligate spending policies.

## Expanding the Tax Base: a) conflict b) immigration

If policymakers are unwilling to cut public spending, it is almost axiomatic that they need to raise more taxes to pay for them in a world in which investors are quickly coming to the conclusion that spendthrift fiscal policies are unsustainable. The old fashioned way of dealing with this problem, let's say before about 65 years ago, was distinctly Roman—governments who exhausted their own domestic tax base would simply find another land to conquer to find more taxpayers. Mercifully, the odds of this option, at least for the developed economies of the U.S. and Western Europe, are extraordinarily low. A more modern approach, however, might entail changes in immigration policy that attract new potential taxpayers. But if the current controversy in Arizona is any guide, this option is also fraught with political controversy and peril. This leaves only higher taxes as the fallback position for politicians that are unwilling to rein in government spending. The problem of course is that the current size of the federal deficit is so large that almost no increase in marginal income tax rates could close the gap. A VAT tax has also been proffered as another potential source of tax revenues. Unfortunately, it has been estimated that the VAT would need to be 20% in the U.S. to eliminate the deficit. Higher taxes are, to be sure, inevitable. **Regretfully, as Hauser and others have observed, federal tax revenues have almost always been equal to 20% of the GDP, regardless of the level of marginal tax rates.** Said another way, taxpayers find a way to keep their tax liabilities constant—higher taxes normally result in lower tax compliance and lots of time spent trying to game the system.

## The Chris Christie Option: Pro-Growth Tax Policies AND Gov't Spending Cuts

Managing Director of Institutional Sales and relatively new Strategas hire, Pat Alwell, has humorously, albeit incessantly, pointed out the irony in the concept that in comparison with former Mr. Universe Arnold Schwarzenegger, it is Chris Christie, governor of New Jersey, that has developed the reputation for having "abs of steel" when it comes to dealing with entrenched special interests and seemingly intractable public spending. In truth, Governor Christie's promise of pro-growth tax policies, that stimulate capital formation, and cuts in public spending has yet to be realized and is far from certain. Still, such a plan would probably be the most market friendly for equity and fixed income investors alike. Sadly, the current populist political winds also render it the least likely. Governor Christie has become something of a phenomenon in recent weeks and, if he can pull it off, could provide a playbook for other enterprising political hopefuls in November.

If we have a non-consensus view, it's that there is a not insignificant chance that we could grow our way out of the problem. Unfortunately, the odds of such an outcome are still probably only one in three. This leaves two other less palatable options—deflation and inflation—for investors about which to obsess. By definition this suggests that economic volatility and the potential for price stability aren't very likely, with obvious implications for earnings multiples. Forced to choose between these two, we believe that policymakers should always choose inflation, preserving some political maneuverability if their policies go awry. We know this is a close call and we, ultimately, may have too little faith in policymakers to stake out principled positions and too much faith in their competence to actually engineer inflation, but, for the time being that's the way we see it. Deflation may indeed be inevitable, but if the history of democracies is any guide, not before currency debasement and inflation are tried first.

**Handicapping the Sovereign Debt Endgame**

| Odds | Outcome<br>Result | How to Play It<br>ETFs | Notes |
|---|---|---|---|
| 45% | Currency devaluation-induced inflation | DBP<br>XLE: OIL<br>IOO; DVY<br>TIP; TIPZ | Precious Metals<br>Energy<br>Dividend paying "Global Operators"<br>TIPS |
| 30% | Growing our way out (an innovation boom) | XLK<br>GEX<br>VLI<br>JDK | Tech stocks<br>Alternative Energy<br>Private Equity<br>Small-Cap stocks |
| 20% | Austerity-fueled deflation (policy error) | PHYS; GLD<br>TLT | Gold<br>Long-Dated U.S. Treasuries<br>Cash |
| 3% | Expanding the tax base (Immigration OR Expanded War) | TLT<br>XLB; XLV<br>XLI; ITA; PPA | U.S. Treasuries<br>Consumer Staples & Health Care<br>War Effort Stocks (Industrials, National Defense) |
| 2% | The Chris Christie (Pro-growth policies AND spending cuts | CYC<br>MUNI<br>MIC | Cyclicals<br>Tax-Free Municipal Bonds<br>Private Infrastructure Funds |

# *The Flash Crash & Its Discontents*

*Originally Published—June 18, 2010*

Of all the questions we get from our clients on the road, the one that has been most difficult to answer, and by extension, the most troubling, has regarded the causes and long-term after-effects of the May 6th flash crash. In today's 24-hour news cycle, two months can seem like an eternity and, as we all know, there has been enough other disconcerting economic, environmental, and political news in the interim to discourage both the seasoned professional investor and the novice alike. But despite the fact that this incident might seem like a footnote in the annals of financial history, we're finding few institutional investors who are willing to accept the idea that such an incident is simply a cost of doing business in the computer age. Large long-only shops in particular view the flash crash, quite correctly it would seem to us, as an existential threat to the confidence of millions of individual savers and investors upon which the future growth of their industry is dependent. After two fifty percent declines in the broader market in the past 10 years and an almost daily diet of news reports of the misdeeds of Wall Street's biggest and most famous firms, the last thing Wall Street needed was its own version of the BP oil spill—a p.r. nightmare that still raises questions about the pace at which technological change can and should be implemented to satisfy the needs of both progress and prudence at the same time.

As strategists and economists, we are hardly experts on the subjects of trading or market structure. As a result, we've done our best to speak to a variety of buy side and sell side traders, officials at both the NYSE and electronic exchanges, and regulators to determine what happened on May 6th and what the implications might be for the investor. Strategas' own traders [9]—John Ghize and Tim Hughes—were invaluable in collecting the data that led us to the following conclusions:

## Fragmentation Has Probably Gone Too Far

With 37 exchanges to which equity orders can be routed, the average free market person might believe that more is in fact more. The biggest problem with fragmentation is that, however, is that, like many other complex systems, it works well until it stops working, at which point it fails spectacularly. Our discussions with a variety of traders suggest that not all electronic exchanges are equal, many

9. In the midst of one of the greatest financial crises in history, Strategas, oddly, it would seem, decided to become a regulated entity by becoming a broker/dealer. We have a small but highly professional agency only equity trading desk standing at the ready to answer any questions about this piece or, even better, to fill any orders you might have.

merely content to execute orders at the prevailing market when things are stable and very few willing to stand in the pocket and take the hit in times of market stress. Exchanges, in our view, should have a fiduciary duty not only to themselves but to the overall strength of the American capital markets. Fragmentation has also made it extremely difficult for the SEC to piece together what exactly happened on May 6th.

## Speed Favors the Trader Rather than the Investor or Issuers

In preparation for writing this piece, we heard no shortage of horror stories about average investors with stop/loss orders in long-term positions see significant wealth destroyed, and tax liabilities accrue, in the midst of that half-hour on May 6th. Of course, for the short-term investor or the professional trader charged with executing orders, speed it would seem is always and everywhere a good thing. But one wonders whether the need for speed serves the interests of the long-term investor or, perhaps more important, the issuer of securities dependent upon the capital markets for funding.

## The Current Financial Regulatory Regime is Fighting the Last War

It won't be surprising to anyone who's seen Congress or the federal government in action over the last several years to learn that the flash crash revealed, according to our contacts and friends who have been had to deal with them in the aftermath of the crash, an almost mystifying lack of understanding on the part of politicians and regulators in their attempts to make sense of the events of May 6th. The result has been an all-too-common half-assed approach to satisfy the media and public at large without doing the hard work of creating safer and more efficient markets.

## The Flash Crash Has Been a Boon to the NYSE

In the past decade or so, it's been hard to find many fans of the Big Board among the ranks of the industry's buy-side traders. This is undoubtedly due to lingering hard feelings about the NYSE's near monopoly on the execution of its listed companies as well as a Moore's law of sorts has made their jobs easier with, it is assumed, less risk. With the advent of Regs NMS and ATS, the Big Board's market share in its listed companies has fallen dramatically, from over 80% to about 30% in the last decade. By all accounts, the Exchange has gained share in the aftermath of May 6th, as some brokers have changed their routing systems to take account not only of speed but also of safety. Reports also suggest that a number of issuers have viewed Exchange membership as a relatively low-cost of insurance against extreme market turbulence. Duncan Niederauer, CEO of NYSE-Euronext appears to have gained traction in his claim that "it's ok, at times, to take the plane off auto-pilot, and have a human being operate the controls."

## High Frequency Trading May Not Have Been the Cause but it Didn't Help

This may be, perhaps, the most controversial conclusion we have come to in this process. For obvious reasons, both brokers and exchanges are loathe to criticize some of their best customers. Still, one wonders the economic and social utility of using computer programs exploit minute discrepancies in securities prices in microseconds. There is nothing inherently wrong with this of course but should remember that equities are long-duration assets and that ultimate function of the market is to allow companies to most efficiently access capital.

In truth, we have yet to find anyone who really knows what happened on May 6th, and it would a dangerous conceit for us to believe that our own conclusions would be anything approaching the final answer on the subject. Still, as a research firm, we believe we have a duty to at least attempt to add some value in answering questions about an event that could have broad implications for the U.S. capital markets. What we fear most was summed up succinctly although somewhat disturbingly this week by our friend and famed market technician Ralph Acampora when looking at a chart we created showing net redemptions of equity funds in the past 17 months—"This chart tells me that we've lost a generation of average investors and that they might never come back." Without real reforms, this would be a great loss not only for New York but for the global capital markets.

# *Gold: Still a Rodney Dangerfield Asset*

*Investment Strategy Viewpoint Originally Published—November 10, 2010*

"It just can't be right," said the 30-something hedge fund manager through a towel after a grueling 45 minutes on the squash courts of the New York Athletic Club.

"I mean, G. Gordon Liddy is trying to sell it to me on Fox News. My orthodontist owns gold—he wears gold, for crying out loud. It just can't be right," he said, shaking his head, his voice trailing.

The case against gold is well-known and, until relatively recently, time-tested. The yellow metal is never ever really consumed, provides no yield, and carries with it storage costs. The polemic surrounding gold, like the inflation vs. deflation debate, is enough to result in bar fights in some sections of this grand city and it's hard to find too many investors who are agnostic about it. You either see it as the barbarous relic of the retail crowd or a necessary hedge against the cupidity of politicians the world over. **Despite the recent run-up in gold, it is, by our lights, too early to fade.** There are now, unquestionably, elements of froth in the market that should give investors pause. **But if there is one fact that is missed among investment sophisticates, it's that investing in gold is still considered a hopeless backwater at most large mutual fund companies in this country.** It is for this reason that we believe that it is not yet over-owned.

**Gold Stocks at Prior Peaks: Then & Now**

| **1980** | **Ticker** | **Name** | **Mkt Value $B** |
|---|---|---|---|
| Largest Gold Company | ANGLY | Anglo-Amer So Afr ADR | 3.7 |
| Avg Mkt Cap of S&P 500 Stock | | | 1.9 |
| Avg Mkt Cap of Gold Stock | | | 0.7 |
| | | | |
| **2010** | **Ticker** | **Name** | **Mkt Value $B** |
| Largest Gold Company | ABX | Barrick Gold | 51.1 |
| Avg Mkt Cap of S&P 500 Stock | | | 21.5 |
| Avg Mkt Cap of Gold Stock | | | 8.7 |

I find a certain irony in the fact that I have two friends in the investment business who, after enjoying great success and fortune managing other peoples' money in the 1980s and 1990s, have been, in their retirement, buying physical gold. They are unknown to each other and are different in many ways save for the fact that they were born in foreign lands—one in Armenia, the other in Cuba. They live in America, not by tradition or family ties, but by choice. Despite the fact that they so obviously believe in the great promise of this country, they have both come to the conclusion that they should hedge their hard-earned fortunes with hard assets. For them, their decision to own gold isn't the result of some ethereal academic exercise, it is based on life experiences most people born in America couldn't possibly understand.

While the hard asset story may seem tired and old to some in the investment business, it is just starting to capture the consciousness of many professional and retail investors alike who thought it was overly alarmist to believe the political class might seek to devalue its way out its own profligacy. This isn't to say that we believe the Fed is intentionally trying to cheapen the dollar. We take the Chairman at his word that he is simply trying to decrease the tail risks associated with deflation. But intentional or not, the net result of further monetary accommodation is the same—weaker purchasing power of the greenback. **Ultimately, we believe the crux of the case for gold is that it's hard to quadruple the size of the Fed's balance sheet and run budget deficits of nearly 10% of GDP and also stick the landing on inflation.** However you might handicap the prospects of either a Reinhart-Rogoff style deflation or efforts to reflate that work too well, gold remains one of the best hedges against the volatility of inflation. In the past century, the asset "worked" in two distinct periods—the deflation of the 1930s and the inflation of the 1970s. Given the uncertainty of global monetary and fiscal policies today, there is probably still room for it to garner the respect it deserves.

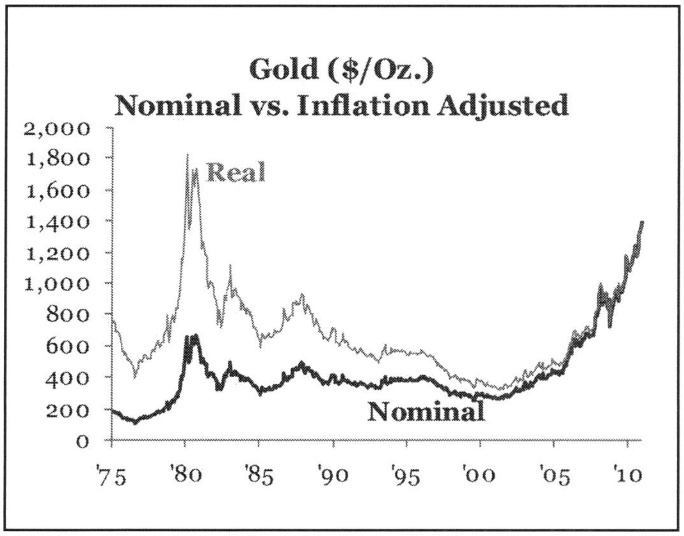


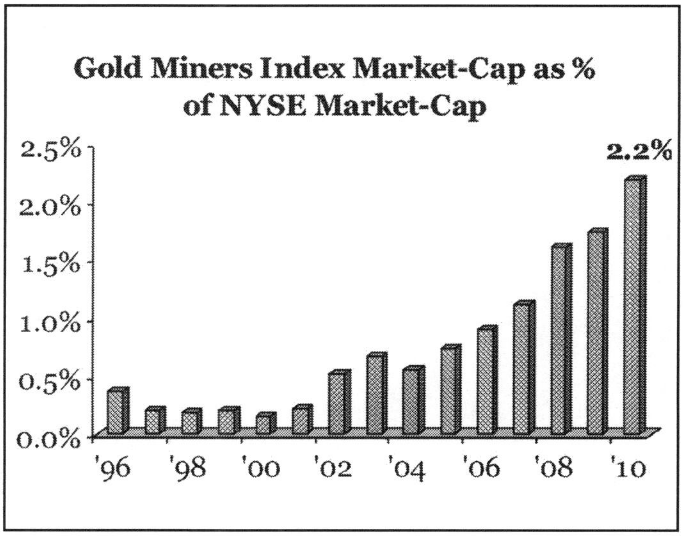

## THE SELF ESTEEM SOCIETY

Availing myself of the pleasures of commercial airline travel each week and frequently subjected to the sullen ennui of the cashiers at Duane Reade here in Manhattan, I had thought that I was well past the point at which the nerve endings of my dignity could register the slightest offense. That was until we decided to place postings for a variety of entry-level jobs in recent months and we started to receive cover letters from recent college graduates that would have made Donald Trump blush in their pomposity. *"The question isn't whether you should hire me,"* started one, *"it's whether I'm going to want to work for you."* Another candidate made it clear that he was *"a caged tiger waiting to enter the arena of the world of finance."* Subsequent interviews with candidates whose cover letters were the least obnoxious often didn't go much better—and regardless of how little ego you may think you have, it's hard to maintain your composure when a 22-year-old kid expresses disgust at the fact that your company doesn't possess green initiatives greater than recycling. Of course, we are a small company and only four years old and our offices have a certain Eastern European DMV-vibe. There is no fish tank, no tragically beautiful receptionist. We know we're not Goldman Sachs but we are, after all, offering these candidates the prospect of gainful employment and a paycheck which, one would presume, might engender some humility among the unemployed.

Of course, most of us are idiots when we first leave college, often not nicked-up enough by the slings and arrows of outrageous fortune to understand how hard life is and how little to which others actually think we're entitled. This all started to make sense to me upon reading a small squib in the paper about how American kids, when compared to their contemporaries in 29 other developed countries, ranked 25th in math, 21st in science, while ranking # 1 in only one category—confidence. I started to think about my late father, as I often do in the quiet of long transcontinental flights. At his core, he was a sweet man with the heart and soul of a poet. But he was a man of different era in which there were no participation trophies. His code was based on the belief that self-esteem had to be *earned and* he had zero tolerance for phonies or pretense of any kind. When confronted with those who had no appreciation for the great opportunities this country afforded, he could make The Great Santini look like Deepak Chopra. The transformation of a society in which prior generations prized an equality of opportunity to one that insists on an equality of outcome seems so much more important now, when the country is again faced with the need to make sacrifices to ensure its long-term fiscal viability and to compete with increasingly aggressive economic rivals. It is in this context that we should all be somewhat saddened by the reaction of those on both the right and the left to the recommendations of the President's Commission on Fiscal Responsibility. Everyone recognizes that, despite our status as a reserve currency, the U.S. cannot sustainably spend far in excess of its means. But when it seems as if we all want the other guy to make the necessary sacrifices we reveal, in the process, our own, although more mature, sense of entitlement. This is, of course, not a uniquely American problem. One doesn't know whether to laugh or cry at the spectacle of 17-year-old French students protesting the fact that their retirement age needs to be extended from 60 to 62 in a country in which the average life expectancy is nearly 81 years old. But without political leadership designed to do the right thing regardless of the electoral consequences, it's hard not to feel that the correlation between the West's sense of entitlement and the price of gold will only grow.

*A NOTE TO FELLOW TRAVELERS: If you ever find yourself on line for one of those body scanning machines and have the choice to go with the traditional metal detector, always choose the metal detector. Besides the fact that you are probably providing cheap thrills to a guy who lives with 20 cats in a room with a big ball of twine and thousands of 50-year old copies of Life magazine, it is a painfully slow process in which you need to take off virtually every article of clothing (belts, cufflinks, etc.) and must stand in the starting position for some obscure African interpretive dance. It's hard not to think that the terrorists have, in some small way, won.*

# BEST ESSAYS OF 2011

## *What the Donald Got Right*

*Originally Published—May 20, 2011*

It may seem like ancient history after the country's collective joy in vanquishing Osama bin Laden, but it wasn't too long ago that there was another outsized personality who was taking his own victory lap. Of course, we'll never know whether the nascent Trump candidacy was simply a side show designed to burnish The Donald's brand or whether it revealed one of the most prominent glass jaws in political history. Like most contact sports, politics is fun until you take that first hit, as Mr. Trump found out at the White House Correspondents Dinner two weeks ago. Still, there is no denying that, for three weeks in April, Donald Trump was a political phenomenon. One could write this off as America's endless fascination with celebrity, but the size and enthusiasm of the crowds he was able to summon suggest that such a characterization would be a mistake. It would be hard to deny that he tapped into a thirst in the American people for a quality that can seem hopelessly outdated in our modern "I'm-o.k.-you're-o.k." society—*pride*.

Generally speaking, Mr. Trump recognized that most Americans believe in their own exceptionalism and are tired of the near-constant focus on the country's defects under the cloak of *change*. More specifically, he expressed, simply and directly, a frustration among most Americans with being pushed around by countries, like China and many oil producing nations in the Middle East, that are (dare we say it?) inferior to America in their pursuit of economic freedom and human dignity. As the richest country on the planet, it's easier to be magnanimous and accept these differences (and the economic disadvantages to average Americans they create) when times are good, but they appear eminently nonsensical, almost traitorous, when times are bad.

Although The Donald never quite precisely expressed it this way, his brief flirtation with a Presidential campaign exposed a simple, fundamental truth:

allowing China to peg its currency to the dollar may be described as many things—practical, far-sighted, etc.—but it is demonstrably not an exercise in free trade. He, almost alone among those seeking the Presidency, has had the courage to question whether the terms of trade we have established with China has been some Faustian bargain that provided a boon to large multinational corporations that have the resources to shift inputs around the globe with relative ease at the expense of many small businesses and high-paying middle class jobs for those without college degrees.

Hundreds of hollowed out manufacturing towns and fractured lives in the Northeast and Midwest stand as monuments to the insistence of the political and intellectual elite that anything described as free trade is always and everywhere in the national interest. In a country with 300 million people, it simply isn't realistic to expect everyone to become a software engineer or find employment manufacturing solar panels. As is almost always the case, the poor pay more. The unemployment rate for Americans over 25 years old without a high school diploma (1.7 million Americans, incidentally) rests at 14.6% compared with a rate of 4.5% for those of the same age with a college degree. Increasingly, economic policies that favor large companies with political pull at the expense of small business that remain at the backbone of American enterprise and employment are heightening the political tensions between the educated and less-educated, the young and the old, and those with accumulated wealth and those who have yet to achieve it. One might say these tensions have been ever-present, but historians would be hard-pressed to find another example in recorded economic history of such a rapid, willing, and vast transfer of wealth.

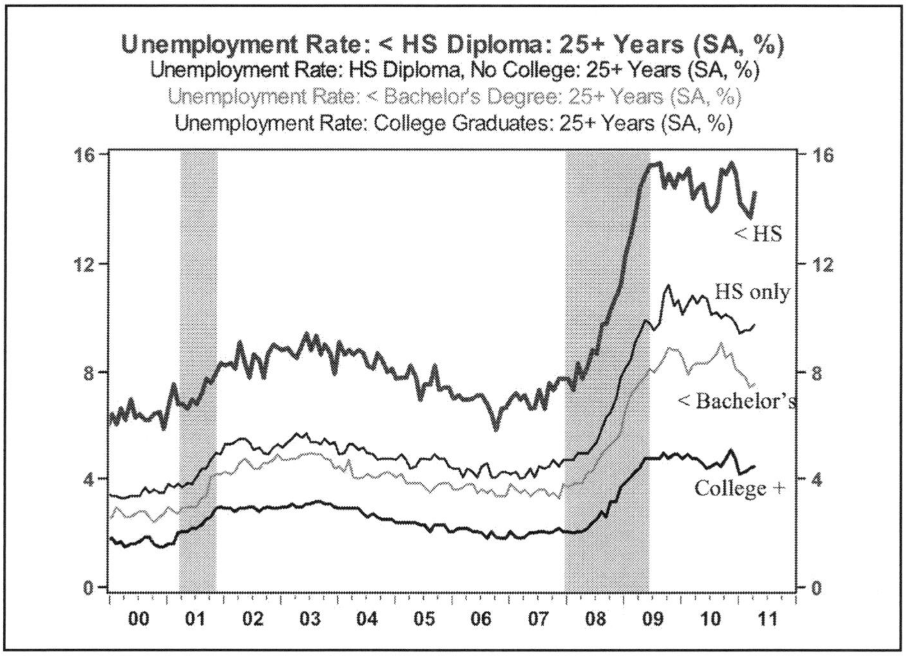

There is no denying that, throughout time, growing protectionist sentiments are often and correctly seen as the last refuge for politicians unwilling or unable to face up to the growing costs of their own fiscal and monetary munificence. When it comes to this period in global economic development, however, social scientists may find it almost mystifying that there hasn't been more debate in the public square about the potential costs of America's current "free trade" system. While this may be attributable to the fact that the benefits of globalization are a protected intellectual orthodoxy of the intelligentsia, big business, and the political elite, one doesn't need to be overly-cynical to believe another politician may pick up on the path to political popularity that Mr. Trump so successfully, albeit briefly, forged. Said perhaps more simply and controversially, this may be a time when protectionist sentiments could gain political traction because they have some merit.

# *Cash: Unsafe at Any Speed Why Vast Cash Hoards Make Investors Want to "Ralph"*

*Originally Published—June 29, 2011*

It shouldn't be all that surprising, in a way, to see a man who has dedicated his life to being a thorn in the side of Corporate America become one of the most vocal champions of shareholder rights. Still, one must admit that it's a little jarring to see Ralph Nader team-up with Carl Icahn to prompt companies to part with their vast cash hoards to enhance shareholder value. Given his recent comments in an open letter to Cisco CEO John Chambers and on CNBC, it's not hard to imagine Mr. Nader with a microphone in his hand and slicked back hair rail "I AM NOT A DESTROYER OF COMPANIES, I AM A LIBERATOR OF THEM!" Of course, the great thing about dividends, ultimately, is that they remind management that it's not their company four times a year. In the aftermath of an intergalactic financial crisis that prompted the Feds to impose greater regulatory scrutiny on the Health Care, Financial, and Energy sectors (more than 40% of the S&P, by the way), it is not surprising that your average corporate chieftain wants to have a greater cash cushion than in years past. New opportunities can present themselves at any time, of course, but let's face it, you're not fooling anyone that you've got a lot of great ideas for new sources of growth with $40 or $50 billion in cash on your balance sheet. Remarkably, since the 1930s, more than 50% of the total return of equities has, on average, been derived from dividends alone. Perhaps more important, academic studies have shown that companies that pay dividends have had higher growth rates than companies that don't throughout time. The mere act of paying the actual owners of the business something imposes a certain level of financial sobriety on the company that's hard to price. In a way, Nader is creating a Tea Party movement for passive shareholders. Perhaps channeling his inner-Glenn Beck, he said recently "shareholders who often call themselves conservatives say to government 'it's not government's money, it's our money.' It's time for those shareholders to say to corporate bosses 'it's not your money, it's our money as owner/shareholders." We published the piece that follows on page 3 two weeks ago, and it's received some attention. Given Mr. Nader's newfound penchant for shareholder rights, we thought it might not be a bad idea to run it once again.

# *Il Cavaliere Inesistente*[10]

# *In a garden in Versilia, a Little European Union*

*Originally Published—August 12, 2011*

As a guy who finds it hard to take a break from his native land's constant stream of "news," my visits with my family to a small beach town near Lucca have become an important source of rest and perspective for me over the last few years. I am never quite sure whether it's the fact that I'm on vacation or the nature of the Italian people that makes me feel so at ease, but I suspect that a couple thousand years of accumulated distrust of the political class has granted Italians such a great appreciation of the important things in life—family meals, friends, sea, sun—that so many of the rest of us, in our frenetic attempts to enrich ourselves, often take for granted. Although the cost of such perspective for Italy may be, perhaps, an over-developed sense of skepticism, most Americans would deem it to be, all in all, a fair trade. Despite more than 30 years of studying the language and the culture, my Italian is most often put to the test, ironically given my diet at home in New York, when I read the menu. As late as the 1800s, Italy boasted as many as 250 different kinds of pasta shapes. Perhaps in a small bow toward modernity and efficiency, the unified land of Garibaldi now has only 55 or 60 different words for pasta depending on who you talk to, enough to confuse all-but-native adult speakers and eerily reminiscent of Charles DeGaulle's famous rhetorical expression of exasperation, "how can anyone govern a nation that has two hundred and forty-six different kinds of cheese?" For 10 days in early July, my sole source of news was the *Corriere della Sera* in the morning with my coffee and a half of the evening broadcast of *telegiornale* before dinner. The primary focus of these admittedly limited sources of information was not on controversy but on information. I avoided America's faux debates with outside "experts" and constant polemics and realized, in the process, how much less exhausting and how much more efficient such an approach to gathering information can be. As luck would have it, my attempt to gain perspective by tuning out was thrown into jeopardy by an almost instantaneous 8% drop in the Mibtel the moment I stepped on Italian soil. In a flash, I was once again confronted by the question of when the bill would arrive after nearly 50 years of profligacy in the Western world.

---

10. The Nonexistent Knight, a novel by Italo Calvino. Premier Berlusconi is often referred to as "Il Cavaliere" in the popular press.

The beauty of visiting one place for a while is the ability to get a sense of its rhythms and rituals. Perhaps the most enjoyable part of our daily life in the Versilia was watching the children amass in the garden of the hotel every night after dinner. In the context of the current financial storm on the Continent, I couldn't help but think that this group of kids from all parts of Europe (my children were the only Americans) represented a miniature version of the EU. Every night a group of French, Italian, and German kids would amass near the bar—the parents sipping their cocktails and getting eaten alive by the mosquitoes while the kids ran triumphantly and happily though the garden of the hotel. Few of life's pleasures come without any cost, and this nightly ritual became reminiscent of the EU in another way—a small number of monetary authorities (the parents) were forced to confront varied, multiple and often wanton fiscal demands of their constituents (their children) that ranged from bottles of Coca-Cola to Italian ices to lollipops to the almost endless variety of treats that kids so desperately want to spend money on during vacation, a period when the parents' defenses are at their weakest. After the first night, it was clear that any real attempts at financial discipline could be completely ruined by the spending habits of a single child. What one wanted, they all wanted, and all, ultimately, received—another disturbing parallel to the problems currently facing Europe's single currency.

The kids got along better than a similar group of adults could be expected to, and the scene would fill even the most hardhearted with a certain sense of optimism about the future. But even among the innocent games of *nascondino* under the Tuscan moon, it wasn't difficult to see the source of so many of the petty arguments and mistrusts among the "adults" in Brussels and Frankfurt. After a couple of evenings it became clear that the French kids thought of themselves as the most refined and sophisticated, the Italians the best entertainers and most clever, and the Germans the most intelligent and rational. (As the only American, my son, Dominic, was largely relegated to the role of happy advisor and confidante.) More than the innocent happiness of childhood, if there was one thing that bound all these kids together it was a collective distrust of a child, a young adult really, from Frankfurt. As the oldest and most confident, he often sought to impose a structure to the children's games that the other kids were all-too-happy to ignore. Watching those kids in the garden was fun, but it did little to soothe my unease about the future of the Euro. The cultural differences on the stage of global finance seemed almost inborn and atavistic when viewed through the lens of those children's games off the Tirrenian. There wasn't a single one of those kids, or their parents, who would ever describe themselves as "European." Ultimately, they were all, at their most cosmopolitan, Italian or French or German; at their most parochial, a Neapolitan or a Parisian or a Frankfurter.

I last visited Europe on business in late May, at which point I became very bearish on the Euro. Frankly, it's hard to spend any time in a beach town in Italy and become more bearish on just about anything. And yet I became more convinced after my stay that the Euro was, at best, over-valued and, at worst, a horribly misguided social experiment. This is due in large part to what seems likely to be, just like in our own little garden in the Versilia, a never-ending tension between those charged with making broad policies and the almost-tribal exigencies of local and individual interests. Premier Berlusconi was conspicuous by his absence during what was a white-knuckle ride for the Italian financial markets in those weeks. *Il Cavaliere* was, by and large, *Il Cavaliere Inesistente*, largely ceding control to finance minister Tremonti who bluntly, and at times colorfully, urged the Parliament to pass a bill seeking fiscal reforms and tax incentives. Without such maneuvers, he warned, the Continent's financial system would meet a fate similar to that of the Titanic, where even the rich would suffer.

Half measures and stop-gap policies may work for short periods of time. But in the absence of dramatic actions based on realistic projections designed to solve the long-term structural imbalances of the Euro, it seems increasingly likely that the markets will impose discipline when politicians are unwilling or unable to do so. Short of the ECB actually deciding to expand its balance sheet and monetize its debt, the odds of recession in Europe, and a full-fledged European-led global financial crisis, have only grown. Trichet's comments last week did little to soothe our fears. The price of gold seems to be telling us all that further monetary accommodation is inevitable.

# *The Difference Between Money & Capital*

*Originally Published—August 26, 2011*

"We've tried the big Keynesian stimulus package and massive monetary accommodation. The only thing we haven't tried is a supply-side solution to solve the nation's unemployment problem," I said plaintively to no one in particular.

"I think you're dead wrong," boomed CNBC's widely-respected economics correspondent. "Look at corporate profits and bloated balance sheets. I think President Obama has engineered the greatest supply side gains ever. Why should we do more to help *them*?"

I used to tell people they were "dead wrong" in the financial markets, but that was before I had lost money on biotech stocks and airline stocks and that "private equity" deal with a medical device company run out of a strip mall off I-17 in New Jersey. Before I learned that in the social sciences arrogance is far more dangerous than stupidity and took to heart Mark Twain's famous observation "it ain't what you don't know that gets you into trouble, it's what you know for sure that just ain't so." In short, I used to tell people they were "dead wrong"—then I turned 25.

The exchange revealed, to my mind, a fundamental difference between those who believe that we need to create more wealth to help the economy and those who simply want to redistribute it. It also revealed the common confusion between the concept of capital and money. It's a common misconception but they are demonstrably not the same thing. A quick definition from an academic website put it this way: "Capital comprises the physical and non-physical assets (such as education and skills) used in making goods and services. Money is primarily a means of exchanging one good for another. Capital is measured in monetary terms, and since money (cash) buys physical assets (for example, buys a factory), capital is often thought of as money. But strictly speaking, they are different concepts." Said another way, capital involves risk and creates jobs. Accumulating money on the balance sheets of large corporations does not.

One of the main reasons the U.S. has been able to engineer unemployment rates of below 4% and 5% while Europe, even when everything is humming, can hardly get out of its own way has been the vibrance of America's entrepreneurial class. Historically, job creation in the U.S. has been driven not by very large businesses but by small businesses that often rely on home equity lines of credit to get started and to expand. Greatly reducing the supply of unsold real estate and also creating some sense of certainty about the regulatory and tax environment might go a long way in bringing the unemployment rate down.

# *Schoolyard Rules & Self-Dealing Damage Confidence, Future Earnings Power of Financials*

*Originally Published—November 26, 2011*

Anyone who's ever participated or watched kids' schoolyard pick-up games knows that the rules are always subject to change, often being set by the most quick-witted, the shameless, or the child who actually owns the ball. Yesterday Johnny insisted that the ball that bounced off of Dominic's book bag was a goal. Today, on defense, he swears that it hit the post. One might think that after 20 years of education and socialization, Johnny, now a Managing Director in structured products at FancyPants & Co. and living in a co-op off Park Avenue, might have developed a greater sense of fair play. Sadly, as we are finding out in the post-financial modernization world, he has not.

Given the problems facing the global economy, it may seem misguided to worry about whether Greece's private sector involvement (PSI) should have triggered payouts on credit default swaps. Still, there's something about the issue, writ large, that might say quite a bit about the current crisis of confidence gripping the global economy and the financial markets. On these pages, we have not been shy in linking the propensity of policymakers to capriciously change the rules for the economy and the markets with the current capital strike. It would seem only fair, then, that we call out Wall Street for changing its own rules on its customers when it suits them. Here again, the biggest loser is the rest of us—the companies and government entities who rely on access to the capital markets.

As a quick reminder, credit default swaps are a form of insurance against a default. The current controversy over what exactly constitutes a sovereign credit default was triggered by the "voluntary" haircuts imposed on Greek debt as a result of both the July 21st and October 26th Eurozone agreements. The organization that will help inform this decision is the International Swaps and Derivatives Association (ISDA), the governing body of the structured products business, which, according to its website, is made up of "a broad range of OTC derivatives market participants: global, international and regional banks, asset managers, energy and commodities firms, government and supranational entities, insurers and diversified financial institutions, corporations, law firms, exchanges, clearinghouses and other service providers."

A closer inspection of the organization's leadership would suggest that this is a charitable description of those who guide its mission—only four of ISDA's 25 officers and directors hail from the buy-side. The rest, somewhat unsurprisingly, is made up of a dog's breakfast of managing directors of sell-side firms that structure these "products" for their "clients." In the tradition of those who peddled the unparalleled investment management services of Long Term Capital Management and the benefits of purchasing subprime mortgage-backed securities, ISDA's own explanation of why a "voluntary" 50% haircut on Greek sovereign debt wouldn't actually constitute a "credit event" comes down to this: "those that disagree with us are clearly too stupid and unsophisticated to be buying these products in the first place." To be fair, a final ruling on whether the Greek PSI will actually result in a credit event could involve the courts for years, but all indications suggest that ISDA will side with those who underwrote, rather than purchased, this insurance.

While this may seem arcane to some, there are serious real-world implications of this latest example of Wall Street's self-dealing:

1. it serves as yet another reminder that the large, modern publicly-traded investment bank is incapable of acting as both principal and agent—at least honorably;

2. in the absence of confidence that the vendors of these products will make good on their markers, real money purchasers of credit products will either choose to sit on the sidelines or demand far higher interest rates to buy them. Speculators will simply short the underlying securities—let's say Italian bonds—to make their trades. In either case, the net result will be a higher cost of capital for those seeking to access the credit markets;

3. the "tails I win, heads you lose" attitude of those who underwrite these products will likely curtail their use and, ultimately, deprive the dealers themselves of an ability to sell what were previously high-margin products to their institutional clients. This may be yet another reason to be cautious on the financials despite already deep discounts to book value.

Few people will shed a tear for buyers of seemingly arcane financial products. If history is any guide, this piece will engender kudos from old-timers and calumny from dealers and recent business school graduates. In truth, I have never read a credit default swap agreement or ever purchased over-the-counter protection against a "credit event." But I have been around long enough to know when something seems wrong, a distinction that is often lost on lawyers but is crucial to keeping the capital markets functioning properly. For dealers, I would recognize that you can only screw your own clients for so long before you damage your own franchise. As the house, sometimes you have to lose to keep the casino open.

# BEST ESSAYS OF 2012

## *In Defense of History—Investing as a Social Science*

*Originally Published—February 10, 2012*

As a middle-aged man who owns an apartment in Manhattan, a brokerage firm, and common stocks, it would be an almost absurd understatement to say that my life is long beta. There's nothing like a global financial crisis (and the red brackets on your statements that accompany it) to make you lay awake at night and think about what you might have missed in all those years of formal education. I was fortunate enough to attend great schools, earning both a bachelor's degree in economics and an MBA, and I've wondered more times than I care to admit in the last few years whether I learned a damn thing. After considerable thought, I've come to the conclusion that the broader, more liberal arts-oriented courses I took in my undergraduate years did far more to help me to adapt to what was deemed to be "economically unprecedented" than the more technical lessons I learned in business school. Not once in the last three years did I feel compelled to develop more complex mathematical models to help me discern what was happening. This was due, at least in part, to an almost immediate revelation that it was these same models that sowed the seeds of the financial collapse in the first place. The financial crisis didn't prompt me to do more math but to read quite a bit more history.

It might be hard to believe, but my decision to attend business school was due in equal measure to the comfort of conformity and to my own romantic nature. I am not exaggerating when I say that I thought that I was about to enter a secret club in which all the secrets of America's captains of industry would be revealed to me. My delusions of what took place at America's business schools were quickly dashed after attending math camp, team-building exercises replete with trust falls in the Poconos, and my first meal at the Anvil Club, a place I imagined to be a leather-couched salon in which professors, smoking pipes and sporting patches on the elbows of their sports coats, would discuss the weighty issues of fiscal and monetary policy and international trade. Only after my first meal there did I realize that it is just like any other public institution cafeteria and that a professor from an elite MBA program wouldn't eat there on a bet.

This isn't to say that business school has no place in one's education as a businessman, but simply that the ratio of what was taught to me about systems, processes, theories, and mathematics to what was taught to me about real people was probably a thousand to one. In fact, it is not an exaggeration at all to say that a graduate from a top business school would never have been even remotely introduced to the likes of J.P. Morgan, Andrew Carnegie, Cornelius Vanderbilt, Jay Gould, or John Rockefeller. Nor would a business school graduate have been taught all that much about the history and theory of the corporation and its relationship and responsibility to its shareholders, employees, local community, or Board of Directors. There is no denying that math and science are critical to America's economic future. One can't help wondering, however, whether too many of our math and science students are using their studies to become financial engineers rather than real engineers, developing innovations that would provide the basis of productivity and the accumulation of wealth and capital that go along with it.

Finance is an important discipline and Wall Street provides an invaluable service to society, breathing life into the dreams that only capitalism can inspire. But a greater recognition that finance is at its heart a social science, with all the uncertainty that marks human interactions, would, no doubt, make would-be financiers more humble, less dangerous, and, by extension, more useful. A greater emphasis on economic history would arm students with a basic humanity that could remind them that, outside of the laws of science, 2,500 years of human history demonstrate that there are few certainties in life and that the atavistic emotions of pride, fear, and greed can turn the seemingly impossible into a stark reality very quickly.

My 9th-grade social studies teacher (even then I guess it was considered outré to call it history) would be happy to know that I remember the first thing she wrote on the blackboard thirty years ago: "those who do not know their past are condemned to repeat it. Santanyana." She would be sad to learn that, some 30-odd years later, I still have no earthly idea who Santanyana was or why he was important. As Michelangelo once said, "I am still learning." Nothing could be more important for those of us in this business.

**WANTED**

$$\mathrm{VaR}_{\alpha}(X) = -\inf\{\chi \varepsilon \mathbb{R} : P(X > \chi) \leq 1 - \alpha\}$$

**DEAD OR ALIVE**

It looks impressive enough to convey confidence, but this equation almost single-handedly brought down the world's financial system.

# *Find The Humanity: Core Curricula of America's Elite Business Schools*

## Wharton

**August Core**

Foundations of Teamwork and Leadership

**Fall and Spring Core**

Financial Accounting

Accelerated Financial Accounting

Fundamentals of Managerial Accounting

Corporate Finance

Macroeconomics and the Global Economic Environment

Accelerated Corporate Finance

The Governmental and Legal Environment of Business

Ethics and Responsibility

Managerial Economics

Management of People at Work

Competitive Strategy

Global Strategic Management

Marketing Management: Program Design

Marketing Management: Strategy

Decision Models and Uncertainty

Operations Management: Quality and Productivity

Operations Management: Supply Chain Management

Statistical Analysis for Management

Management Communication

## Harvard

**Term 1 Courses**

Finance I

Financial Reporting and Control

Leadership and Organizational Behavior

Marketing

Technology and Operations Management

**Term 2 Courses**

Business, Government, and the International Economy

Strategy

The Entrepreneurial Manager

Finance II

Leadership and Corporate Accountability

## FIELD Courses

Field 1

- Individual skill building to develop leadership intelligence
- Leadership exercises, peer feedback, and personal reflection

Field 2

- Globalization, including a required global immersion experience during the January term
- Value creation at the product or service level in a global context

Field 3

- Integrating the course through the design and launch of a microbusiness

# *Ports in a Storm—Investment Books in Defense of History*

The financial crisis and its attendant anxieties led me to read the following books over the past three years:

***The Forgotten Man*, Amity Shlaes**
More than the standard hagiography of FDR and his economic policies, Ms. Shlaes dares to wonder whether the New Deal did more to lengthen the Depression than to shorten it. It would be almost impossible to read her account of the Roosevelt Administration's treatment of large and small businesses alike and not see some passing resemblance to today's regulatory environment.

***The Lords of Finance*, Liaquat Ahamed**
As much as we'd all like to think that an invisible hand will turn the world's economic rudder in the right direction, Ahamed's book reminds us that economic circumstances are often shaped, at least in the short-term, by all-too-human economic policymakers, with their own weaknesses, egos, and conceits.

***The Mystery of Capital*, Hernando de Soto**
The esteemed Peruvian economist explores a central paradox—why does capitalism thrive in some countries and fail miserably in others? Drawing an important distinction between money and capital, de Soto believes title rights and a solid legal foundation are central to the capital formation process.

***The Panic of 1907*, Robert Bruner & Sean Carr**
Perhaps even more interesting because it was written by the dean of one the country's best business schools, this is a highly readable account of a panic so great and dangerous that it led eventually to the formation of the Federal Reserve System in 1913. In the absence of a central bank, one shudders to think what the impact of this crisis might have been without the steady hand of J.P. Morgan.

***Pictures of the Socialistic Future*, Eugene Richter**
Written nearly 60 years before any practical, real-time, example of a socialistic society was evident, historians continue to be amazed at Richter's ability to lamp almost perfectly a society based on equality of outcome rather than equality of opportunity. While a work of fiction, *Pictures* turned out to be remarkably prophetic.

***This Time is Different*, Kenneth Rogoff and Carmen Reinhart**

Somewhat more academic than the other tomes on this list, *This Time is Different* became an instant classic in the study of what happens to societies in the aftermath of credit cycles that happen with such regularity that one wonders if you might actually be able to set your watch to them.

***When Money Dies*, Adam Ferguson**

Perhaps the definitive historical work on the hyperinflation of Weimar Germany, Ferguson poignantly depicts the impact that deficit spending and massive currency devaluation can have on a "developed" society's social fabric.

*Strategas has a more comprehensive reading list for those who are interested.*

# *Facebook and the "Death of Equities"*

*Originally Published—May 25, 2012*

As is often the case on sunny Fridays in the spring and summer, there was a little bit of a circus-like atmosphere on our sales and trading desk last week. It was the end of a long week of travel and client events and our people were content to stay in the office, get some administrative work done, and daydream about the beautiful weekend ahead of them. People were happy and someone conceived of a "call the close" contest for Facebook's IPO. In a rare occurrence, we actually turned the sound up for CNBC and Bloomberg and enjoyed the spectacle of one of the most widely anticipated IPOs in more than a decade. Based on the almost universally breathless comments from the press on this momentous occurrence, it didn't take me too long to realize something I found surprising—*it seemed like almost everyone in our shop was rooting against Mark Zuckerberg and the stock.*

It would be one thing for me to be skeptical of the hoodie and the hype. I was the oldest guy in the room; I still use a briefcase, shave and wear a suit every day of my professional life, and most importantly believe that access to America's capital markets is a privilege rather than a right. It is quite another thing to see 25-year-olds who were recently intense users of Facebook take the under. Part of this can undoubtedly be traced to the human impulse toward envy. After all, as Nobel Prize winning economist Charles Kindelberger put it, there is nothing so disturbing to a man's soul as to see a friend get rich. But I sensed something deeper in the jokes and dark humor about the stock's disappointing debut. It was hard to describe but it might be best summed-up as a certain wistfulness—for the older folks, a sadness for what America once was and for the young people just starting out, a sadness about what they may have to rely upon for their future.

This isn't meant to be an indictment of Mark Zuckerberg or the company. Facebook is a terrific American story and should be celebrated. What seemed off were the plaintive calls of the financial media to see the man and the company as some sort of savior for a global economy still coming to terms with a financial crisis that has, at its core, nearly 60 years of fiscal profligacy. It seemed to be too much pressure to place on a 28-year-old kid and a company whose main role is to entertain rather than educate. With close to $16 trillion in Federal debt financed short-term at an average interest rate of 2.2%, the world's largest economy and only superpower, the inventor of the airplane, the transistor, the telephone, and fast food, America was reduced, it seemed last Friday, to pinning its hopes on a website that, ironically, is banned from use at all of the brokerage firms in the deal.

Revelations about how the IPO was handled on the part of NASDAQ, Morgan Stanley, and the issuer itself have only heightened the public's distrust of Wall Street as an insider's game at a time in which confidence in the markets is sorely lacking. Over the past five years, over $1 trillion has flowed into bond mutual funds while roughly $400 billion has been redeemed from equity funds. Two 50% declines in stocks in the past decade and serial misdeeds on the part of Wall Street and Corporate America have led many individual investors to conclude that they will begin to see a number on their statement that is roughly equivalent to the one they saw the month before. In this environment, it isn't hard to imagine a new "Death of Equities[11]" cover of a weekly news magazine. Herein lies both the immediate risk and the long-term opportunity of stocks. **We are often asked what will lead to a rekindling of the love affair between the public and publicly traded equities. After much thought, it has come down to this—the public will only consider equities once they start to lose money in bonds.** In an era of financial repression, this might take a long time but this moment will arrive just the same.

In the history of human interactions, there are few things more cliché than societies who find themselves in deep fiscal trouble. Sadly, Mark Zuckerberg isn't likely to be the answer to all of what ails us. Generally speaking, there have been four methods through which societies have sought to get themselves out of debt. Up until 1945, going to war was the method of choice. In Roman fashion, a country would wage war on a neighbor and, if successful, take its natural resources and raise taxes on the newly conquered. This approach is considered politically incorrect now, plus Mexico seems scary. War's kissing cousin in dealing with fiscal problems at home was a devaluation of the currency, which, a little bit like drinking alcohol, seems like a great idea at the time but only leads to new and greater problems down the road. Another method, which is often a policy mistake rather than a choice, is deflation. But since standing in the pocket and taking the hit runs counter to the impulses of the modern politician and today's central bankers, the best, yet most difficult to achieve, choice remains growing oneself out of the problem, not with more public spending, but with productivity. Since it can be argued that too much time on the internet does more to diminish productivity than enhance it, America needs something more. A greater reliance on the country's natural blessings of population growth, natural resources, and freedoms might be a good start.

---

11. *BusinessWeek* ran a cover story entitled *The Death of Equities* on August 13,1979.

# *America—Like No Place on Earth*

*Originally Published—June 8, 2012*

In front of a flat screen television in Philadelphia this week, I wondered aloud whether Scott Walker's victory in Wisconsin wasn't in some way a PATCO moment for America—a meaningful signal that the structure of the U.S. economy was changing, and as far as corporate America and by extension the equity markets were concerned, for the better. Hyperbole is at the heart of the media's attempts to make 24-hour news coverage always seem relevant or important and **so one must be careful to draw too many long-term conclusions from the blow to collective bargaining in a traditionally blue state**. But when one pairs this event with the fact that voters in San Diego and San Jose, California also chose to vote down richer pension benefits for state and local workers, it's hard not to believe some underlying trend has been established. Perhaps the sleeping giant of the American taxpayer, sickened by GSA boondoggles, a variety of money-losing gambits on companies like Solyndra, and other examples of corporate welfare and crony capitalism, has been awakened and is now more than a little cranky.

As *The Wall Street Journal* pointed out in an editorial this week, some of the changes that have taken place in Wisconsin since Governor Walker took office are nothing less than stunning. AFSCME membership has dropped from 63,000 to 29,000 in less than two years, an indication that the value proposition of union dues is far less attractive when the union no longer has a monopolistic power to negotiate contracts for state and local employees. **It would be dangerous to extrapolate the events in Wisconsin to a broader mandate for the desire for long-term cuts in Medicare and Social Security**. But, at the margin there seems to be a growing trend for taxpayers to expect value for their tax dollars, expecting their public servants to have a greater interest in the public welfare than in establishing a long and lucrative retirement.

A friend suggested that perhaps the events of the past week were more akin to California's Proposition 13 in 1978. In what many believe to have been an important harbinger for Ronald Reagan's victory in 1980, Howard Jarvis and Paul Gann convinced Golden Staters, increasingly alarmed at the prospects of having to sell their homes to simply pay their property taxes, to write into law limits on the ability of municipalities to continue to levy ever-increasing assessments on homeowners. Proposition 13 is still extraordinarily controversial in California to this day although most concede that is was one of the first important battles in the taxpayer revolt movement.

If these developments in Wisconsin and California are any indication of the general electorate's desire for reform, there is some hope that the long-awaited bottom in valuations is at hand. Assured that they have seen the zenith of the uncertainty surrounding capital formation, companies might start to regain enough confidence to make long-term plans to turn their vast cash hoards (which are inert) into capital which, one hopes, is productive. **Recent events should also be seen as an unalloyed positive for the future of municipal finances, although these will need to be fought town by town and county by county.**

While France appears to have learned a different lesson from the current near-death experience of the devolution of the Euro by lowering the retirement age from 62 to 60 just this week, The Steiger Amendment from the 1970s and union reform in the bluest of blue states today confirms that political miracles are still possible in America. While it is virtually impossible to imagine large groups of people in Rome or Athens or Madrid rallying to defend the benefits of limited government, there are still millions of Americans, lacking cynicism, who believe firmly in the founding principles of this country and, nearly 250 years after its birth, are still willing to fight for them. The desire to deal with long-term structural problems before they metastasize into incurable ones is ultimately this country's great and unique strength. Despite its blemishes, the U.S. is still the greatest show on Earth.

# *The Palio Factor*

*Originally Published—July 13, 2012*

As loyal readers of these pages know, my family and I take a week every July and visit the same seaside resort in Italy to reconnect with our heritage, take a break from work and school, and become reacquainted with one another after what is usually an exhausting first half of the year. Superstitious to a fault and possessing a great respect for the Fates, I approached my annual trip this year with a sense of foreboding, wondering whether my arrival would be accompanied with the type of vicious and rapid market sell-off that greeted me last year. My fears weren't eased when Delta Airlines lost my luggage (naturally, my wife's *bags* showed up a.o.k.). Years of experience traveling to the old country left me with only some vague hope that any would-be thief would take a look at the size of my clothing, feel guilty about robbing someone with an obvious pituitary problem, and return them. As luck would have it, my lost luggage did show up two days later, but only after I was forced to buy certain essentials in a town that isn't remotely acquainted with the idea of every-day low prices. 500 euro later and I was the proud owner of a pocket t-shirt, a pair of pleatless shorts, and a bathing suit that constricted my prostate in ways I never thought possible. Wondering whether I had somehow mistakenly bought a beautifully tailored and colorful truss and possessing a new appreciation for falsetto in tow, I proceeded to wander about the town and talk to my old friends among the local population. My conversations were all dominated by what one might describe as the ascendancy of the three Marios—Monti, Draghi, and Balotelli, two economists and a soccer star of Ghanaian descent—who all signaled what was perceived to be Italy's growth as a society and its importance in the European Union.

My fears about a market sell-off were almost immediately put to rest when yet another summit (the 19th by our count) produced an agreement for the European Stability Mechanism to inject money directly into troubled banks rather than having to funnel it through its constituent national governments. Certainly this was one step closer to European integration but it was a far cry from a Eurobond solution that had the potential to kick the can not only down the road but perhaps down the autobahn. A 7% rally in the FTSE Mibtel on the last day of the quarter led many Italian newspapers to treat the agreement with a sense of euphoria, one going so far as to say that Germany had suffered two consecutive losses to the Italians in as many days—one on the football pitch on Thursday, the other in the halls of Eurozone headquarters in Brussels the day after. Italy, of course, subsequently lost to Spain, but the pride lingered, perhaps because both the *azzurri* and Mario Monti had achieved far more than what anyone had thought likely.

Since my trip last year, talk of "lo spread," or the basis point differential between 10-year German Bunds and Italian BTPs, has become ubiquitous in the popular culture and is now often used as short-hand for all of the attendant anxieties of a financial crisis that is almost four years old. Our favorite town is hanging in there economically, mainly because it is supported by Italians who are price inelastic and Russians whose fortunes are tied to the price of oil. The local merchants are accustomed to having their fortunes tied to the vicissitudes of the global financial markets but there is little question that things haven't been the same since the financial crisis started.

Italians are a warm and fun people but nowhere on Earth will you find strangers so willingly disposed to letting you know just how tired they are of the fecklessness of their own elected officials. Complaining about the political process, and finding ways to circumvent the sometimes-capricious nature of its legislation is, in many ways, second only to soccer as a national pastime. A unified Italy, it should be remembered, is itself a relatively new concept, achieved ultimately only in 1861, the product of an older, yet more successful, political and currency union brought about by Garibaldi. Great differences, polictically, economically, and culturally, between the northern and southern parts of this beautiful peninsula and its large islands persist. To this day, it is rare but not unheard of to find those who believe the *Risorgimento* was an act of colonization rather than of unification. I am no expert on European politics or culture, but I've been regularly visiting Italy for 40 years and know enough about its people, culture, and mores to know that, after nearly two millenia of misplaced confidences in politicians, the distrust of the political elite is almost atavistic among Italians. If there is a political infrastructure the average Italian distrusts more than his own, it is one in Brussels that seeks to make policies that cover 500 million people among 27 disparate countries who, until about 70 years ago, had been relentlessly at war with one another for centuries. And so it becomes clear that the Euro was always the product of the desires of a political elite that altruistically sought to eliminate war rather than any grass roots desire on the part of the average citizen to seek some undefined concept of a Greater Europe.

Despite the wishes of an academic and political class to eliminate any traces of the nationalism that so injured the Continent throughout history, the latest summit and my observations did little to convince me that nationalistic tendencies are on the wane. Lest one think that such tendencies are a thing of the past, I can't say that I was all that surprised to see a magazine article about a group of Roman merchants who have started to issue their own scrip as an alternative to the Euro. A greater indication of the growing resentment of the populace towards its elected officials has been the political phenomenon of Beppe Grillo, a comedian so disgusted with politics that he started his own political party, the Five Star Movement, that is dedicated, as near as I can tell, to little other than being a recepticle for protest votes from other Italians who feel the same way. People didn't take him or his nihilistic message all that seriously until he started winning. More than 250 *Grillini* have been elected to local political posts across the country.

Ultimately, there was nothing that summed up my dim hopes for the sustainability of the Euro better than the spectacle of Italy's most famous horse race, Siena's medieval Palio. Held continuously since 1656 on July 2nd in honor of Madonna of Provenzano and August 16th in honor of the Assumption of Mary, the Palio may be one of the most brutal and vicious, yet beautiful, contests in all of sports. Remarkably, this relatively small city of 54,000 boasts 17 separate districts that each possess their own allies and archenemies. There are few lengths to which each of the city's districts won't go to win the race and incidents of bribery, blood doping, and post race violence are not only common but expected. And one has to wonder, if the citizens of an ancient walled city of 54,000 can't get along, what chance does Europe as a whole have?

# *Desperately Seeking Political Inevitabilities*

*Originally Published—October 9, 2012*

Given the messiness of the democratic process in the 21st century, one could be forgiven for wondering whether the consent of the governed is slowly but surely being overwhelmed by a 24-hour news cycle, endless snap polls, and never-ending political spin. At our election conference in New York a month ago, legendary pollster Scott Rasmussen, aside from preventing many of our Republican guests from hurtling themselves into traffic in despair, made one elegant and hopeful comment about America that resonated with our audience above all others—our people are always far ahead of our politicians. Whether it was the Stamp Act, the Declaration of Independence, or the Civil Rights movement in the '50s and '60s, the politicians have often shown themselves woefully inadequate at leading the people in the important secular issues of the day. It has been the voters that have elected politicians to reflect their will on a variety of economic, political, and social issues throughout history.

In thinking about the broad array of policy issues facing voters here and abroad, I started to wonder where the citizens of the world might be ahead of their elected officials and what investment implications that might have. In some ways, it's more obvious in Europe, where the Euro may be one of the greatest examples in the history of democracy of an "eat your peas" approach to governing in which an entrenched political elite with expensive tastes has strong-armed its people to do something they really never wanted to do in the first place. For those interested or hopelessly bored, the English version of the German weekly magazine *Der Spiegel* is often a good read and gives the average ugly American some insight into the hearts and minds of Europeans, or, well, German Europeans anyway. And so it was that, at the suggestion of a friend and a client, I read an article that listed, in almost stereotypical German fashion, the most "dangerous" politicians for the survivability of the Euro, a conglomeration of both famous and obscure somewhat-extreme elected officials from both the left and the right. What was most striking about the list of politicians who populated the list were their ages. With the exception of Silvio Berlusconi, who—as we all know—likes to associate himself with younger people, these Euroskeptics were all virtually youngsters between the ages of 38 and 50.

The broader point of this, it seemed to me, was that the political elite that was most insistent in creating their Utopian vision of greater Europe in which war would be impossible is now in the twilight of its political influence. Younger generations of Europeans who have not seen the horrors of a land war on the Continent have no such yearning to create yet another layer of bureaucracy from which a variety of rules, regulations, and taxes come not from their local capitals but from Brussels. A lifetime of traveling to Italy has taught me that the regional differences in countries that outsiders see as unified are so great that the concept of greater Europe seems an absurd fiction. It's hard enough to get many Italians to describe themselves as Italian, much less European. Garibaldi's "Italy" was only unified in 1861, it should be remembered. Sadly, we see more and more examples of regionalism in Europe every day—in just the last two months, we have seen the wealthier regions of Catalonia in Spain and Wallonia in Belgium seek greater independence if not outright secession. The greater point in all this is that when times get tough, there is a natural human impulse to become more provincial, not more cosmopolitan.

**Der Spiegel: Europe's 10 Most Dangerous Politicians**

| | Name | Age | Position |
|---|---|---|---|
| 1. | Alexis Tsipras | 38 | Leader of Greece's leftist Syriza party |
| 2. | Markus Söder | 45 | Bavarian Finance Minister |
| 3. | Silvio Berlusconi | 76 | Former Italian Prime Minister |
| 4. | Marine Le Pen | 44 | Leader of the Far-Right Front National in France |
| 5. | Timo Soini | 50 | Leader of the True Finns Party, Member of European Parliament |
| 6. | Alexander Dobrindt | 42 | General Secretary of Conservative Bavarian Christian Social Union (CSU) |
| 7. | Nigel Farage | 48 | Leader of U.K. Independence Party (UKIP), Member of European Parliament |
| 8. | Heinz-Christian Strache | 43 | Head of Austrian Freedom Party |
| 9. | Geert Wilders | 49 | Head of the Dutch Freedom Party |
| 10. | Viktor Orbán | 49 | Hungarian Prime Minister |

And so one wonders what the future of the single currency concept will be in a period in which the virtues of the Euro are difficult to discern for the average Hans, Pablo, or Spiros on the streets of the Continent. Strategas' Chief Economist, Don Rissmiller, has only half-joked that the "good outcome" for Europe may be, ultimately, that it becomes Japan—that is to say, the Eurozone stays intact but its standard of living erodes slowly over a long period of time. For the aforementioned political elite on the Continent, this might be seen as an acceptable trade-off for peace. The problem, of course, is that sooner or later, the people themselves may have a different vision of their own future. My business trips to Japan over the years have led me to believe that it would be hard to translate the word *kamikaze*, in spirit and meaning, into any romance language. While the Land of the Rising Sun is made up of a single, largely xenophobic culture in which social conformity stands as a virtue, Western Civilization is different. The same impulse that has made it so great—an unshakeable belief and respect for the rights of the individual—also stands as the Euro's long-term Achilles' Heel. In the short-term—say, over the next few years—it would make little sense to fade the survivability of the Euro—the fix, as they say, is in. The Continent's elected officials are committed to preserving the currency, and the ECB has made it clear, practically speaking, that its balance sheet will swell to whatever size is necessary to preserve it. No, the great risk to this grand experiment will come in the future, perhaps well into the future, at the ballot box.

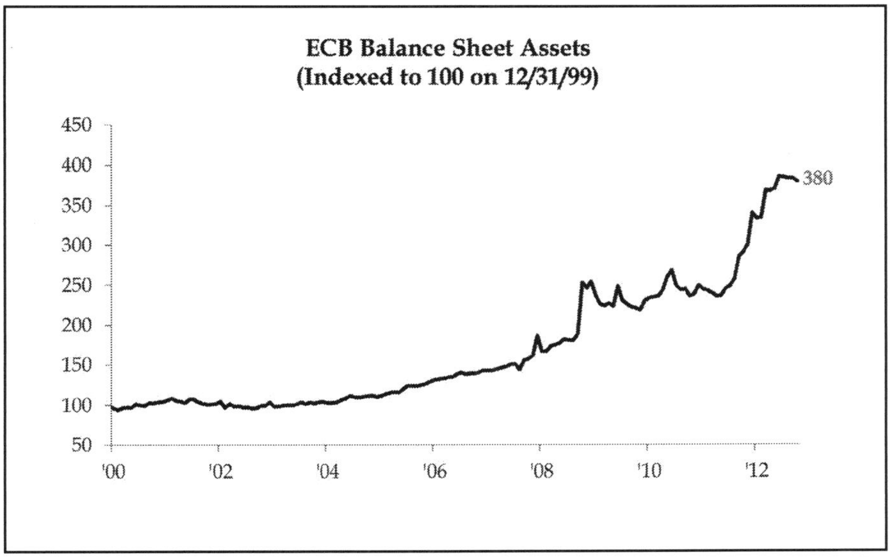


While it can be argued that the stakes of our current Presidential election are high, Americans, mercifully, face no such existential questions about their future. Still, there is one issue with broad economic and financial market implications in which the public seems well ahead of its elected officials—the use of natural gas and its potential to render the country energy independent. Of all the structural problems facing the U.S. economy, the most serious and most difficult to correct in terms of our future growth may simply be the fact that, three years after the financial crisis, we are still overwhelmingly and dangerously dependent upon consumption. Popularly defined as the sum of Consumption, Capital Spending, Government Expenditures, and Net Exports, or GDP=C+I+G+(X-M), many institutional investors are surprised to learn that nearly 71% of America's GDP is still driven by consumer spending. Given all the economic and financial drama in the context of significantly higher unemployment over the past few years, our continued dependence upon consumer spending may seem hard to fathom. This is, of course, until one considers how much "G" (or government spending) was used to support "C" (or consumption) over the past few years. Whether it was a tax credit for first time homebuyers, cash for clunkers, or cash for caulkers, the Administration's solution, it seems, was to prescribe as medicine largely what got us sick in the first place. At least for now, the odds of using fiscal policy to smooth out any future economic weakness are exceedingly long regardless of who wins the election three weeks from now. In the future, economic growth in the U.S., it would be safe to assume, will be far more dependent upon capital spending and exports (I and X) if we'd like to grow.

There's nothing wrong with this, of course. This is an approach to economic growth that served us well in the decades immediately following the end of World War II. The problem now, however, is that less than 15% of our economy is in manufacturing and, unlike in the postwar period, our global competition in this sphere is steep. Given the size of our debts and unfunded liabilities, growing our way out of our structural problems may be the only effective way of dealing with them. The way America chooses to grow also has important implications for the social fabric of the nation. As the chart below shows, there is a yawning gap between the unemployment rates of those who are college-educated and those who are not. At 4%, the unemployment rate for those with a college degree remains remarkably low. Those without a high school diploma, on the other hand, are three times as likely to be unemployed and face an unemployment rate of 11%. For some, such a discrepancy leads to a rather pat belief that everyone should pursue higher education. This is, without question, a consummation devoutly to be wished but seems unrealistic in a country of 310 million people. Maintaining a large and vibrant middle class was less of an issue 40 years ago when those who didn't get a college education could earn a nice living in manufacturing. As many of these activities were offshored, many of these same people could work in the trades supporting housing in the '80s, '90s, and first part of the '00s. Unfortunately, as it stands now, there is no natural industry to soak up such a large population of potential workers.

While it could be claimed that there is potentially no shortage of candidates for the role of America's leading industry, the most obvious, it would seem, would be to take advantage of the vast natural resources with which America has been blessed. With natural gas prices hovering around $3.30 in the U.S. and LNG prices of $18 in the world's third largest economy, Japan, the market's invisible hand is screaming for domestic production of natural gas for export. While

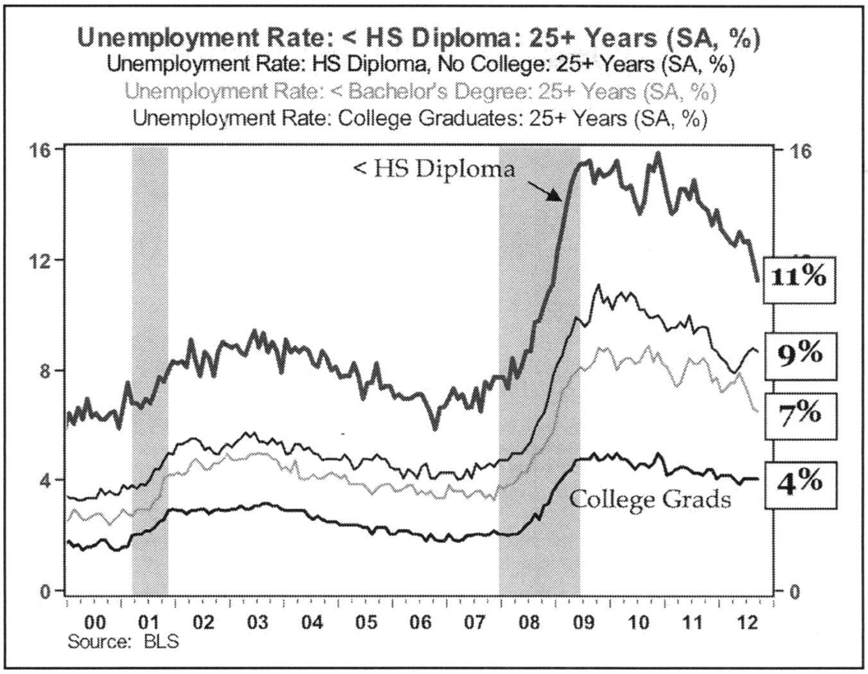


**Population Breakdown by Education (25 Years & Over, 2011)**

| | Thous | % Total |
|---|---|---|
| Less than HS Diploma | 25,040 | 12% |
| HS Grads, No College | 61,911 | 31% |
| Less than Bach. Degree | 53,250 | 26% |
| College Graduates | 61,343 | 30% |
| | 201,543 | 100% |

the U.S. has fewer than 60 billion barrels of proved natural gas reserves (only about 4-5% of the world's total), the Department of Energy has estimated that nearly 400 billion barrels are recoverable using existing technologies. Of course, drilling can be controversial and there are environmental concerns which must be balanced with the desire for economic growth. But here, too, the polling suggests that the American public is far more in favor of shale gas as a potential step-function productivity enhancement for the country than are its political power brokers. While there is very little daylight between Republican A and Republican B when it comes to energy policy—that is to say, it's a "drill baby drill" party—the differences among Democrats are far greater. While there is no doubt a large and vocal environmental lobby within the party, there are also large numbers of rank-and-file union Democrats in blue states that poll almost exactly like Republicans when it comes to the issues of fracking and energy independence. In this regard, there may be far more bipartisan support for greatly exploiting our natural resources to create a vibrant export industry or to make our own manufacturing more competitive than is popularly believed.

The answers to these weighty issues will come, as they say, in God's time. This might not make them investable in the short-term, but for those with truly long-term time horizons, it would seem that European equities might be a value trap while U.S. stocks an incredible bargain.

# *The Fiscal Cliff Through the Eyes of a Small Company*

*Originally Published—November 16, 2012*

My partners and I often joke that if we were really lynx-eyed forecasters, we would have been far too afraid to start our new venture in September of 2006, on the precipice of the financial crisis and an intergalactic bear market. The irony, it turned out, was that dislocations in the economy turned into an opportunity for a little company doing macro research. Long/short hedge funds in particular had become accustomed to being able to be wildly successful without needing to know much about the Fed, interest rates, inflation, or Washington's shadow over the financial markets. That all changed when Bear Stearns failed. We survived and at times have prospered. We have 45 people now in research, sales, trading, and operations, with offices in New York and Washington. Along the way, we started a trading desk and became a broker/dealer, which was a good move, and established an office in Geneva, which was not. We've learned more about financial regulation (and, incidentally, attorneys' fees) than we ever thought possible. As part of the normal course of business, we've been audited by both FINRA and the SEC with clean bills of health at the cost, mainly, of untold man-hours to make sure that we were in compliance and had enough documentation to prove it. It's all been part of the great parade of entrepreneurship, and I wouldn't have traded any of it for a minute.

We've also learned quite a bit about managing employee benefits, and the increasing volatility in the costs associated with them. We pay 80% of our colleagues' health care premiums for adequate although admittedly unexceptional health care coverage. We do the best we can with the resources we have. In each of the last two years, we received letters informing us that the health care premiums for our employees would increase by 18% and 24%, respectively. That immediately led us to cast about for cheaper coverage with, it can be assumed, an inferior standard of care at some point in the future. Ultimately, our premiums went up an average of 6% each year, about three times the rate of inflation, if one ignores the time, effort, and stress associated with changing coverage. We can afford to continue to pay for private insurance now, but I'd be lying if I said with confidence that we would never consider paying the government "fine" if it ever turned out that we could not.

And so here we are now, contemporaneously commentators and participants in the drama that has become the debate over the fiscal cliff. We have been consistent in our belief that an avoidance of most of the cliff categorically did *not* mean that there would be no fiscal drag next year. As it stands now, an opening bid for the drag would be $185 billion in 2013 (an expiration of the payroll tax cut and extended unemployment insurance benefits plus the stipulated tax increases on capital gains, etc.), although it takes less than an active imagination to see the price tag reach $266 billion if one assumes only that marginal tax rates are raised for those making over $250,000 per year. The sky is currently filled with enough trial balloons about the potential resolution of the fiscal cliff to blot out the sun. Of the four ways government can principally influence the economy for better or worse—fiscal policy, regulation, monetary policy, and trade—it appears that investors will continue to be forced to rely on monetary policy for help. Taxes will undoubtedly rise for some, and the one effective way the federal government could effectively ease more—regulatory policy—seems less likely now than ever before. The Wall Street law firm Davis Polk has created a new business of simply keeping track of the seemingly infinite number of rules that will need to be written to complete the process of financial regulation put into place by Dodd-Frank. Sadly, only 33% of the 398 required rulemakings have been finalized. (Only 265 rules to go!) Another 33% have yet to have even been proposed. Is it any wonder the Fed has had trouble turning excess reserves into effective monetary stimulus?

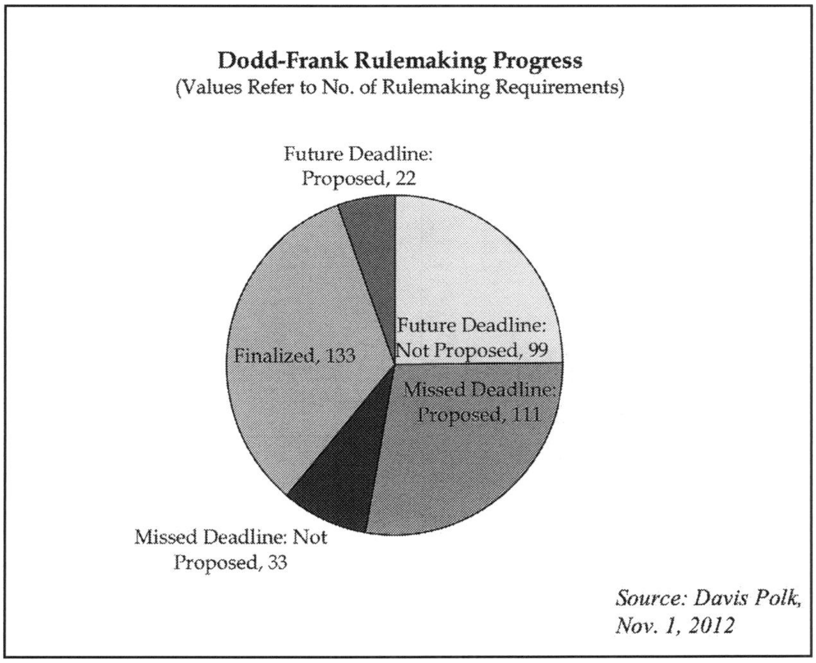


What are we doing as a company in light of this uncertainty? We've put on hold business expenses short of pencils, and any capital spending we were considering, including an update of the men's bathroom some have begun to call "the latrine." Instead of calling clients and focusing on our research, we are scheduling, probably in vain, conference calls (read fees) with our attorneys and accountants to try to create contingencies against potentially bad outcomes for us in the tax code. It has forced us to ask ourselves questions that seem at odds with economic growth, like, are there any unintended consequences of employing more than 50 people?

If there has been a myth that seems to have been perpetuated during the Presidential campaign about business owners, it seems to me, it's that we all whistle into work every day, arrive, have our secretary bring us a cup of coffee, and promptly light a cigar with a $20 bill. All this without any concerns whatsoever about our competitors, the welfare of our employees, the needs of our clients, new entrants into our industry, the opportunity costs of roads not taken, or an innumerate variety of initiatives from regulators and tax collectors. It's hard not to think, at times, that Andy Grove was right when he said that "only the paranoid survive." Being a competent businessman these days, much less a good one, is largely an exercise in near-constant anxiety punctuated by less frequent episodes of joy and disappointment. Business owners are at times well-paid for their efforts, but it is naïve to believe that they feel for a moment that their financial futures are secure. Perhaps we're too close to the "cliff" conceptually to be objective about its impacts on our business. Maybe we'll be lucky and it will largely be a non-event. But I can say that in the six years we've run our business, we've never felt confident enough to buy green bananas. Until we know what the rules of the game are, we're unlikely to buy any bananas at all.

# *The Euro's Achilles' Heel—Democracy*

*Originally Published—March 22, 2013*

No one can doubt the noble intentions and sincerity of Europe's political elite when it first hatched the idea of a single currency in the aftermath of World War II. After all, atavistic, almost tribal, impulses among the many nations of the Continent had led to unfathomable human suffering for hundreds of years. Like many of the best laid plans of man, however, the Euro has started to reveal itself to have a tragic flaw—the consent of the governed, the latest examples being the reemergence of Silvio Berlusconi and the emergence of Beppe Grillo's 5 Star Movement as political players in the world's 6th largest economy and the recent rejection by Cyprus' parliament of a "deposit tax" imposed upon the tiny island nation's by the greater euro zone. While German politicians have patronizingly derided Grillo and Berlusconi as "clowns" and pushed the deposit scheme in Cyprus as a necessary discipline to maintain the viability of the currency union, an objective outside observer might see them simply as reflections, symptoms really, of the unfulfilled promises of a currency regime that, if truth be told, was never all that popular with the people in the first place. The realistic must, at a certain point, recognize that the longer a true economic recovery in Europe remains elusive, the harder it will be to convince the man on the street that the concept of a greater Europe is in his own best interests.

While the Euro has weakened meaningfully in recent weeks, it has strengthened meaningfully versus the dollar since ECB President Draghi warned the global financial markets that the central bank had the wherewithal to deal with any and all future liquidity crises. His "believe me, it will be enough" speech on July 26th put the low in the Euro by removing, at least for a time, the existential threats surrounding the single currency. Interestingly enough, the mere mention of further easing proved to be enough to keep the markets in line. In contrast to the balance sheets of the Fed, the Bank of Japan, and the Swiss National Bank, the amount of assets on the ECB's balance sheet has actually declined in recent months, another culprit in the Euro's strength. With Eurozone unemployment reaching previously unforeseen heights and few truly pro-growth fiscal solutions from European politicians on the horizon, one wonders whether the currency will be the only escape valve for Europe's sclerotic economy. Sadly, nary a word has been heard on either side of the Atlantic about lowering taxes or regulation on business nor has any policy emerged that had even a passing chance of increasing private sector production while shrinking the demands of an ever-growing public sector. While the fix may be in for the short-term to save the Euro via interminable monetary accommodation, the longer-term risks of a rupture within the European Union appear only to be increasing.

As he is a comedian by trade, it is easy to lampoon Italy's Beppe Grillo and his grillini as "clowns." But earning 25% of the vote in a country of 60 million people is no easy task and is unlikely to be a fluke. His "grillini" tend to be well-educated young men and women who have become dissatisfied with the career politicians that serve them and point to broader demographic cracks within Europe. An example of these schisms may have first been revealed in the German weekly Der Spiegel last summer when it published its list of Europe's "most dangerous politicians" when it came to the future of the Euro. What was striking to the casual observer of the article was how young all of the Euro-skeptics were in comparison to the political elites charged with saving it. That is to say, younger generations for whom a land war in Europe now seems an abstraction don't feel the same need to lash their fortunes to the mast of foreign peoples who largely share only a common geography. Europe's historical balkanization should encourage the political elites interested in the survivability of a single currency in Europe to stop deriding those who disagree with them and start taking seriously the sources of their frustration. Only economic growth through structural reform will satisfy the concerns of the people about the unintended consequences of the single currency.

# *The Match Gets Closer—The Potential for a Melt-Up in Financials*

*Originally Published—May 10, 2013*

Chairman Bernanke has been nothing if not unambiguous. In stark contrast with his predecessor, who seemed to take unusual pleasure in being opaque, "Helicopter" Ben has been remarkably consistent and clear: if a central bank faces the uncomfortable choice between inflation and deflation, it should always choose the path of inflation, so much easier to control, the thinking goes, than the alternative. Scrambling for a solution to a financial crisis in modern democracies deathly afraid of pain or catharsis, the Chairman has been calling audibles, not just to his own team, but to everyone on the field and in the stadium. Quantitative easing sounds just technical enough to obfuscate the nature, and the consequences, of expanding a central bank's balance sheet with complete transparency. With the benefit of hindsight, Bernanke appears to have made the right call—five years after the financial crisis and it still appears as if the greater risk for the global economy remains deflation. But while the gas tank of excess reserves appears to be a safe distance away from "the single spark that can light a prairie fire," there are some signs today that the match of animal spirits may be getting closer to igniting a new credit cycle. While this may eventually result in higher final goods prices, the more immediate result may, in fact, be ever-higher prices for riskier financial assets, especially the common stocks of financial institutions forced to take more risk in an era of financial repression.

As our chief economist Don Rissmiller has pointed out, the "normal" progression of inflation goes something like this: an increase in money growth leads to higher incomes which then leads to higher final goods prices which then eventually leads to higher prices of financial assets. In the current cycle, excess money growth has been transmitted almost directly to the inflation of financial assets, ironically exacerbating the income disparity so often used as the primary argument to seek expansionary monetary and fiscal policies. Without the growth in incomes, final goods price inflation has been anemic, except of course for those items, like, let's say like massive condominiums in New York, which benefit from the wealth effect from rising securities prices.

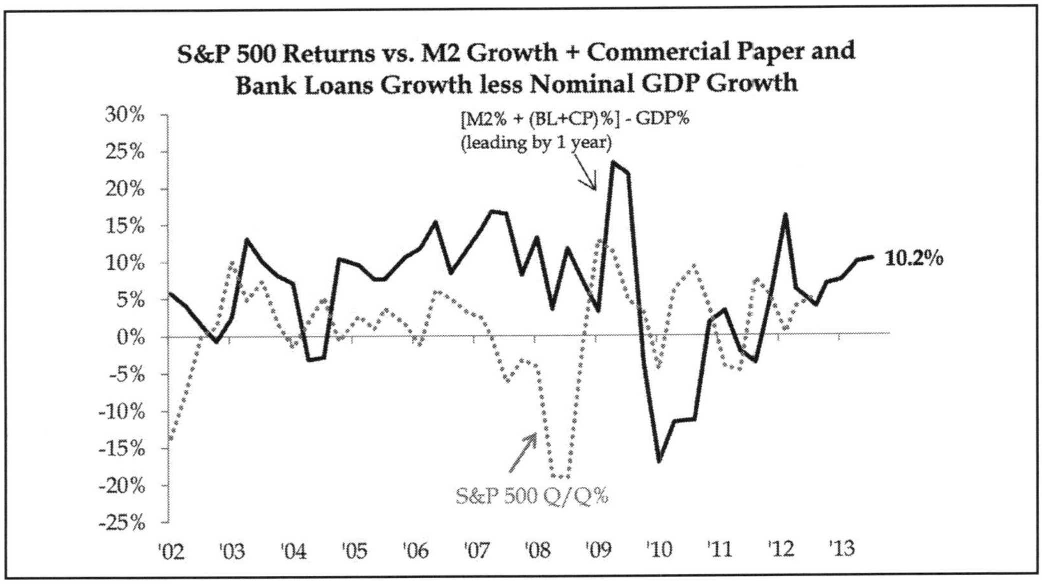


Consistent readers of our work know that "financial repression" the basis for our belief that equities will continue to benefit from the T.I.N.A. factor (there is no alternative). The term was first coined at Stanford in the 1970s and was recently popularized by Carmen Reinhart. Despite its rather ominous and highfalutin sound, the term is simply used to identify the practice of sovereign debtors in the modern era to use any and all means necessary pay negative real interest on their own debt, *regardless of the rate of inflation*. After World War II, the U.S. employed interest rate caps for this purpose. Today, it appears, the Fed is the instrument of this approach—Chairman Bernanke and his merry band of central bankers have bought about 60% of the net new issuance of Treasurys in just the last two years. **The net result of financial repression is that investors must take more**

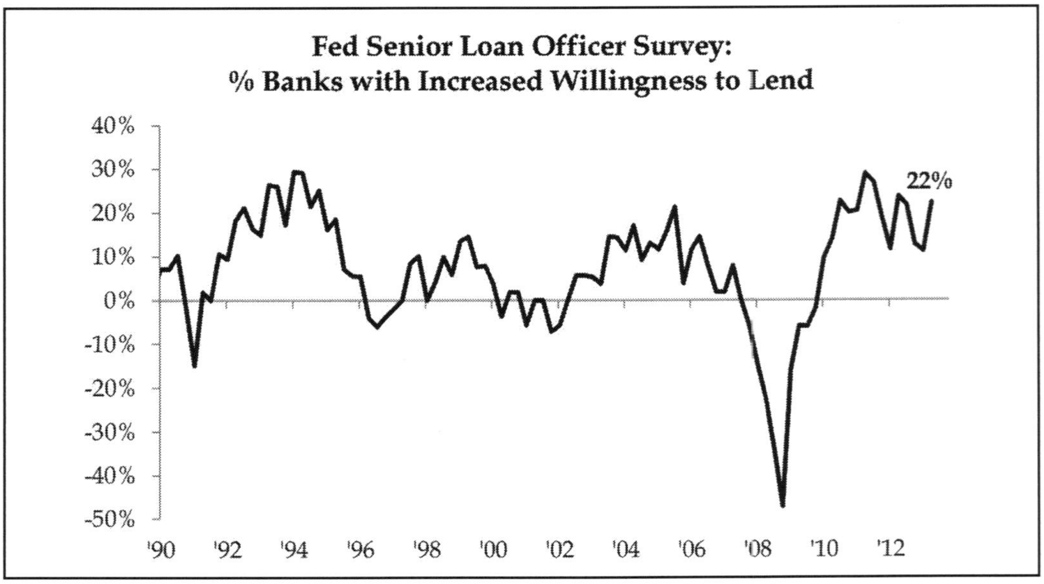

**risk to achieve the same return. Perhaps more importantly, banks too must take more risk to maintain the same level of profitability.** While the wholesale cost of funding remains near zero, the ability of banks and other financial institutions to play the yield curve has become more difficult as long-term interest rates have fallen.

Of course, in a fractional reserve system, loan growth is the basis for monetary expansion. Commercial and Industrial loans have strengthened meaningfully as have auto loans. If there are laggards in loan portfolios they remain tied to housing. Mortgage lending has started to bottom but home equity lending, often the source of funding for small businesses, is still declining sequentially. Given the degree of new and yet-to-be-written regulatory reform for the industry, not to mention the fact that the searingly difficult experiences of the financial crisis are still fresh in the minds of financial executives, it is not surprising that banks have been less than eager to risk making the same mistakes that got them into this mess in the first place. But while the mind may be willing to be prudent, the flesh, in our view, will be weak. (We thought we were in an alternative universe a few weeks ago when we heard President Obama imploring banks to ease their lending standards.) This week's Fed Senior Loan Officers Survey suggests that, little by little, banks are becoming more comfortable with the idea of taking on more risk.

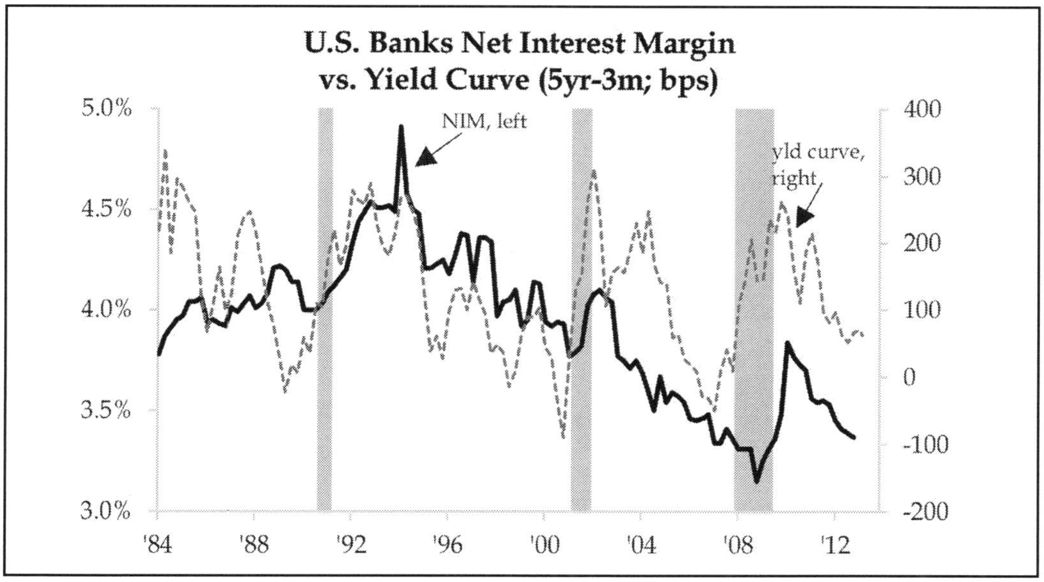


While financial repression is likely to remain a relentless impetus to expand lending, there are other reasons why we are having an intense internal debate about the virtues of going overweight a sector that has caused so much pain. They include:

1. The economy is improving at precisely the time banks may need to lower their lending standards

2. With housing prices bottoming, banks have probably over-reserved for bad loans

3. Aside from the big money center banks, the sector may be the most inoculated from financial problems abroad

4. The stocks are "cheap" by historical price-to-book metrics

5. Excessive and still-murky regulatory environment is likely to prompt a wave of consolidation, especially among smaller regional banks

Wall Street law firm Davis Polk has calculated that only 37% of the rules that must be written as a result of Dodd-Frank have actually been completed. As then Federal Reserve Governor Kevin Warsh put it in a speech in 2008, the concept of liquidity has less to do with the availability of capital and much more to do with the concept of confidence. Confidence takes time. As a result we have decided to punt for the time being, maintaining a market weight in the sector with an eye to overweighting it at the slightest indication that regulatory burdens may ease. Strategas' President and Sector Strategist Nicholas Bohnsack favors regional banks with simple business models and a local focus over the larger Wall Street Diversifieds. He has noted that when the sector is performing in-line with the market, outperformance is generally found further down the capitalization spectrum. More specifically, Regional Banks will likely face less scrutiny and fewer regulatory restrictions than their larger counterparts.

# *A Lax Dad's Lament*

*Originally Published—May 24, 2013*

> *"Actually a pretty nice little Saturday, we're going to go to Home Depot. Yeah, buy some wallpaper, maybe get some flooring, stuff like that. Maybe Bed, Bath, & Beyond, I don't know, I don't know if we'll have enough time."*
>
> *Frank the Tank from the movie Old School*

So, while I had the good fortune of traveling to my beloved Italy last week for a conference with two Fed Presidents (they don't known when the Fed will exit QE either, by the way), I can't say that it was exactly a milk run. Over two and a half days, my colleagues and I traveled from Newark to Frankfurt to Milan and were jammed with meetings with precious little time for much leisure. I arrived home on Friday afternoon, exhausted, and I got reacquainted with my family to prepare for another journey the next day—to the annual Eli Jamboree Youth Lacrosse Tournament in beautiful New Haven, Connecticut. I love spending time with my son and I love watching him play lacrosse but I must admit that I have asked myself on more than one occasion why, as a resident of a metropolitan area of more than 12 million people, I have to travel anywhere for a 10-year-old to play competitive athletics. But such is life as a parent these days. The good news, of course, is that the "Jamboree" starts at 8:30, which for a city resident meant that we needed to be in the car by 6:15 if we had any real chance of being there 45 minutes before game time, a team rule. No sense in getting any more rest than I need to, plenty of time to sleep in the afterlife. The "Jamboree" is well-organized, but it involves 7 short games on any one of 8 fields, requiring the parents, caravan-like, to lug equipment, donuts, and Gatorade for 22 boys from field to field over the next four hours. Dead-tired, I was sleep-walking most of the time. But the boys played well and I did have something to which I could look forward; I was going to reward myself with a trip to, it is claimed, one of the best pizzerias in the country after the games had ended.

And so, after the tournament was over, my son Dominic and I walked back to the car parked at the Yale Bowl, I opened the trunk, put all his gear in the car, and proceeded to do something I hadn't done since I was in high school—I locked the keys in the vehicle. Of course, when I did this a quarter century ago, I used a metal wire hanger to jimmy the door open and I was on my way within a half-hour. An annoyance, but hardly something that would ruin your day. Regretfully, fancy

Teutonic automobiles don't take too kindly to jimmying of any kind these days, and, through a comedy of errors, I found myself with a car in "lock down" mode. The famed manufacturer's Roadside Assistance, I was to find out, was neither roadside nor particularly assistant. The car disabled, I was informed after about 45 minutes of talking to a variety of pulseless individuals and soulless automated prompts that my only options were to either stay in a hotel so a key could be FedEx-ed to me the next day—again in New Haven—or have the car towed to one of two dealers, neither of which would have a service department open on Saturday to help me out. Getting home from there would be up to me. This was shaping up to be a beautiful little Saturday, let me tellya. About an hour later, Louie's Towing (a pseudonym for reasons that will become apparent) showed up to take the car to a dealer that wouldn't help me until Monday. (A quick reminder, towing an all-wheel drive is harder than towing front or rear wheel suspensions.) Fed up, and requiring more patience of a 10-year-old than I had a right to, I asked Louie how much it would cost to tow the car all the way back to the City. His eyes lit up like a child's on Christmas morning.

*"Five bucks a mile plus a dollar a mile for the axles plus tolls."*

Ok, so we're 73 miles away and it's going to be about $500 bucks, a reasonable price for my stupidity.

*"Done."*

So Dom and I hopped in the cab of this guy's truck, got acquainted with his pit bull "Hammy," and proceeded to put the hammer down on one of the most beautiful and traffic-less highways in the lower 48—I-95. Hammy's "spot" was where passengers would normally put their feet and, not wishing to anger him, we decided to put our legs on the dashboard. Louie speaks at a decibel level that would be reasonable, let's say, on the deck of an aircraft carrier, and we were, over the next two and a half hours, regaled with stories about a variety of bar fights, lawsuits, ex-wives, and jail. Classic Vinyl was cranking in the background and every once in a while Louie would take a call on speaker from any number of characters and degenerates that would tell him their stories about various bar fights, lawsuits, ex-wives, and jail, many of which would earn an NC-17 rating. Did anyone else know that the Triborough Bridge charges double for commercial vehicles plus additional tolls for each extra axle? Yep, the last knee to my coin purse was forking over a $31 toll to the Port Authority. Good times.

And so, we arrived home, exhausted, about six hours later, and I poured myself a Jack Daniel's and thought, as I am wont to do after such episodes, about what I could learn from the day as it relates to investing and business. I came to a simple conclusion—no product is strong enough or exclusive enough to withstand lousy service. My automobile is the sum result of more than 100 years of institutional knowledge, superior engineering, and masterful design. Thousands of people had a hand in its construction and it is clearly a testament to human genius and progress. Sadly, all of that was ruined by the fact that there wasn't a single human being on the other end of the phone willing to help out a customer in need, despite promises to the contrary at the point of sale. And I thought about my own business and vowed to make sure we never lose a customer through the unforced error of indifferent service. Constructing a product people want to buy is difficult and not easily replicable. Good customer service is easy in comparison, it simply requires effort. It is a wonder, then, why so few companies, especially on Wall Street, place any emphasis on it. And so I'd like to ask all of you who have read this piece thus far to call me right away if you ever find yourself unsatisfied with our service at Strategas on any issue no matter how small. Have a wonderful Memorial Day weekend.

# *Raiders in White Hats Shareholder Activism as an Investable Theme*

*Originally Published—June 7, 2013*

Perhaps it's a foolish consistency on our part, but we believe that all the hand wringing and gnashing of teeth with regard to Fed tapering is premature. By continuing to increase the size of its balance sheet, the Fed is, after all, easing aggressively. Recent economic data would suggest that the chances of deflation are just as likely as inflation and Chairman Bernanke has been steadfast in his adherence to financial repression (low or negative real interest rates for an extended period) to spur economic growth. While there is no shortage of talking heads postulating on what the Fed might do next, a former voting member of the FOMC gave me some advice at the end of his term that has served me well ever since. "Jason," he said, "unless the person talking about Fed policy is bald and has a beard, you're best to ignore him." The major consequence of financial repression, as we have started to see, is that it forces **all** economic actors to take more risk. Investors have to buy riskier financial assets, banks may need to, Ye Gods, make loans to maintain net interest margins and profit growth, and companies must get more aggressive to achieve profit growth in a period of low nominal GDP. Low business confidence and high cash hoards are some indication that companies have thus far been more comfortable in attempting to wring ever more operating leverage out of their businesses than in potentially riskier attempts to seek greater organic growth. The emergence of a number of "shareholder activists," however, may be making any number of C-suite executives wonder whether holding extra cash is all that safe, at least as far as their own jobs are concerned. The emergence of corporate gadflies may also be a signal that risk aversion has reached its apex.

In the '80s they were known as "raiders." The popular media often portrayed them as either one of two differing although similarly distasteful caricatures. The first, as parasites who, phalanxed by a team of lawyers filing 13Ds, would just as soon accept greenmail than take any long-term interest in shareholder value. The second, as sadistic corporate Darwinists, who took unusual pleasure in breaking up companies and firing workers to realize outsized short-term profits. Of course, all caricatures are based in part on fact, and there was no shortage of actors, in real life or in the movies, who were willing to play to type. What was often missing from these reports, however, was any discussion of the long-term impact raiders actually had on shareholder value, management practices, and local communities. Greenmail was too often seen as a harmless bribe to maintain the status quo while divestitures were too often viewed as an unfortunate by-product of an overly harsh capitalistic system. Missing was any discussion of the decline in the price of the common once the purported greenmailer went away or whether, after nearly two-decades of serial acquisitions, corporate America needed outside agents of change.

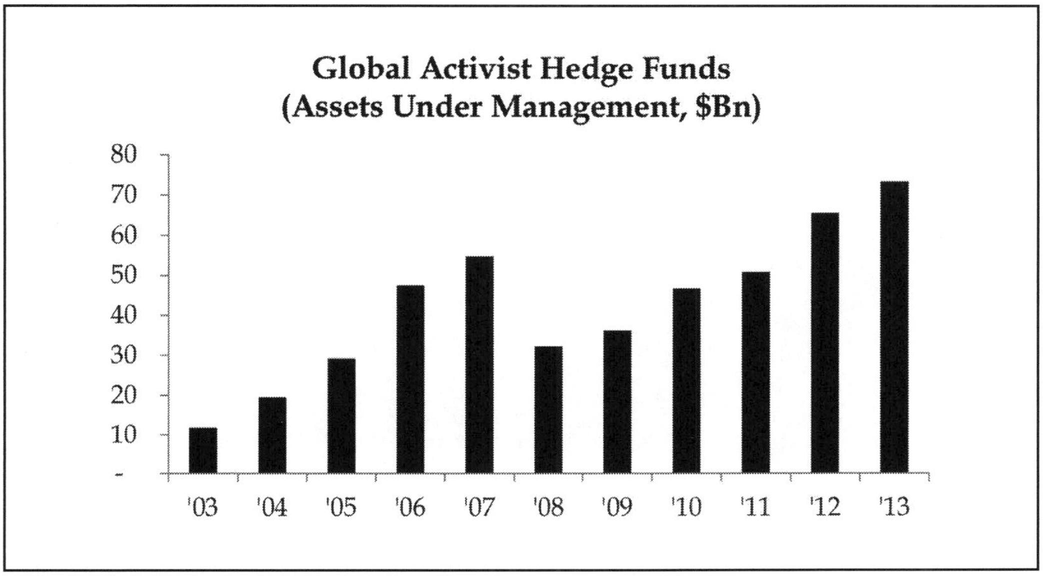


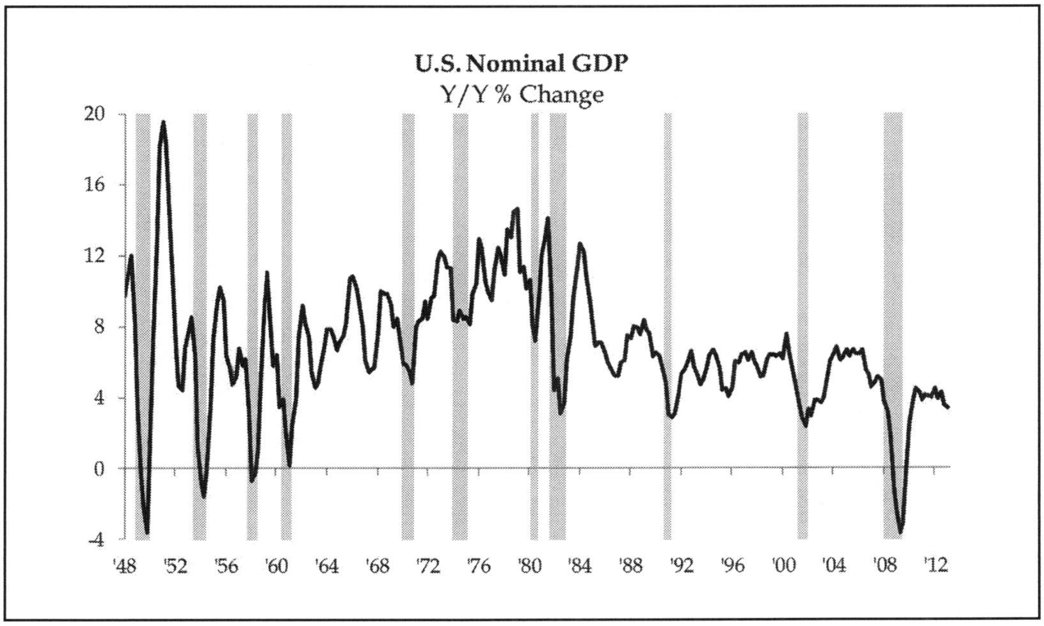

Of course, it has become a Wall Street laugh-line to describe some raiders of yester-year as present-day activists. A cynic might attribute this to more effective p.r., but to be fair, the raiders of old are more clearly working for the benefit of shareholders today. While large institutional investors like mutual funds and pension schemes tended to side with company managements in years past, they are increasingly welcoming the "help" of activist managers in unlocking shareholder value. Pressure to encourage changes in strategy at companies like Timken, Dell, Apple, and Proctor & Gamble, while all initiated in the activist community, were all ultimately supported by large and high profile long-only investors. This is due in large part to the increasing sophistication of the arguments they make and, perhaps more importantly, their efficacy. Most recently, Dan Loeb of Third Point Management used his 6.5% stake in Sony to argue publicly that the company should break itself up. According to FactSet SharkWatch, there were 241 activist campaigns in 2012 targeting a change in company strategy or board membership, up from 187 in 2009. About one-fifth of these campaigns were waged against companies with more than $1 billion in market value. On how things have changed during his career, Carl Icahn said, "In my early days 25 years ago, CEOs would routinely sue me to deter me from waging such battles. They don't sue me anymore. Now they know I am not going away and I usually win." Indeed, according to data from the Hedge Fund Research Institute, activist hedge fund strategies have outperformed more traditional funds by a wide margin in the last few years.

Two themes have emerged during the explosive growth in the alternative investment community: 1) many of the very best hedge fund managers have launched long-only funds with long lock-up periods; and 2) there has been a convergence of traditional hedge fund and private equity strategies. Both of these trends suggest that a lot of smart people have determined that their real edge is not in outsmarting an increasingly crowded investment landscape on XYZ's next quarter but in discerning long-term value. They also suggest that shareholder activism may, in fact, become its own asset class. Of course, there is a place within the various performance indices that rack hedge fund performance for event-driven funds that might, for example, bet on the outcome of a proposed merger. But, true shareholder activism is obviously less passive, with the various players seeking to, at the very least, influence the outcome of an investment, and, if possible, to determine it.

One of the central ironies of the growth in the hedge fund industry is that it has likely contributed to the long-term decline in volatility of stocks in the aggregate. It seems clear that, with so many investors using the same information, short-term opportunities are "arbed" out of the market very quickly. The average holding period for stocks is a little more than a year today, down from 8 years in 1960. The recent decline in volatility and sheer difficulty of achieving sustainable outperformance may encourage investors of all stripes to take a longer-term, and perhaps more activist, role in the future of their investments.

How the level of cash, the growth and convergence of alternative asset classes, and the decline in volatility will converge to ultimately impact stocks is unknown for, as noted above, only prudent and well-considered activism will boost long-term shareholder value. But it seems to be a good bet that an increasingly antsy investment community will put pressure on companies now more than ever before to boost returns. The bottom line is that Gordon Gekko is tan, rested, and ready. He has eschewed suspenders, yellow power ties, and his downtown office and now instead prefers to ply his trade in Zegna slacks and a cashmere sweater from his smallish long-short fund in Greenwich. Whether he is acting out of self-interest or for more altruistic reasons may be irrelevant. With a sense that many large-cap growth stocks are undervalued or under-managed, the average shareholder may be happy to have him on his side. The companies listed below may be particularly attractive.

**Top 25 S&P 500 Non-Fin. Companies by Cash & ST Investments on the Balance Sheet**

| | Company | Cash ($Mil.) | Sector | | Company | Cash ($Mil.) | Sector |
|---|---|---|---|---|---|---|---|
| GE | General Electric | 89,781 | Industrials | INTC | Intel | 17,073 | Technology |
| MSFT | Microsoft | 74,483 | Technology | MRK | Merck | 16,022 | Health Care |
| GOOG | Google | 50,098 | Technology | QCOM | QUALCOMM | 13,493 | Technology |
| CSCO | Cisco | 47,388 | Technology | HPQ | Hewlett-Packard | 13,240 | Technology |
| AAPL | Apple | 39,137 | Technology | UNH | UnitedHealth Group | 13,057 | Health Care |
| PFE | Pfizer | 35,346 | Health Care | IBM | IBM | 11,993 | Technology |
| ORCL | Oracle | 33,407 | Technology | BA | Boeing | 11,853 | Industrials |
| F | Ford | 32,010 | Discretionary | MDT | Medtronic | 11,071 | Health Care |
| JNJ | Johnson & Johnson | 21,668 | Health Care | DELL | Dell | 10,905 | Technology |
| AMGN | Amgen | 21,271 | Health Care | FCX | Freeport-McMoRan | 9,595 | Materials |
| WLP | WellPoint | 20,857 | Health Care | HUM | Humana | 9,539 | Health Care |
| CVX | Chevron | 19,048 | Energy | EBAY | eBay | 9,402 | Technology |
| KO | Coca-Cola | 18,428 | Staples | | | | |

*Source: Compustat; as of 6/6/13*

# *What Have We Learned?*

*Originally Published—September 20, 2013*

Last week, on the 12th anniversary of 9/11 and virtually the 5th anniversary of the failure of Lehman, I had drinks with some buddies at Rothmann's to reminisce. Despite some of the hits we had all taken in the intervening years both personally and professionally, we could all consider ourselves lucky. We were all employed and were at peace with the fact that Wall Street changed and was less fun than in the "good old days." All of us cases of arrested development to some degree, we all oddly attempted to adopt an air of mature responsibility. The guys who usually drank the hard stuff drank beer and we all decided to leave earlier than we normally would to get home to our families. Even at our advanced respective ages, I thought in the cab on the way home, perhaps we were finally turning into men. Maybe it was only natural given the industry's transgressions that both its sinners and the righteous would need to suffer in equal measure for it to be granted some greater metaphysical absolution. In 2013, there was little doubt that we all had to work harder to achieve similar results, if we were fortunate enough to have jobs at all. This was a good thing, I thought. Maybe we were at the point at which we might all realize that our true rewards might come in the next life.

**Then vs. Now: Lehman Failure vs. Mar-'09 Bottom vs. Today**

| | Day Before Lehman Failure | March '09 Bottom | Today |
|---|---|---|---|
| S&P 500 | 1,252 | 677 | 1,722 |
| Dow Jones Industrial Average | 11,422 | 6,547 | 15,637 |
| Employed (NFP, Thous.) | 136,377 | 132,106 | 136,133 |
| U.S. Deficit 12 Mo. Rolling ($BN) | -455 | -923 | -679 |
| Total Public Debt Subject to the Limit ($BN) | 9,620 | 10,890 | 16,700 |
| Financials Sector (% S&P 500 Mkt Cap) | 15.3% | 8.9% | 16.4% |
| 10-Year U.S. Treasury Yield | 3.7% | 2.9% | 2.7% |
| Federal Funds Rate | 2.000% | 0.125% | 0.125% |
| Fed Balance Sheet Assets ($BN) | 1,007 | 1,992 | 3,658 |
| S&P 500 Operating Earnings (LTM, $BN) | 610.5 | 431.6 | 885.7 |
| S&P 500 Operating Margin (LTM) | 6.5% | 4.7% | 9.0% |

I arrived home and had dinner with my wife and kids, telling them the story once again of my experiences on 9/11, remembering the City's collective sadness and attempting to suspend the memory of a friend from Georgetown, Tommy Galvin. I retired to my study after our meal to read through a few e-mails and watch a little television. Earlier in the day, I received a message from an earnest young woman in the Private Wealth department of "Bulge Bracket, Inc." It was the third time she solicited a meeting with me to demonstrate how her team "who have 50 years investment experience including 43 years at Bulge Bracket oversee more than four billion dollars" for their high net worth clients. She mentioned her experience helping the needy in Third World and the fact that she, too, had attended my alma mater for her MBA. The former fact was intriguing, the latter, at least to my mind, completely inconsequential. After her third entreaty, I wrote her back:

> Ms. Efficient,
>
> I am currently very happy with my financial advisor who also happens to be my best friend from business school. With that proviso, if you'd still like to come and visit I'm sure I could find a half-hour to chat.
>
> Jase

Although I now have my own office, I have never felt comfortable spending much of my time at any place other than with our salesmen and traders. I see how hard they work to attain new clients for my own firm and, given my own continuing efforts to build a career in the business, I have always tried to maintain a certain grace with those who strive. I've made thousands of cold calls in my career and still pitch new business at every opportunity. We try (how we try!) to never take for granted our clients and potential clients. I understood and I gave in.

Ms. Efficient's response, regretfully, showed me that perhaps things hadn't changed on Wall Street as much as I had hoped or thought. Obviously whatever perspective and humanity she might have attained in the Sub-Sahara had been completely obliterated by business school and her work at a bulge bracket firm. Her offer of a meeting turned into a conference call along with a reminder that "we have quite high minimums here—$10 million of investible assets…to start a relationship." I had long ago been granted the wisdom to ignore the simple slights, humiliations, and degradations necessary to survive a life on Wall Street. But on this night, of all nights, I couldn't help myself. I wanted to rage against an industry that insisted on ignoring its more noble roots in favor of a variety of behaviors that had gotten us into trouble in the first place. Before I had a chance to reconsider, I fired off my screed in an effort to score one for the good guys:

> This is a remarkably irritating exchange and reminds me of why most people can't stand Wall Street in general and [your firm] in particular. I receive no psychic benefit from saying that I "work" with someone from [Bulge Bracket, Inc.]. You contacted me, obviously with a blast e-mail, and now seem to be worried about the fact that I might waste your time. You've only succeeded in confirming my worst suspicions of your firm and in establishing my solemn promise to myself that I will never work with it in any capacity. I don't know how old you are but I have a suspicion that you are far younger than I am. Please do a little reading—perhaps even a little thinking—on what it means to be a fiduciary. Then reevaluate why you are in the business to begin with. Do you really love it—as I do—and see it as a long term path to doing well for your clients and for yourself or are merely caught up in the idea that you work for [Bulge Bracket, Inc.]?
>
> Please, please, lose my e-mail address,
>
> Jason DeSena Trennert

It saddens me to no end to see the government picking on arguably the best large financial institution in the world. This is, no doubt, expensive, distracting, and counter-productive for the economy as a whole. But I wonder whether a greater obstacle than the regulators of our business exists—the confidence of the public. It appears that we have miles to go before we sleep.

**Net Flows into Mutual Funds ($BN)**

| | Year | Equity – Domestic | Equity – International | Bond | Money Mkt |
|---|---|---|---|---|---|
| 2008-2012 | 2008 | (148.8) | (80.3) | 29.1 | 644.9 |
| | 2009 | (29.4) | 27.6 | 379.6 | (583.6) |
| | 2010 | (81.2) | 57.8 | 235.6 | (529.0) |
| | 2011 | (132.5) | 4.2 | 125.1 | (16.6) |
| | 2012 | (156.0) | 2.8 | 303.6 | (0.3) |
| | ***TOTAL*** | ***(547.8)*** | ***12.1*** | ***1,072.9*** | ***(484.6)*** |
| 2013 YTD | Jan | 18.4 | 19.4 | 32.8 | (11.1) |
| | Feb | (1.4) | 15.6 | 20.3 | (31.6) |
| | Mar | 2.3 | 12.5 | 16.1 | (58.3) |
| | Apr | (1.4) | 5.8 | 12.1 | (24.4) |
| | May | (4.0) | 9.4 | 12.2 | 28.3 |
| | Jun | (6.6) | 6.6 | (59.9) | (17.1) |
| | Jul | 8.4 | 9.7 | (16.7) | 26.6 |
| | Aug | (2.2) | 8.8 | (29.1) | NA |
| | ***TOTAL*** | ***13.3*** | ***87.8*** | ***(12.3)*** | ***(87.5)*** |

*Despite losses in his bond funds, the average investor isn't embracing equity funds the way many would have expected or hoped.*

# *Three Wise Men from the East(Side)*

*Originally Published—December 20, 2013*

While the velocity of money continues to decline, it appears as if the velocity of activity on the sell-side is accelerating. In a low-volatility, high-correlation world, commission budgets get squeezed and small brokers like Strategas must work harder to achieve growth. Of course it seems as if we've been all saying the same thing for years, but the hyperactivity of the holiday season also seems to be greater, which compounds the stress of what should be a joyous time of year. And so it was a great pleasure earlier this week to be invited to Byron Wien's annual luncheon to discuss the market and economic outlook for the year ahead. The participants are largely comprised of Wall Street legends who have proved themselves in both bull and bear markets with a few of the young strivers like me thrown in for good measure. The food is good, the atmosphere of Blackstone's offices is inviting, and the discussion stretches one's mind about non-consensus investment ideas.

It was well into the evening on Tuesday and I found that the afterglow of Byron's annual luncheon was being eroded little by little by the crush of responding to e-mails, buying Christmas presents on-line, and starting on a Christmas card list that seemed impossibly long. Feeling a bit like a self-exiled Bob Cratchit, I looked over our sales and trading desks and saw that the only two people left in the office were me and a brand new salesman we had just hired named Luke. A little depressed, I decided that enough was enough. As I began to walk out I could see that Luke was reading Strategas' trusty sales manual, a group of reading materials and processes I've collected for more than 20 years. I had forgotten that smack in the middle of this tome we use to inculcate new colleagues on the firm's ethos were pieces from three of the participants of Byron's luncheon that day—an immortal investment essay from Byron himself and two Harvard Business School cases about Ed Hajim and Jack Rivkin, respectively. In that somber holiday light of a December evening, I took considerable comfort in seeing a young man learn, perhaps for the first time, valuable lessons that only accompany the skinned knees of experience.

Seizing the moment to remind myself of the lessons that have shaped the way we've built our firm and gain some much needed long-term perspective, I fished out my own copy of the sales manual and thought you might like to relearn some of them with me. Many of Byron's investment essays have taken on "classic" status and more than a few have been immortalized between hard covers. Discovering Freud in Salzburg is a particular favorite but Byron's essay *What Portfolio Managers Want From Institutional Salespeople* is still as relevant today, perhaps even more, than it was when it was first written in 1993. As the proprietor of a for-profit research shop, I am more than a little embarrassed to admit that our copy is a bootleg version that bears, for reasons I can no longer remember, the fax stamp of Atalanta Sosnoff. Byron highlights immortal truths and characteristics of great salesmen and sell-side analysts. Key to the relationship between the buy-side and sell-side, he believes, is the concept of empathy. Too many brokers, Byron notes, sell what they have rather than attempting to understand what the client wants. While this will always be true when it comes to product, it is even more important today when it comes to research. At least in the old days, sending out research actually incurred some cost—postage or fax line charges. Today, the marginal cost of sending out another e-mail is zero. As a result, portfolio managers are inundated with hundreds if not thousands of e-mail messages a day. Contrary to what many had predicted, the value of a good institutional salesman has only increased with the usage of technology to deliver information.

The Harvard Business School case *Furman Selz: A Tale of Two Acquisitions* and the story of its indomitable leader Ed Hajim has also guided us as a partnership to put in place a culture and a mechanism through which all of our colleagues believe their futures are lashed to the mast together. (Ed, it should be noted, sits on our Advisory Board.) Of course, finding people who *want* to view their future this way is harder than it might sound. While it has become almost cliché, we have found that younger people these days are looking for immediate payoffs and can get uneasy during the frequent "broken plays" that characterize life on modern Wall Street. Recruiting great people will forever be a critical element in building a first class investment firm. In the case, Ed said, "the secret to attracting top talent to our firm was excitement. We were growing, we were exciting, and you were a shareholder." Ed's experiences at Furman Selz are a great reminder of why the classic Wall Street partnership was perhaps the greatest risk model ever devised, putting VAR and CVAR to shame in its elegance. Ed's good counsel has prompted us to become a far more professional business, especially when it comes to management committee meetings and our interviewing process.

The final entry from one of the wise men at Byron's luncheon was the story of Jack Rivkin's tenure: Harvard Business School case *Lehman Brothers: Rise of the Equity Research Department.* The story is an inspiring one that demonstrates how a combination of hard work, esprit de corps, and proper training can turn young analysts into impactful superstars. The case quoted one of the beneficiaries of Jack's training program: "we went through all the different aspects of what our job entailed: from stock picking to how to talk to the press, how to talk to the client, how to talk to the salespeople. We learned how to do all this to our best ability and build our franchise molded to our strengths. And the camaraderie that they built was unbelievable." We've stolen Ed's "no-jerk" policy and have built a great research team.

Divining the future path of securities' prices will forever be a dangerous game. Like reading, having good mentors reminds you that you are not alone. Your pursuits, successes, and failures have been experienced by men far greater than you. Despite a total return in the S&P 500 of nearly 30%, there are few investors I know that don't feel as if 2013 has been a difficult year. The indices have been hard to beat and a wall-of-worry market has offered few new opportunities to put money to work at truly compelling prices. While we're all prone to bouts of nostalgia at this time of year, I've found that the time between Christmas and New Years to be a critically important time for me to derive some long-term perspective and to try to remember lessons forgotten. Three wise men, it appears, will forever remain an important feature of the Christmas season.

# BEST ESSAYS OF 2014

## *The Holy See as a New Economic Power*

*Originally Published—January 10, 2014*

What do *Time, GQ, Esquire,* and *The Advocate* have in common? They all named Pope Francis their 2013 Man of the Year. (In the case of *Esquire* it was actually best-dressed.) Few guys on Wall Street would quite raise such an achievement to the level of winning golf's Grand Slam, but it is, by any standard, a difficult distinction for any human being to achieve in the same year. While actors have always been warned to avoid working with children or animals given their ability to steal a scene, businessmen have long been warned to stay away from politics and religion when talking given the potential to offend current and potential customers. And so while this is a tricky piece to write for someone who considers himself both a committed Catholic and a committed capitalist, it seems as if the potential investment implications of the new Pontiff are too large to ignore.

The 266th Pope of the Catholic Church, Jorge Mario Bergoglio has, as Pope Francis, captured the imaginations of people of all religious faiths and political beliefs. Although some might attribute the Pontiff's popularity with his de-emphasis on potentially divisive social issues, it is arguably his outspoken support for the poor and his willingness to shun the typical accoutrements of a head of state that have garnered the most attention. In a world in which the town council members of Bell, California felt comfortable voting themselves salaries that approached half-a-million dollars, it is somewhat refreshing to see a guy who is officially in charge of the spiritual lives of 1.2 billion Catholics drive a 1984 Renault 4, 4-door stick shift, preferring to wear a simple cassock instead of the ermine-trimmed mozzetta used by prior Pontiffs. In one of his first official acts as Pope, he humbly kissed and washed the feet of 12 prisoners in Rome to underscore his role as a servant to the disenfranchised. In just the past week, he largely eliminated the honorific of "monsignor" to all but a few priests in an effort to abolish the "clerical careerism" that has come to characterize the Church.

But it is perhaps his first official act as Pope—his choice of the name of Francis—that may hold the most significance for investors looking to divine economic and social trends. As the first Jesuit priest to be named Pope, it was surprising to those who follow the Holy See to see that he eschewed the names Ignatius and Xavier. He chose Francis in homage to the famous Saint from Assisi because of his willingness to bring *"an idea of poverty against the luxury, pride, vanity of the civil and ecclesiastical powers of the time."* (Italics and underlining added.) It is this commitment to the people themselves, not to the trappings of power that come with "serving" the people, that appears to have most angered both conservative and liberal critics alike. In his recent Apostolic Exhortation, *Evangelii Gaudium*, Pope Francis urges us to reject a "new idolatry of money" and a "financial system which rules rather than serves." Some conservatives see this as a direct indictment of capitalism while a more charitable interpretation of his comments would suggest that his Argentinian origins lead him to believe that it is the unholy alliance of politics and money that pose the greatest risk to alleviating the scourge of poverty. It should be remembered that Milton Friedman was famous for making the distinction that he saw himself as "pro-market" rather than "pro-business" given the penchant of large politically-well-connected businesses to benefit most from the growth in government. Indeed, a look at the relationship between income inequality (the GINI coefficient) and per capita income suggests that higher standards of living accrue, ironically, perhaps to some, to those countries that possess greater differences between rich and poor. This may be scant solace to human beings who care more about relative outcomes rather than absolutes but it bears study.

The most important investment implication of all this is that, like it or not, populist sentiments in a time of stubbornly-high unemployment are only likely to grow. Disciples of monetarism and the belief that heavy debt-loads hinder long-term economic growth (Reinhart-Rogoff) have taken major hits within the academic world and in the media. The election of New York City Mayor Bill de Blasio and SeaTac, Washington's decision to institute a $15 minimum wage are further indications of the willingness of politicians to try to equal the playing field *de jure*. The ranks of those standing to support austerity seem to be shrinking, their political influence waning. Nearly every day, the news headlines show another European country's government rethinking cuts now, especially in light of the Fed's decision to pare back its bond-buying program. Could another fiscal stimulus program, perhaps centered around infrastructure spending in the U.S. and Europe be far behind? As Strategas' Chief Economist Don Rissmiller has noted, if you thought it was historically tough to fight the Fed, try fighting the Pope.

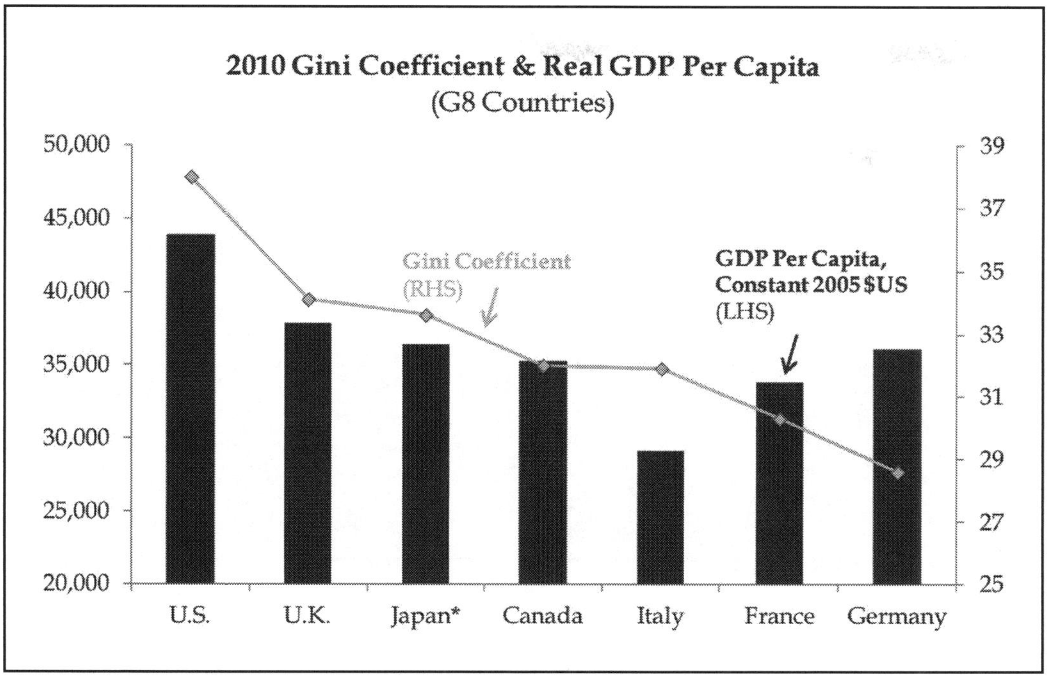


**Uses 2009 Gini Coefficient.*
*Source: OECD. Chart excludes Russia.*

# *Assorted Thoughts on Michael Lewis' Flash Boys*

*Originally Published—April 4, 2014*

Let me start by saying that I have yet to finish reading Mr. Lewis' book and that, at the same time, I am a long-time fan of him as a writer. Perhaps hoping that these biases might cancel each other out and attempting to respond to an increasing number of client questions on the subject of high frequency trading, I decided to write this week's essay on the subject despite the fact that I know I have both incomplete information and a lack of expertise on the subject at hand. Loving the great arena of Wall Street and fascinated by the subject in an odd week in which I haven't been on an airplane, I've watched as much coverage of the book as I could muster starting with Steve Croft's piece on 60 Minutes, to the almost-too-painful to watch food fight between the book's chief protagonist Brad Katsuyama and a representative from the BATs exchange, to, finally, Mr. Lewis' hour-long interview on the book on Charlie Rose. Possessing an extraordinarily competent group of traders here at Strategas and, as a result, access to some of the largest buy side traders on the Street, I've spent the last several days talking to as many people as I could on the subject. All the big investment banks have market structure experts and this piece isn't meant to compete with their expertise, simply to try to relay the thoughts of a number of experts on the subject. There was a surprising degree of consensus on the normative judgments on the issues at hand but a greater level of disagreement on the style in which Mr. Lewis told his story.

## Here are the points in which there seem to be broad consensus among traders:

1. If there is a chief complaint of Mr. Lewis' book it is his liberal use of the term "rigged" to describe a market in which trading costs have come down and spreads have narrowed. ***Not one*** of the traders I spoke with justified the ability and willingness of some high frequency traders to use predatory tactics to front run customer orders via the use of technology to increase the speed at which data was transmitted. Still, ***all*** of the buy side traders I spoke with thought that the current system was far better than the "license to steal" that existed under the old specialist system. "The 'skim' in those days could be measured in eighths and quarters rather than pennies," said one. "It's not perfect but it's better."

2. There is a broad agreement that the current system is an unintended consequence of the regulatory apparatus of the exchanges that was put into place with the creation of Reg. NMS, Reg. ATS (which allowed the creation of dark pools), decimalization, and the maker-taker model which allows brokers to get rebates for routing orders to particular venues. All of these developments have added to the fragmentation and complexity of the markets.

3. The largest active money managers have been thinking about these issues for years and there is a sense in which technology itself is already rendering obsolete the ability of some high frequency traders to game the system and, concomitantly, make money. As an example, some high frequency shops are using microwaves rather than fiber optic cable to transmit information. According to a Purdue University study, the profits of HFT firms have fallen from $5 billion in 2009 to $1 billion last year.

4. Most feel that the greatest risk of the current system is its complexity and its resulting fragility. Market wide circuit breakers and the newly implemented limit up limit down rules should curb any material sell off in the markets but another "Knight capital event" or "programming glitch" is still possible.

## Here are my opinions based on these conversations:

1. While it would be easy to scapegoat dark pools and the new exchanges for the lack of confidence individual investors have in the stock market, there is a broader lack of confidence in all public institutions that has made both the average guy and largest corporation unwilling to take risk. Michael Lewis' accusations don't help but mutual fund flows would suggest that the individual lost confidence in the system a long time ago. Two fifty percent declines in 10 years, the flash crash, and a series of scandals among big businesses, government officials, religious institutions, and universities have all contributed to an increased skepticism that can only be eased through the passage of time and genuine attempts to do the right thing.

2. Regulators are still woefully behind in addressing the problems with the exchanges they have largely created themselves. My conversations with senior NYSE officials revealed a shocking lack of understanding of market structure among top regulators. One told me that, in the immediate aftermath of the flash crash, a conversation with the SEC made it apparent that the regulator was shocked to learn that the Exchange only had a market share of 25% of the trading of listed equities. (It has since fallen to 12%.)

3. It is a fool's errand to confuse volume with liquidity and there is a sense in which the outrage directed at high frequency traders is driven by the same emotion that drove the anger toward the old specialist system—the unsettling feeling one gets when we see other people get rich. At least the specialists of old had to stand in the pocket and be the buyers of last resort during past market dislocations. It's not easy to find bids from "market makers" today when all hell breaks loose.

4. The exposure of the current system makes it virtually impossible for large financial institutions, regulators, and politicians to accept the status quo. Already number one on *The New York Times* best seller's list, *Flash Boys* is likely to result in class action lawsuits, new regulations, legal action from regulatory bodies, and perhaps even a Tobin Tax on financial transactions. "It's legal" is not a good excuse for questionable behavior. This is a distinction often ignored or purposefully blurred by lawyers. While it may work in a court of law, it won't work in the court of public opinion.

5. In free markets, it should be theoretically impossible to make profits consistently without taking risk. The fact that some HFT firms have been able to do this suggests that there is a problem.

Lastly, I think it's important to note, from a purely sociological point of view, that the trading community has been ground zero for the move toward disintermediation. The aftermath of the financial crisis hasn't been easy on anyone who makes their living on Wall Street, none more than traders on the floor of the Big Board and countless numbers of sell-side traders. For those of us who grew up in the business, who love it, and see its social utility, these are people, not statistics. I admire Michael Lewis for his ability to explain arcane but interesting subjects—e.g. mortgage backed securities, the scouting process in Major League Baseball, high frequency trading—in a way that is both amusing and comprehensible. To those who believe that Lewis is making hyperbolic claims only in an effort to sell books I would say simply, as someone who doesn't know him personally but has followed his career, that I believe he is an honest broker who is trying to right something he believes—that we should all believe—is wrong. His use of inflammatory speech to make his point suggests that we're all salesmen in some way and that just because we're selling something doesn't mean that it has no value. As de La Rochefoucauld once said, "hypocrisy is the homage vice pays to virtue."

# *Dividends: The Sweetest Poison Pill in an Age of Activism?*

*Originally Published—May 9, 2014*

In a testament to the power of public relations, yesterday's corporate raiders have reinvented themselves as "activists." Some of the rough edges have been shaved off and in many cases the transformation has been greatly aided by the fact that they are right. Carl Icahn's open letter to Warren Buffett in *Barron's* criticizing Coca-Cola's compensation plan was extraordinarily well-reasoned and elegant, almost bordering on inspiring. You know the world has changed when Carl Icahn wins a round in the avuncular contest against the Sage from Omaha. Activist strategies have been among the best performing parts of the hedge fund complex in recent years and, as a result, are attracting more money than ever before. The flows have been so strong that activists have had to pursue larger and larger game. According to *Activist Insight*, nearly twice as many companies with market caps of greater than $10 billion found themselves as targets in 2013 than in 2012 (42 versus 23, respectively.) As an example, Apple, one would think, would be among the few companies in the world that could have told Old Carl to take a walk. Of course it didn't quite work out that way, the company is so desperate to avoid criticism that it issued bonds twice, bought back shares, and agreed to split the stock in just the last year, despite the fact that it has more than $150 billion cash.

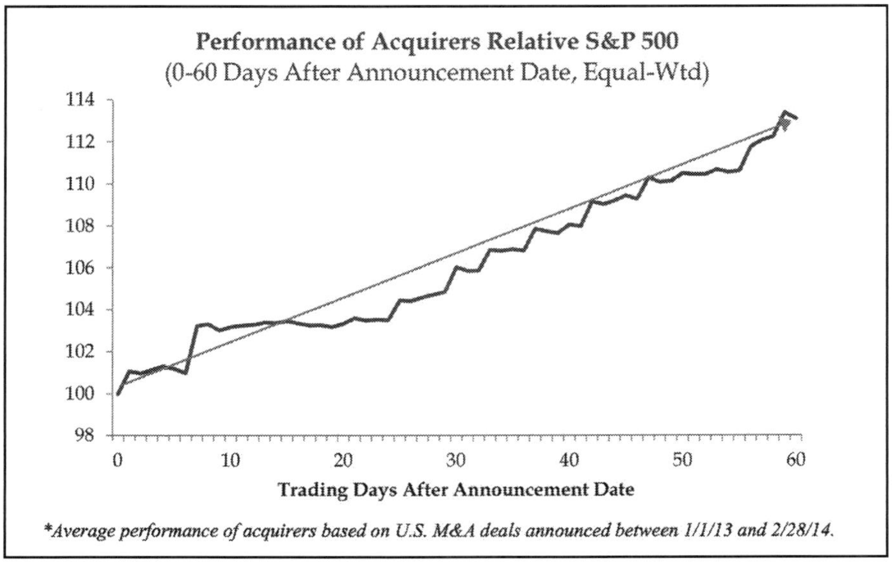

In investing, as in golf—and life—we all must play the ball as it lies. You won't find us making any value judgments about this phenomenon. We simply believe that activism is the free market's response to the fact that no one buys a large cap technology company with the expectation that it will become a bank and a bad one at that. If there is a criticism of the Fed's massive expansion of its balance sheet it could simply be that it has done more to prompt economic actors to take *financial* risk than *economic* risk. Said another way, a combination of the perpetually low interest rates, tax increases, and heavier regulation has made it far easier for companies to decide to buy back stock rather than make greenfield additions to a plant. Capital spending requires genuine long-term rather than temporal confidence, a little bit like the difference between marriage and dating. This has been wonderful news for the *rentier* class but less helpful for those who don't own the means of production. In an environment where public company CEOs are given less time to deliver, it seems only natural that most executives would do exactly what they are incentivized to do.

As the table from Partner and Sector Strategist Nick Bohnsack indicates, companies who have used their cash to buy back stock and repair their balance sheets have outperformed those who have invested in capital expenditures. A restless activist class will only put more pressure on companies to believe they need to use it or lose it. In recent months it appears that many companies have decided that acquisitions are one way to keep the barbarians at bay.

**First Quintile Cash Outlet Performance**

| Outlet | '08 | '09 | '10 | '11 | '12 | '13 | YTD '14 |
|---|---|---|---|---|---|---|---|
| Balance Sheet Repair | -41.0% | 46.2% | 23.3% | -5.4% | 22.7% | 44.8% | 4.2% |
| Payment of Dividends | -34.1% | 23.5% | 17.9% | 9.7% | 15.6% | 29.3% | 3.9% |
| Capital Expenditures | -45.3% | 51.8% | 19.0% | 2.0% | 15.1% | 24.9% | 1.5% |
| Mergers & Acquisitions | -44.9% | 27.6% | 24.8% | -1.0% | 15.4% | 25.9% | 1.0% |
| Share Repurchases | -32.8% | 41.6% | 15.4% | 6.9% | 18.1% | 40.3% | -0.1% |
| **S&P 500 Index** | **-38.5%** | **23.5%** | **12.8%** | **0.0%** | **13.4%** | **29.6%** | **2.0%** |
| Cash/ST Investments | 3.6% | 0.5% | 0.5% | 0.4% | 0.2% | 0.0% | 0.1% |

**Backtest Parameters: Share Repurchase**—Quintiles S&P 500, rebalanced monthly, based on the company's dollar value of share repurchases over the trailing twelve months as a percent of average shareholders' equity. **Balance Sheet Repair**—Quintiles S&P 500, rebalanced monthly, based on the Y/Y in debt as a pct. of avg. debt outstanding, with lower values ranking better (LVRB). **Payment of Dividends**—Quintiles S&P 500, rebalanced monthly, based on the TTM dividends paid vs. TTM dividends paid, lagged 1-year. **Capex**—Quintiles S&P 500, rebalanced monthly, based on Y/Y pct. chg. in capex. **M&A**—Quintiles S&P 500, rebalanced annually, by cash portion of transaction as a pct. of avg. total cash.

Indeed, companies announcing acquisitions since January 2013 have outperformed the market by an average of 113 basis points in the 60 days after the announcement since the start of 2013. According to Dealogic, companies announcing takeover are up an average of 4.6% the day after a deal's announcement, the biggest post deal pop on record. Again, we make no real value judgments on this. When the cost of capital is likely to remain low for a long time, almost anything you do with your cash will be seen as accretive. History has shown, however, that hastily arranged unions especially among large companies rarely enhance shareholder value. We wonder whether a sweeter poison pill might be increasing dividend payouts to shareholders. The Lord only knows there's room—despite record dollar levels of dividends, the S&P 500 payout ratio remains near all-time lows at 33%.

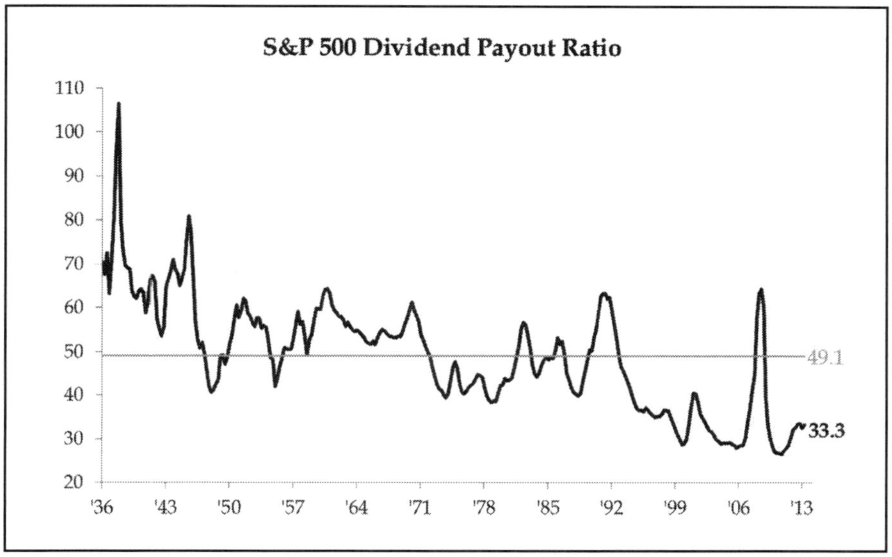


Poison pills were originally conceived of by Marty Lipton of the noted M&A firm Wachtell Lipton in the early 1980s, paving the way for corporate managements to employ all manner of tactics to foil takeover artists, greatly adding to the richness of Wall Street's vocabulary by introducing into the financial argot such terms as "shark repellent" and "golden handcuffs." Predictably, these strategies were ultimately abused, employed to keep ineffectual managements in place in spite of the best wishes and best interests of their public shareholders.[12] One also wonders why dividends aren't seen as the sweetest poison pill for long-term investors—at

12. Although the legality of such poison pill protection was at times in question, the 1985 Moran v. Household decision upheld its place in corporate law. The irony is a 2001 study by CFO magazine found that for every company with such defenses that was able to ward off a takeover, there were 20 other companies with poison pills that accepted takeover offers.

once, a dividend wards off short-term raiders intent on stripping assets, aligns the interests of shareholders and managements, and, perhaps most important, reminds executives that it isn't their company four times a year.

The good news is that, in the *short term*, almost anything a company decides to do with its cash, aside from just holding onto it, is good for equities and will likely be bad for corporate credit one day. Whether prudent or not, M&A activity, increases in dividends, share buybacks, or capex tend to make investors in equities feel good and are, almost always, deleterious to corporate spreads. While the normative case for dividends is, generally speaking, strong, experience suggests that M&A will be the winner in corporate sweepstakes for an outlet for cash. By our lights, there are three main reasons why this is so: 1) as in 1995, a slowdown in profit growth generally leads companies to want to buy growth through acquisition; 2) there is a certain immediacy and magic bullet quality to acquisitions that shuts people up regardless of the long-term consequences for the company; and 3) it's simply more fun. In all my years on Wall Street, I have never heard of a bulge bracket firm giving a CEO a ride on a G-5 or buying him dinner at Smith & Wollensky's for announcing a bump in the dividend. This may be precisely why more long-term investors should start demanding them.

# *In Defense of Active Management*

*Originally Published—August 22, 2014*

Let's be clear—a sell-side boutique extolling the virtues of active management will never be in line for a profiles in courage award for investment research—passive managers, after all, will never be placed in the pantheon of great commission payers. Still, our friends and clients who deal with both high net worth investors and large fiduciaries like pensions, foundations, and endowments are reporting ever-greater numbers of those who question the wisdom of paying management fees for products which, at times, underperform. While the claims that active investment is dead haven't reached the status of *BusinessWeek's* "Death of Equities" cover story in 1979, such calls are being repeated more frequently and at higher decibel levels. Charley Ellis just published what was tantamount to an obituary for the money management industry in the latest issue of the *Financial Analysts Journal* and just yesterday the *Wall Street Journal* highlighted the penchant of individual investors to eschew stock pickers in favor of indexation.

It is incumbent upon the dispassionate financial analyst to rejoice not in a rationalization of his chosen profession but in the truth. There is no question that the democratization and widespread diffusion of information and the sheer size of the money management industry has made it more difficult to add alpha. But it should also be stated that while indexation may look particularly attractive in a period of financial repression, when near-zero percent interest rates dampen volatility and increase correlations, it is unlikely to appear as prudent in a period in which the invisible hand of free markets is able to assert itself. In short, betting on indexed funds to consistently outperform active money management requires, in part, an expectation that quantitative easing will never end. Such a conclusion would also suggest that the free enterprise system is superfluous. Despite what can sometimes appear to be a disposition suggesting otherwise, central bankers are not omniscient gods. It is in the turbulent times that the talented fund manager can most easily add alpha and prove his or her worth.

By our lights, the case for active over passive management rests on five basic pillars: 1) the size of indexed assets may sow the seeds of its own lackluster performance; 2) higher interest rates and the end of financial repression will widen the differences between winners and losers; 3) low nominal growth environments create winner-take-all markets; 4) more complex financial instruments and systems are likely to make markets less efficient than the academics would have you believe; and 5) the prospects for peak profit margins and multiples in the next few years should benefit the skilled stock picker.

## Size of Indexed Assets as its Achilles' Heel

One of the central ironies of passive investing is that the public's desire to index increases in periods of maximum risk and decreases in periods of maximum opportunity. In the first six months of the tech-crazed year 1999, for example, nearly 70% of the money invested was placed in indexed funds. Although it may seem to be a minor point, active managers may also have an edge over their passive competition simply because of the way in which the indices themselves are constructed. Indexed assets have grown from $100 billion in the early 1990s to almost $2 trillion today. As Professor Jeremy Siegel of the Wharton School has pointed out, this hyper-growth in passive investing often forces companies to enter benchmarks at inflated prices, lowering future potential returns. As an example, Yahoo! went up 64% between the day its entry into the S&P was announced and the day it actually went into the Index. The S&P itself found that shares entering the 500 rose 8.5% on average between the time their admission into the S&P was announced and the effective date of their entry. Siegel has postulated that lower bid-ask spreads might offset the impact of this premium but would probably not be enough to completely offset it.

## Higher Interest Rates and an End to Financial Repression

Many an investment ship has foundered on the rocky shoals of expectations that interest rates would normalize. Of course, as it says in the Good Book, we know not the time or the hour. Still, any reasonable student of financial markets would need to bet that German Bund yields of 1% and 10-year U.S. Treasury yields of 2.4% are unsustainable, even in an era in which inflation is low. After all, the central tendency for 10-year Treasury note yields has been historically around the level of nominal GDP—currently around 4-5% in the lower 48. Quintupling the size of a central bank's balance sheet as the Fed, Bank of England, and Swiss National Bank have done may have forestalled economic disaster but it has also made both individuals and corporations alike more interested in taking financial risk than economic risk, especially in a period of political volatility and regulatory hyperactivity. Barring some deus ex machina development, the costs of such monetary munificence will become visible, creating opportunities for portfolio managers to exploit them.

## Nominal vs. Real and Winner-Take-All Markets

Perhaps the strongest argument for active management rests with the fact that index investing unnecessarily exposes investors to performance-crushing returns on stocks of marginal companies. While this is always the case, it is the prospect of weak ***nominal*** growth (real growth and inflation) that widens the differences between winners and losers across all industries and provides fertile ground for winner-take-all markets. The bottom line is that, in nominal terms, anything less than 5% GDP is going to feel an awful lot like a recession for equity investors. This is for no other reason than the fact that revenues, expenses, debt payments, and profits are all made in nominal rather than real terms. When one considers the fact that nominal GDP growth has averaged 6.7% since 1960, our forecast for 4-5% nominal growth over the next few years suggests that there won't be enough seats at the table for weak companies, especially if interest rates rise. This has major implications for how portfolios should be constructed. While we believe a recession is unlikely any time soon, the Fed, to our knowledge, has not outlawed the business cycle. In difficult economic environments, outperformance ultimately becomes a function of avoiding the worst stocks rather than owning the best ones. In the first half of 2007, for example, owning the worst performing 50 stocks in the S&P 500 was painful. In the second half of that year, it was career threatening. In such economic environments, the ability to gain market share becomes critical and volatility increases dramatically. Since 1960, the S&P has traded in a range of 36.3% in years when nominal GDP was less than 5%, versus 24.1% in years when nominal GDP was greater than 5%.

## Complexity & The Myth of Efficient Markets

Despite the best efforts of regulators to increase the "transparency" of the financial markets, there is always a certain sense in which they will also be fighting the last war. It is unlikely the CDO squareds will provide the basis for the next black swan event, but new candidates appear to be invented all the time. The rapid growth of high frequency trading, the asymptotic rise in the number of ETFs and ETNs, record corporate debt issuance, and the fact that there are now over 5,000 private equity funds managing over $3.5 trillion (unlevered) all might come to mind. A big part of Ellis' argument against active management is the growth in the number of financial professionals and the sheer size of the industry itself. It is much more difficult for one professional to beat another professional, the thinking goes, rather than the comparatively uninformed individual, a circumstance that was the hallmark of the money management business in its nascent stages. Of course, this largely ignores the fact that professionals, academics, "quants," and other expensive experts seem to come close to torching the entire financial system with increasing and frightening regularity. Can one really claim, in the aftermath of the financial crisis, that financial "modernization" made markets more efficient? French psychologist Gustave Le Bon, a man many consider the intellectual father in the study of crowd behavior put it this way in his seminal work *The Crowd*:

> *In the case of everything that belongs to the realm of sentiment religion, politics, morality, the affections, and antipathies, etc. The most eminent men seldom surpass the standard of the most ordinary individuals. From the intellectual point of view an abyss may exist between a great mathematician and his boot-maker, but from the point of view of character, the difference is often slight or nonexistent.*

Globalization and the continued proliferation of complex financial instruments and systems suggest that the tails in the financial markets will remain as fat as they have always been. This creates enormous opportunities for the truly active long only manager and the hedge fund alike.

## Peak Profit Margins and Earnings Multiples

Finally, active managers should benefit from the fact that both price earnings multiples and profit margins are destined to peak in the next several years. While the '80s and '90s were salad days for Wall Street, a drop in the Fed Funds rate from 19% in 1981 to 1% in 2003 probably had a lot more to do with the wealth created in our industry than any improvement in the intelligence, talent, or diligence of its practitioners. How often can you expect earnings multiples to quadruple in the space of two decades? Is it realistic to expect such a wonderful tailwind when short term interest rates are quite literally starting from zero? And while a case can be made that profit margins may be less mean reverting than they have in the past due to the growth of asset-light, IP-heavy sectors like technology, health care, and financials, the yawning gap between corporate profits and wages as a percentage of GDP will not, as we all know, be sustainable. If we are indeed in a "second machine age," the potential disruption of traditional American industries will occur faster than the index's ability to capture them. Those companies most able to adapt to these changes are likely to gain the most market share.

Finally, it should be stated that those who most greatly extol the benefits of indexation are also some of the greatest defenders of the Yale Model. It seems an inconsistency to continue to pour money into super-active high fee vehicles like hedge funds while seeking ways to limit exposure to lower fee active managers at traditional long-only managers. In short, a rising tide is unlikely to lift all boats in a period of higher interest rates, unprecedented technological change, and greater economic volatility in the next couple of years. Instead, the equity markets will become far more Darwinian, exposing significant and growing differences between the best and the worst stocks, and the balance sheet will become just as important as the income statement. Such periods provide great opportunities for active managers and long/short hedge funds alike to disrupt the current love affair with indexation.

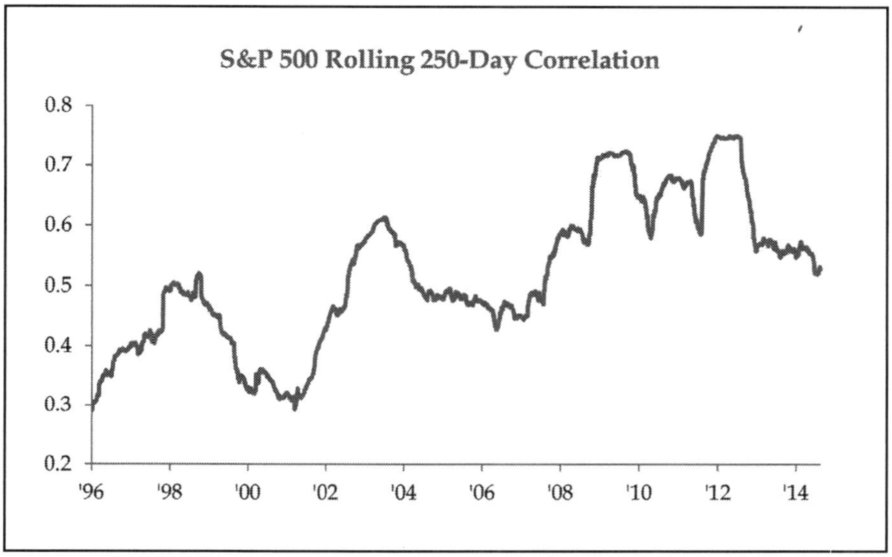


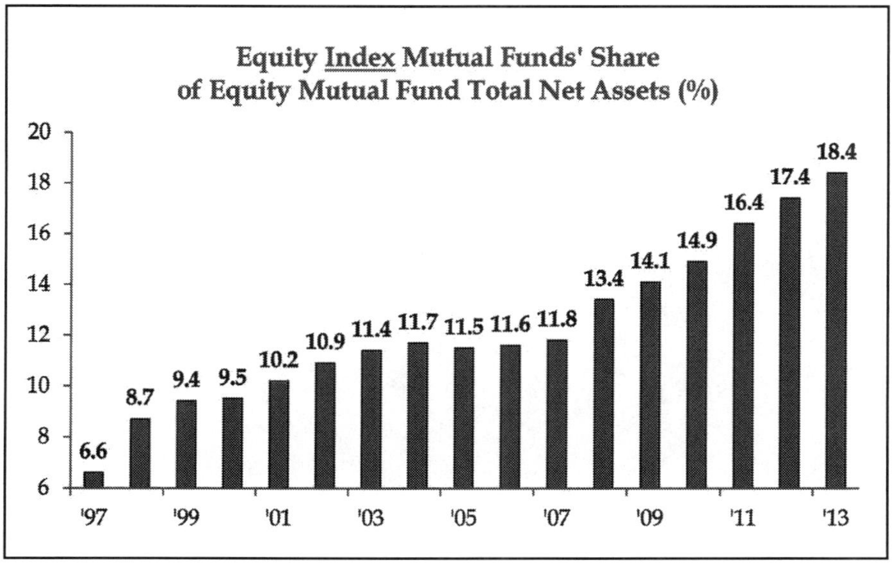

# *The Bull Market No One Loved*

*Originally Published—November 12, 2014*

In some ways it's difficult to know what's harder to believe—the fact that the S&P has reached 40 new highs this year or that a 24/7 media who, let's put it charitably, is desperate for content, has left the story largely unreported. In many ways, this may be one of the most unloved bull markets of all time—it's certainly the least captivating expansion of wealth I've witnessed in my 25-year career. Perhaps it's too difficult a comparison, but it wasn't too long ago, in the salad days of the late 1990s, that new highs were greeted by Wall Street with giddy celebration—marching bands, the releasing of doves, free hats, etc. Today, it barely warrants a mention on the nightly news. While it may be understandable for the average individual investor to have lost interest in stocks after witnessing two major bear markets and serial misdeeds on the part of Wall Street over the past 15 years, it is somewhat more puzzling that professional investors also still look at the current bull with a jaundiced eye. Many still refer to the 200% gain in the S&P 500 over the past 5 ½ years as a "rally," a mirage in a desert of what many believe *should* be subpar returns. The books that offered the new-era optimism that was a part of the zeitgeist of the 1990s have been replaced with far more dour tomes like Thomas Piketty's *Capital in the Twenty-First Century* and Michael Lewis'

**Top 25 Years by # Of Closing All Time Highs** (Since 1928)

| Rank | Year | # All Time Highs | Rank | Year | # All Time Highs |
|---|---|---|---|---|---|
| 1 | 1995 | 77 | 13 | 1996 | 39 |
| 2 | 1964 | 62 | 14 | 1965 | 37 |
| 3 | 1928 | 53 | 15 | 1999 | 35 |
| 4 | 1961 | 52 | 16 | 1968 | 33 |
| 5 | 1987 | 47 | 17 | 1972 | 31 |
| | 1998 | 47 | | 1986 | 31 |
| 7 | 1955 | 46 | 19 | 1983 | 29 |
| 8 | 1997 | 45 | 20 | 1959 | 27 |
| | 2013 | 45 | 21 | 1954 | 26 |
| 10 | 1929 | 43 | 22 | 1958 | 24 |
| | 1985 | 43 | | 1980 | 24 |
| 12 | 2014 YTD | 40 | 24 | 1991 | 22 |
| | | | 25 | 1992 | 18 |

*Flash Boys*, both of which have as their central premise the idea that capitalism and the financial markets are rigged. (It should be noted that, according to Kindle statistics, Piketty's *Capital* may be the least read book purchases of all time.)

I've thought a lot about the reasons behind this apathy and revulsion to a development that should be greeted with, at the least, good-humor rather the persistent cynicism that seems to cast a shadow on just about everything in public life these days from politics to entertainment to sports. I've come up with three reasons for the shift in thinking:

**1. Investors and corporations are still scarred by the financial crisis.** This is, of course, perfectly understandable. It's one thing to worry about the value of your securities, but it's quite another to worry about the value of your cash. When a company like General Electric has trouble accessing the commercial paper market, its managers are unlikely to ever forget it. For the individual investor these sentiments are evidencing themselves in a penchant for bond market mutual funds, which have seen net inflows of $1 trillion since the start of 2008, over domestic equity market funds, which have, almost remarkably seen outflows of more than $500 billion during a durable and powerful upward move in stocks. Corporations are evidencing their risk aversion in other ways, most notably a penchant for share buybacks and debt refinancing over capital expenditures. Companies are also seeing it as a badge of honor to eschew stock splits. The average of a stock in the S&P 500 has never been higher. This hurts trading volumes (damnit!) and exhibits an indifference to the individual investor that is shockingly different than anything anyone has seen in recent years.

**2. Cognitive Dissonance Example #1: Weak recovery, strong markets.** By the standard measures of economic recoveries (employment, manufacturing and trade sales, industrial production, and personal income less transfers), this has undoubtedly been a subpar recovery. Of course all market participants have been taught that the economy is not the market and the market is not the economy. Still, it seems as if there is a widening gap between the performance between two concepts that should share some passing familiarity.

**3. Cognitive Dissonance Example #2: "Bad" policies, good outcomes.** Generally speaking, there are four ways in which government policy can influence the economy—fiscal policy, monetary policy, regulation, and trade. If there is an irony about the policy mix as it stands today, it is that its benefits have accrued to the "wrong" people and done little to ease the plight of the common man. A combination of easy monetary and tight regulation helps the super-rich even more. In such a circumstance, those with deep pockets and aided by a cast of

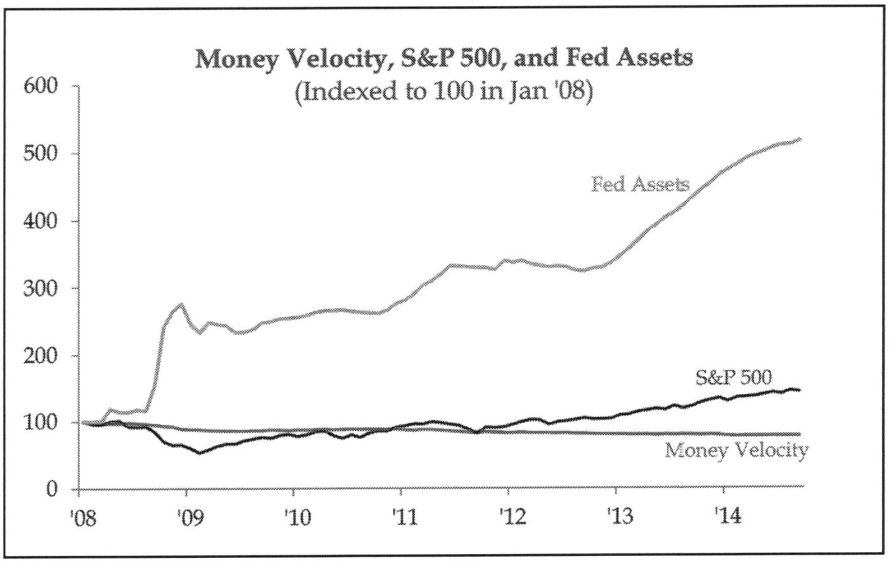


accountants, lawyers, and financial consultants are best able to take advantage of free money. For those without such blessings, prosperity becomes something of a museum piece—not hard to see but impossible to possess.

**Uses of Cash: Pre-Crisis High, Post-Crisis Low, vs. Now**

| Use of Cash | Pre-Crisis High | Post-Crisis Low | Current | % Chg Low To Current |
|---|---|---|---|---|
| Buybacks (TTM, $BN) | $589 | $138 | $533 | 287.3% |
| M&A (TTM, $BN) | $1,024 | $336 | $858 | 155.4% |
| Bond Issuance (TTM, $BN) | $2,737 | $766 | $1,468 | 91.8% |
| Dividends (TTM, $BN) | $252 | $193 | $333 | 72.3% |
| Capex (SAAR, $BN) | $1,982 | $1,584 | $2,227 | 40.6% |
| Non-Financial Corporate Profits w/ IVA & CC Adj (SAAR, $BN) | $1,078 | $655 | $1,260 | 92.3% |
| Non-Financial Corporate Cash (TTM, NSA, $BN) | $5,043 | $4,894 | $6,440 | 31.6% |

The good news in all of this, of course, is that this level of skepticism probably suggests that the bull market will continue for a long time to come. As legendary investor Sir John Templeton once said, "Bull-markets are born on pessimism, grow on skepticism, mature on optimism and die on euphoria." The Achilles' heel to our T.I.N.A. thesis remains the emergence of inflation. While wages seem to have bottomed, we are still far away from the 4% year-over-year increase in wages that tends to signal the end of economic expansions.

# BEST ESSAYS FROM 2015

## *Longing for a More Liberal Use of the "F" Word*

*Originally Published—March 6, 2015*

I remember well an early spring morning more than 20 years ago when I attempted to study for CFA Level I. About 45 minutes into the ethics section and I was snoring and drooling on my newly-purchased text books. Two hours after that and I was at the driving range working on my short game. I repeated the exercise in vain the following Saturday and a year and a half later I was at business school. I realized that I possessed little ability for self-directed study when the temperature broke 60. I was reminded of the whole affair recently when the good folks at the Virginia CFA Society invited me to speak about our investment outlook a few weeks ago. It was a beautiful affair at one of Richmond's most storied and beautiful private clubs and took on, in a way, the air of some great medieval ball for people that knew their way around a financial calculator. Before my speech began, the Society congratulated and saluted the new charter holders and thanked, touchingly, the spouses and significant others that undoubtedly had to suffer with them throughout the whole grueling process. Shortly afterwards, the CFA Institute's Bob Luck shared with the crowd a bittersweet message about the state of the financial industry. The good news is that the number of those achieving and pursuing the CFA designation has grown at a rate that would make any investment banker long to take this non-for-profit organization public.

The bad news is that, according to a 2013 survey conducted by the CFA and public relations firm Edelman, the industry suffers from a poor self-image. In a question posed to 2,100 individual and institutional investors, only 53% expected investment managers and 52% of financial services firms to do what was right. The expectations were only slightly more optimistic among institutional investors themselves at 61% for both types of firms respectively. According to the same

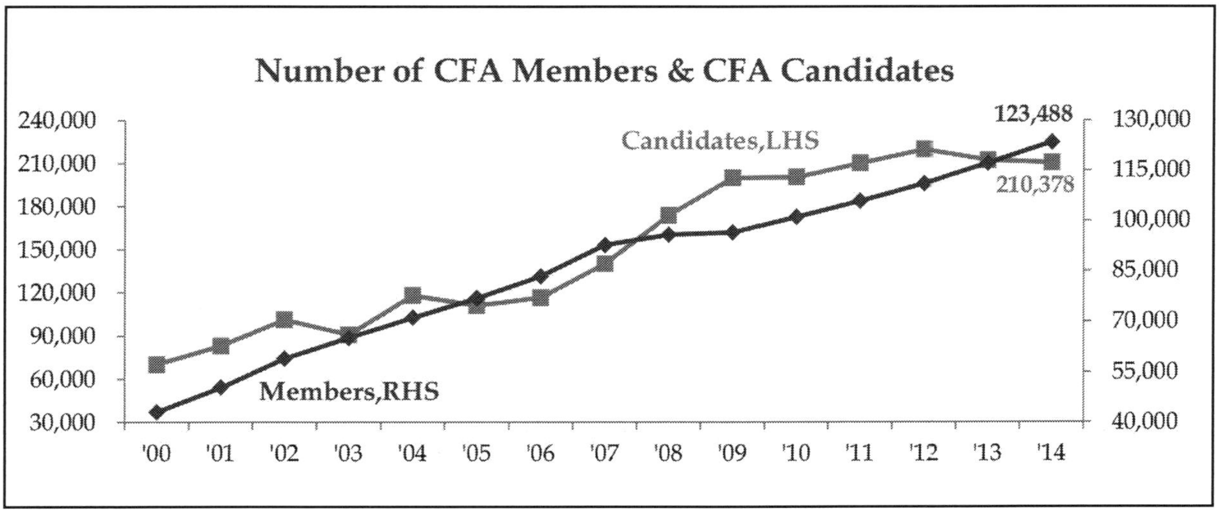


study, the financial services industry ranked last among the public's perceptions of trust. Some of this criticism is no doubt deserved. The financial crisis along with serial misdeeds among individuals at large investment banks and other "financiers" will linger in the minds of investors for a long time to come. Of course, political opportunists and the media are all-too-happy to exploit the prurient interests of a popular culture addicted to scandal. The greatest casualty of "news" relegated to 140 characters at a time appears to be the truth. The phenomenon certainly leaves little room for nuance or context. Our political class, similarly, seems more interested in retribution than reform, not bothering to consider for a moment that the circumstances that led to the financial crisis had many willing participants, not only among unscrupulous financial professionals but also among the general public and our elected "officials." As the chart below indicates, the financial

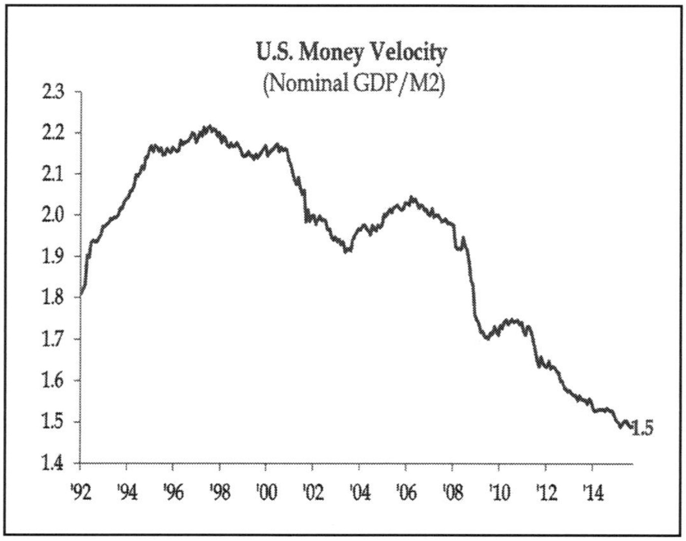


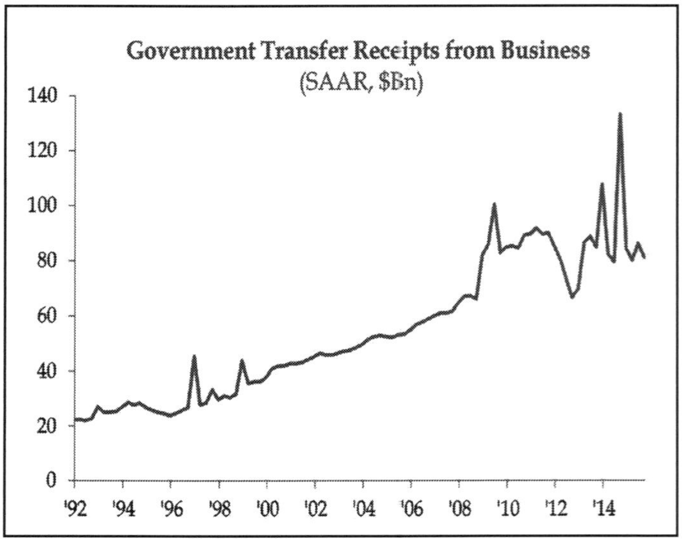

industry continues to pay dearly for its sins, more than six years after the bottom. Is it any wonder, in this sense, that the velocity of money continues to decline despite unprecedented monetary accommodation?

This is, perhaps, only one of many factors contributing to the malaise my partners and I have noticed among our buy-side clients to say nothing of our sell-side colleagues. Despite record highs in the indices, there is a fear that the business is in secular decline. Volumes and commissions are down and the ability to add alpha in the context of a perpetual zero percent interest rate policy seem to be few and far between. Among active managers, the fear seems to be most broadly centered on the growth of passive investments. But as the table below shows, net inflows into domestic equities among mutual funds and ETFs have been a scant $8.6 billion in the past six years. More than $1.2 trillion has flowed into bond funds. (For reference the market capitalization of the S&P 500 is roughly $19 trillion.) Much of this may be attributed to the emotional scars that accompany a financial crisis but at least part of it must be attributed to a perception that financial industry professionals have abandoned their roles as *fiduciaries*.

*An "f" word of a different sort, a* ***fiduciary*** *is expected to put the needs of his client before his own. It is the highest standard of care at either equity or law.*

**Net Flows into Mutual Funds + ETFs ($BN)**

| Year | Equity | | Bond | Money Mkt |
|---|---|---|---|---|
| | Domestic | International | | |
| 2009 | 3.3 | 65.3 | 417.2 | -539.1 |
| 2010 | -34.5 | 98.3 | 262.0 | -524.7 |
| 2011 | -86.1 | 28.4 | 163.7 | -124.0 |
| 2012 | -78.4 | 58.5 | 358.5 | -0.3 |
| 2013 | 122.1 | 204.3 | -59.0 | 15.2 |
| 2014 | 81.3 | 132.1 | 94.5 | 6.3 |
| *TOTAL* | 7.7 | 586.8 | 1,236.9 | -1,116.6 |
| YTD '15 | -106.4 | 199.9 | 60.0 | -18.4 |

Anyone who has worked at a financial firm has asked herself where her loyalties lie—with her firm or her clients. The answers aren't always easy but it seems as if these questions became more difficult after investment banks were no longer partnerships and became public companies. Dismantling Depression era laws like Glass-Steagall didn't help. It is, naturally, very difficult at this point to put the toothpaste back in the tube. Still, the public's perception of Wall Street must be seen in some way as an existential threat to the active management industry. When people let you down, there is a natural human tendency to avoid other people. So far, this phenomenon hasn't extended to the much-vaunted managers of bond funds but it inevitably will. Who then will be left to blame?

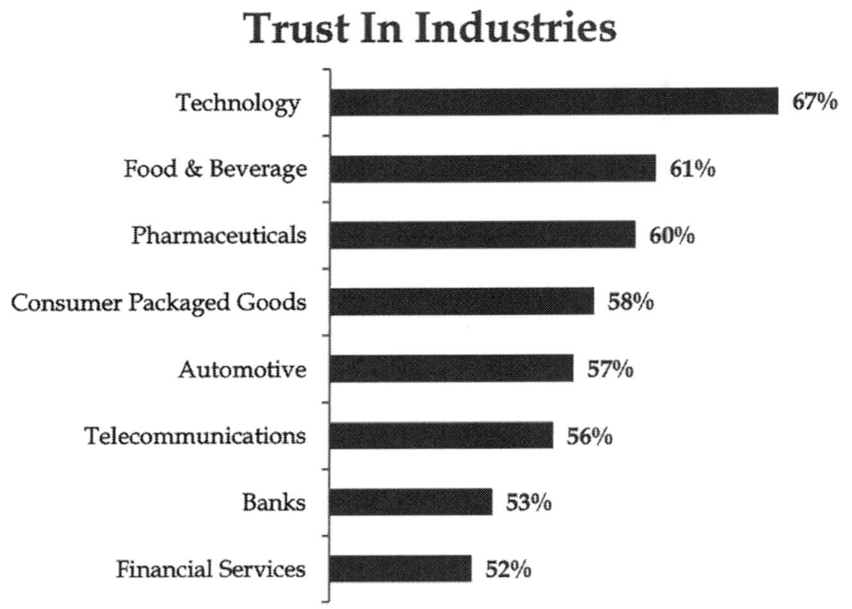

Investors were asked whether they trust the above industries to do what is right.
Source: CFA Institute & Edelman Investor Trust Study 2013

Wall Street, like any business, has had and will continue to have its fair share of parasites and scoundrels. But the ability to raise capital has breathed life into the dreams of the likes of Vanderbilt, Rockefeller, Carnegie, Ford, Jobs, and Gates. In that way this business—our business—is prototypically American. And despite what the popular press might have you believe, Wall Street is not solely comprised of soulless overachievers with no conscience. It's an industry that is made up of hundreds of thousands of regular people who take the subway and the Long Island Rail Road and Metro North to work every day, who worry about paying the mortgage and sending their kids to college. The Lord knows that Jamie Dimon has enough to worry about but one wishes that there was someone else that might be able to fight back and extol the virtues of an industry whose virtues have far outweighed its sins. The CFA Institute is a natural choice. Its curriculum starts with ethics and it is clear from the many events I have attended throughout the years that the subject is central to its mission. The industry should try to start to fight back in the public sphere—not to defend the indefensible behavior of a few but the noble work of the many.

**Top Attributes that Build Trust in an Investment Manager**

| | |
|---|---|
| 53% | Has Transparent and Open Business Practices |
| 52% | Takes Responsible Actions to Address An Issue or A Crisis |
| 51% | Has Ethical Business Practices |
| 48% | Delivers Consistent Financial Returns to Investors |
| 47% | Offers High Quality Products or Services |
| 33% | Has Highly- Regarded And Widely Admired Top Leadership |
| 20% | Creates Programs That Positively Impact The Local Community |
| 18% | Is an Innovator of New Products, Services or Ideas |

Investors were asked: how important is each of the above attributes to building your trust in an investment manager? Source: CFA Institute & Edelman Investor Trust Study 2013

# *Creative Destruction in the Money Management Business*

*Originally Published—August 7, 2015*

*"So let me understand your business a little better. You sell your research to large institutional investors in exchange for commissions?"*

"That's right, sir," I nodded affirmatively. "We have clients all over the country and the world really. Mutual funds, hedge funds, RIAs, endowments…"

*"And you and your partners pay ordinary income tax rates on your profits?"*

"Ummm…..yeah," I said a little confused. "We're an LLC and so our distributions are taxed as income. That's right. It's a pass-through."

*"Hmmm," said a master of the private equity universe ponderously, shaking his head. "To be honest, that doesn't sound like a very good business."*

"Well," I said to the man who by all accounts is one of the good guys in his rarefied circle of merry money makers, "it has its moments, just like any other business."

There are times in business life when you find yourself talking to people who are so successful and have been winning for so long that they appear to have escaped the gravitational pull of life and thus can't imagine anyone who has chosen to pursue a different path. They have largely avoided the slings and arrows of outrageous fortune and forgotten the sting of defeat and the persistent urgency of one of the most reliable concepts in finance—reversion to the mean. I remember well two such conversations in my career. The first occurred in Santa Clara, California in 1999. I was in town in an effort to get a large semiconductor company to participate in the company surveys we conducted at ISI. A standard part of the pitch was that it was a completely anonymous survey, our results and research would be provided for free, and that it was weekly. There were certain cyclical industries, like the airlines for instance, who saw the benefits of the exercise right away and signed up immediately. Within a week six major carriers agreed to participate and within a month it was being used in some fare pricing models. Companies with managements that had either forgotten or never experienced tough times were harder to convince. Their growth, it was believed, was *secular*.

*"Listen," said the head of research at the semi manufacturer, "ASPs for personal computers have been about $2,000 for the last 15 years and it looks like it's going to stay that way. Your economic research is interesting but really has no bearing on our business. I'm afraid participating in your survey would be a waste of time for you and for us."*

I nodded in glum acceptance, said my goodbyes, and wondered whether he might just be right. Within a year we all found out the "new economy" was just as cyclical as the old one. Average Selling Prices for personal computers now rest comfortably at $415, about one-fifth of where they were in 1999. Global sales of PCs in 2014 were just over three hundred million units, roughly 3x what it was at the time of my meeting. Total revenues for the business have thus fallen over 40%.

Another such conversation occurred with a large publicly-traded homebuilder in 2005:

"How's business Sam?" I asked excitedly.

*"If it were any better," he said confidently and forcefully "they'd make it illegal."*

Little did either one of us know how close his words would come to being prophetic. My conversation with the nice man who stands astride the private equity world like a Colossus had the same feel to it, I have to say. Free markets aren't always efficient, of course, and the wheels of its rough justice can be painfully slow to turn. The decision of CalPERS to divest itself of hedge funds in 2014 is seen here in Manhattan as alternatively a harbinger of price discovery in the money management business or simply the latest example of "big, dumb money doing the wrong thing at the wrong time." Whatever side of the fence one might oneself, I have yet to hear a convincing argument to a simple question—

*How can long only managers charging their clients 75 basis points for their money management services be subject to "price discovery" when institutions charging 2 and 20 can avoid it?*

Three or four years ago, the answer to this question would invariably rest on the argument that the higher fee structure allowed the alternative asset manager to hire the best talent. After 5 years of unimpressive performance, few might be willing to make such a claim today.

The best way to eliminate the "corporations short-termism" so derided by political opportunists at the start of the 2016 Presidential race is not, in my opinion, to change the definition of what constitutes a long-term capital gain, it is to eliminate completely the tax on dividends—a reminder to management that they don't actually own the company four times a year. A little bit like Milton Friedman, I am for lower taxes at any time for any reason. I believe that the tax rate on dividends should be zero and that their double taxation may be the single

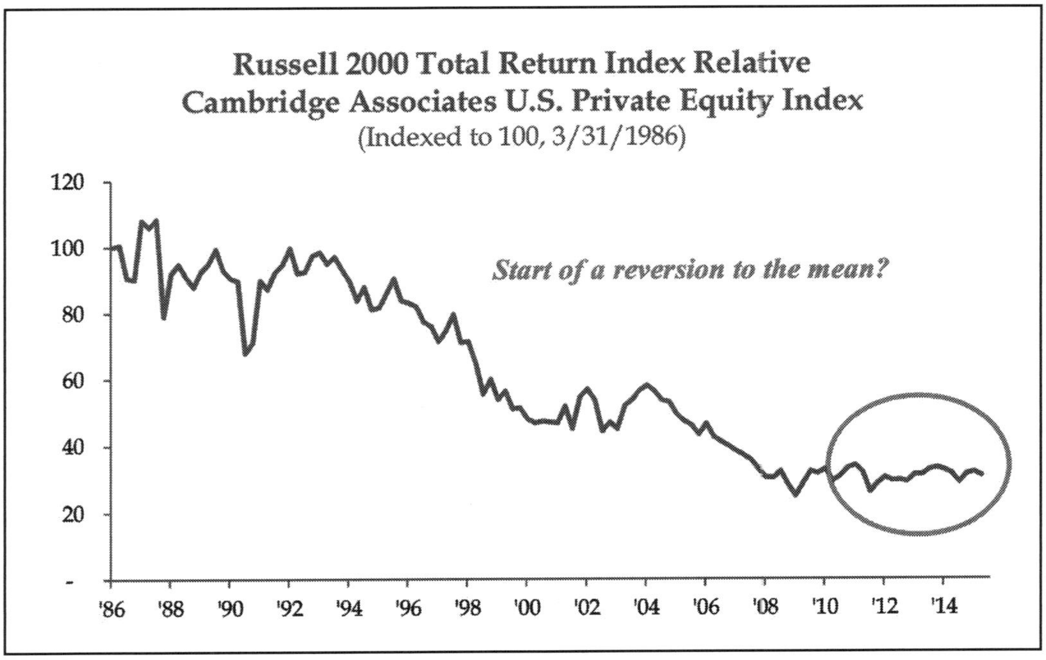


dumbest thing in a tax code—a remarkable achievement for a scheme that tips the Toledos at over 3 million words! Every businessman wants advantages other don't have and all capitalists love free markets when they're starting out. All seek to close the doors behind them once they achieve dominant market positions or have earned through political influence advantages unique to themselves. This is human nature and as such it applies to all of us. Enough money and political influence can forestall the inevitable for a while—but not forever.

The good news it appears is that we are at a point in the cycle at which money center banks and investment banks should do well. Charge-off rates are near 20-year lows for the likes of J.P. Morgan and Wells. The average FICO score for mortgage lending was 727 in June. A steeper yield curve and somewhat easier lending standards could lead be a boon to the earnings of certain financials. The bad news is that there are other firms that appear to be increasingly in the crosshairs of both regulators and consumers. CalPERS just admitted that it had no idea what it is actually paying its private equity managers because of the opacity of carried interest. Increasingly large fiduciaries are coming to the conclusion that their actuarial assumptions may be impossible to achieve. It is only natural upon reaching such a conclusion to seek to cut costs in any way possible—high fee products run by people who have become impossibly wealthy are natural targets. Sadly, the political zeitgeist of the time will likely make these firms easy targets for regulators looking for scalps with deep pockets. The big money center banks and the investment banks have had their turn in the barrel. Now, I'm afraid it will be the large publicly traded alternative money managers. "Calpers' total bill [when carried interest is included] is likely to be astronomical. People will choke when they see the real number," said a finance professor at Oxford. At Strategas we have a bias to be overweight more traditional financials and underweight relatively new ones dependent upon favorable tax treatment of capital gains.

Several alternative asset managers did not start trading until more recently: Apollo on 3/30/2011, Oaktree on 4/12/2012, Carlyle on 5/03/2012, Ares on 5/02/2014, and Fifth Street on 10/30/2014.

| Traditional | |
|---|---|
| BLK | BlackRock |
| STT | State Street |
| BEN | Franklin Resources |
| TROW | T. Rowe Price Group |
| IVZ | Invesco Ltd. |
| AMG | Affiliated Managers |
| LM | Legg Mason |
| EV | Eaton Vance |
| WDR | Waddell & Reed Financial |
| FII | Federated Investors |
| **Alternative** | |
| BX | Blackstone Group |
| KKR | KKR |
| CG | Carlyle Group |
| OAK | Oaktree Capital |
| OZM | Och-Ziff |
| APO | Apollo Global M |
| PSEC | Prospect Capital |
| ARES | Ares Management |
| FIG | Fortress Investment Group |
| FSAM | Fifth Street Asset Mgmt. |

# *America the Beautiful*

*Originally Published—August 14, 2015*

There was a certain point in my career at which I decided to stop complaining about how unpleasant commercial airline travel was and to develop a Zen-like attitude to the seemingly endless indignities and inconveniences. Part of the new attitude was the realization that New York City, for its pretensions of cosmopolitanism, was pretty provincial in its own right. Traveling, I realized, was extraordinarily helpful, essential really, for a job that requires some recognition of major themes and economic trends. At least that was the rationalization I used as I embarked upon a trip to Florida to find my mom a suitable place for her to escape what is likely to be another brutal winter in the Northeast.

She's approaching 80, and while in relatively good health, can no longer drive (a relief for the citizens of Smithtown on Long Island), has little interest in cooking or food at all, and has, sadly, let her status as a widow isolate her to the point where even her own Neapolitan obstinacy is giving way to the practical considerations that accompany getting older. Even she, after 10 years, is recognizing that there is a statute of limitations on grieving. Making matters more difficult (naturally), an immigrant's pride prevents her from accepting from her eldest son (and only child!) even a modest condominium as a gift. An attractive and kind real estate agent pulled up the screen in the conference room of the 48,000 properties for rent or sale were reduced precisely to one when the list of my mother's requirements were factored-in. (The greatest obstacle, it appeared, would be a condo association's acceptance of Paolo, my mom's 10 pound Maltese.)

Driving up and down the inter-coastal highway A1A for three days was a revelation in and of itself. Any signs that there was an epic real estate bust have long since been erased. Cranes are ubiquitous and the new condo towers are shouting from the sandy shores of the Atlantic with increasing urgency. The number of buildings and communities along the coast is, for the practical purposes of the would-be buyer or renter, infinite, with a range of prices to match. We went through two tanks of gas in the course of four days searching high and low for a rental. This was no pleasure trip, let me tell you. As luck would have it, the Westin just off I-95 north of Miami had a transformer blow and was reduced to generator power, the service elevator, and cold food. Half a sandwich, a glass and a half of Chardonnay and my mom felt like turning in at around 7:30. A part of a modern chain, there was nothing about the hotel that would indicate to a kidnapped traveler where in America they might be. Not the names, cities of origin, or passions of the staff proudly displayed on their name tags, and certainly not the faux moderne décor with its bloodless textures, fabrics, and colors impossible to find in nature found in hotels in the vast expanse that is America. Wide-awake, bored, and not being able to stand the hotel's sterility for another moment, I hopped in my rented Impala and drove to the nearest restaurant that had outdoor seating and what appeared to be a lively atmosphere. I didn't venture far and, somewhat predictably now that I think about it, wound up at a Hooters about a mile and a half away. After my chicken wings and a Coors Light, I started to ponder what I might learn from the trip. My Dad taught me a long time ago that humanity often comes from observing others. The crowd was a dog's breakfast of modern American characters—there were quite a few tubby, sunburned older blonde guys in Hawaiian fishing shirts who carried their libations by inserting their index fingers into the mouths of their beer bottles. There was a corn-bred beauty who appeared to be about six feet tall with her boyfriend, a Latin guy who looked to be about 5'5" 150 pounds. A chihuahua that was the spitting image of the dog in the Yo Quiero Taco Bell ads rested comfortably in his lap. There were two guys who seemed so nervous and spoke so furtively that they could be reasonably thought to be taking their vacation from the Viet Cong politburo, an extraordinarily large human being that looked like the actor Ving Rhames, and me, an impossibly tan, fancy-pants dude, taking notes on a paper towel between sips of beer and attempting to catch the action of the three major baseball games being shown simultaneously. (I would have been thrilled with the label "eccentric," a euphemism for "crazy" sometimes reserved for those in button-downed shirts and sports jackets smoking a De Nobili cigar at a Hooters west of I-95.)

This was America, I thought—a collection of people from different backgrounds trying to have some fun and make a few bucks. There was no pretension, just a group of people free to choose what might make them happy. It could have been just about anywhere in the U.S. The trip was evocative of many themes, I thought—the greying of America, the country's almost limitless ability for renewal, its embrace of immigrants, the prototypical melting pot of cultures, styles, and beliefs that make up a modern empire, and our (my) risk of obesity and excess.

My thoughts then drifted, as they often do, to business and what we're trying to accomplish here at Strategas. I started to think about creative destruction and the risk of success. I wondered why I knew very little about Hooters as a corporation while any regular viewer of CNBC would know more than it ever cared to about

Buffalo Wild Wings. Were the owners simply content in its niche—pretty girls serving pub food? Clearly the brand has a value and a head start. Did it realize that by the standards of today's popular culture, Hooters uniforms seem almost puritanical and about as scandalous as a nun's habit? Could it survive given the never-ending supply of casual dining establishments if its food didn't get better—not better *for* you mind you, simply better? I decided that no business, even one in the business of chicken wings and cheap thrills, can stop innovating. Everybody has to be excellent at something other than growth. The essence of capitalism, and thus America, is in serving the needs and wants of others.

# *Donald Trump is Underowned*

*Originally Published—August 28, 2015*

It's often been said that the most dangerous words in the investment business are "it's different this time." To be sure, few good things happen after uttering those words, but I've found more immediate pain meted out by the markets when I say "the market is wrong." One would imagine such thoughts sometimes occur to the cottage industry of political punditry, but if one looks at the phenomenon that has become Donald Trump's bid for the Presidency, it seems few see the irony. If Donald Trump were a stock (need you ask what the symbol would be?) it would be hitting new highs despite a series, maybe even as a result, of analyst downgrades and downward earnings revisions. Since Trump's speech announcing his candidacy (perhaps one of the most interesting if not the most hilarious political speeches of all time), a series of political pundits have continued to write his political obituary, always after the latest shocking thing he has to say. Never has anyone in modern political life been so insistent on sticking his thumb into the eyes of political correctness and not been destroyed by it. As a result, nearly three months after the IPO, TRUMP is hitting new highs, large institutional investors are underweight in their positioning, and the shorts are finding it hard to borrow the stock. In essence, all the "experts" are saying the "market" is wrong, with predictable results.

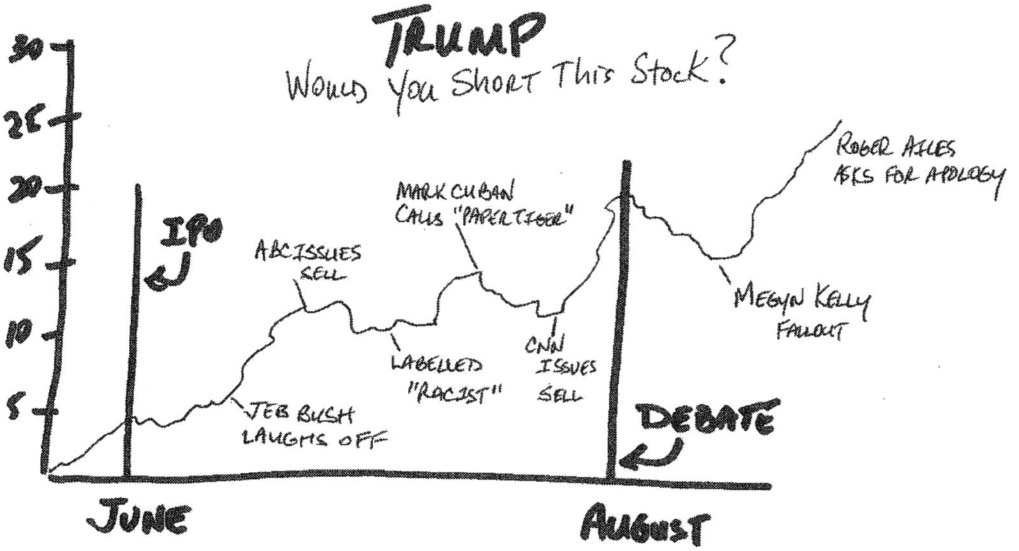

My continued skepticism of pundits and other expensive experts (myself included!) came into clearer focus for me this summer because I yielded to temptation and accepted invitations to fundraisers for two would-be Presidential candidates. Yes the silly season of the election process has started, even for Republicans in Manhattan. On consecutive days, I attended events for Rick Perry and Mike Huckabee. I found both to be likeable enough fellows. What was surprising however was not what they had to say, it was the reaction of the City's conservative political commentariat to their respective candidacies. Perhaps it comes with the territory with the fourth estate but their private comments revealed a shockingly depressing level of cynicism and an utter lack of respect for "the man in the arena." Ultimately, it seemed, they were dismayed that both candidates would be unable to check off every box on the checklist of conservative policy orthodoxy. The subject of Donald Trump as a viable candidate was seen as so absurd as to not even be discussed. "He's not even a Republican!" they hissed, without acknowledging for a moment that this political amateur was beating them at their own game by every conceivable objective measure. Woe is the person that fails to recognize the genius of the elite, conservative and liberal alike.

In my own bow to political correctness, let me say that this essay is no endorsement of Donald Trump as a candidate or some of the outrageous things he sometimes says. I'm simply seeing his success thus far as another example of being able to make outsized gains with variant perceptions and non-consensus views. While there is a market and economic parallel, there is a market and economic implication as well. As recent market action put more clearly into focus over the past week, people, average people, are starting to wonder what has really been meant by the term "free trade." Although it may be the most efficient way to allocate resources in its purest form, free trade is never politically popular. But what people have wondered with China's ascendancy is whether a country of that size can decide to peg its currency to the dollar and not act, prima facie, in an anti-competitive fashion. Sure, it's been great for big businesses with political influence, but what about the rest of us? Has the ability to buy everything from tube socks to flat-panel screens at near cost been worth it for the country as a whole? We're optimistic about the market in the intermediate term—the risk-reward for the S&P looks exceedingly attractive and we believe a recession is unlikely for another year or two. It is thus hard for us to foresee a long-lasting bear market. That being said, the events of the last week would suggest that either such unhappy occurrence would redound positively on the candidacy of The Donald, the only candidate in both political parties that has been consistent in his criticism of trade agreements that favor big businesses and those with political influence at the expense of everyone else.

His wealth (does it really make a difference if it's $3 billion or $12 billion?) gives him a certain flexibility other candidates can't replicate. His other great virtue, and an underappreciated one by the literati at that it seems to me, is that the man is genuinely funny. Of all the books I've read, I can only remember three so humorous that tears of laughter scalded my face—Frederick Exley's *A Fan's Notes*, Anthony Bourdain's *Kitchen Confidential*, and Rick Reilly's *Who's Your Caddy?* Reilly's literary device was to carry the bag for a variety of tour pros and celebrities and devote a chapter to each. His experiences looping for Deepak Chopra and Donald Trump are wet-your-pants funny. Chopra, despite his quest for inner peace, would utter, often invent, curse words that would make Tony Montana blush with every wayward shot. The Donald was the apotheosis of every man's (well perhaps every 15-year old boy's) dream. Reilly wrote, in a chapter entitled The Search for True Trumpaliciousness:

> *You do not interview Trump. You just try to be in the Doppler radar when his tornado blows by and sucks you in. You needn't even ask a question. Trump will take over from here. Your job is to simply try to keep your hat on and your Bic working. At the end of a 12-hour day, you will be spit out of a black stretch limo on a Manhattan street corner, unsure of what you've seen, your notes scattered, your mind severely Trumped. So you try to piece it together. Was it real? Any of it? So many lies. So many truths. So much bullshit. So much beauty. It all rolls into one colossal Trumpalooza.*

In my career I've been tempted to try to short stocks that have many of the same characteristics. It feels right, even sensible. Unfortunately, it's also often very expensive.

# *Red Dawn*

*Originally Published—September 25, 2015*

Committed capitalists of a certain age could be forgiven for wondering whether a more modern version of the 1980s film *Red Dawn* was unfolding here in the U.S. over the last week. For those of you unfamiliar with the picture, it recounts the story of a group of Midwestern high school students who band together to defend their mid-western town from invading Soviet forces. With a cast that includes Patrick Swayze, C. Thomas Howell, Charlie Sheen, and Lea Thompson, it still remains a mystery to me that the Academy of Motion Pictures failed to recognize its genius when it was released in 1984. It's one of those movies so bad it's actually good. WOLVERINES! Although somewhat less dramatic, a more modern invasion of statists seems to have taken place in the U.S. recently—the Federal Reserve appears as if it wants to add to its already considerable responsibilities and act as central banker to the world while the Democratic front runner for the 2016 presidential race tweeted her desire to set drug prices. Two of the country's most prominent economists, and Nobel laureates at that, released a book on Tuesday entitled *Phishing for Phools*, which attempts to deliver a "fundamental challenge" to the wisdom of free markets. "As long as there is profit to be made," our intellectual heroes intone, "sellers will systematically exploit our psychological weaknesses and our ignorance through manipulation and deception." Presumably, the fact that one of the authors happens to be married to Janet Yellen should be of no particular concern as long as the rest of us can rely on the "help" of the intelligentsia to figure it all out. It reminds me of the late Barton Biggs quip that Long Term Capital Management might have been able to withstand the addition to its staff of one Nobel Laureate, but that once the fund hired its second, it was doomed. As luck would have it, the free market was represented by a creepy little dude who thought he would be a more sympathetic character as a pharmaceutical profiteer than as a hedge fund manager. (With this logic, is there any doubt that he will seek a seat in Congress?) The arrival of China's President Xi, 159 other U.N. clowns, and a loveable but admittedly left-leaning Pope, and I felt a strong desire to return to 1984, when Reagan was our President, Milton Friedman was my hero, and Alex P. Keaton was a role model. If there is an investment conclusion in all this, it is that until free markets are allowed to operate independently, the financial markets will likely continue to be held hostage to the utterances of those with the greatest political clout. The most recent volatility may just be the beginning, especially as we enter the silly season of American presidential politics.

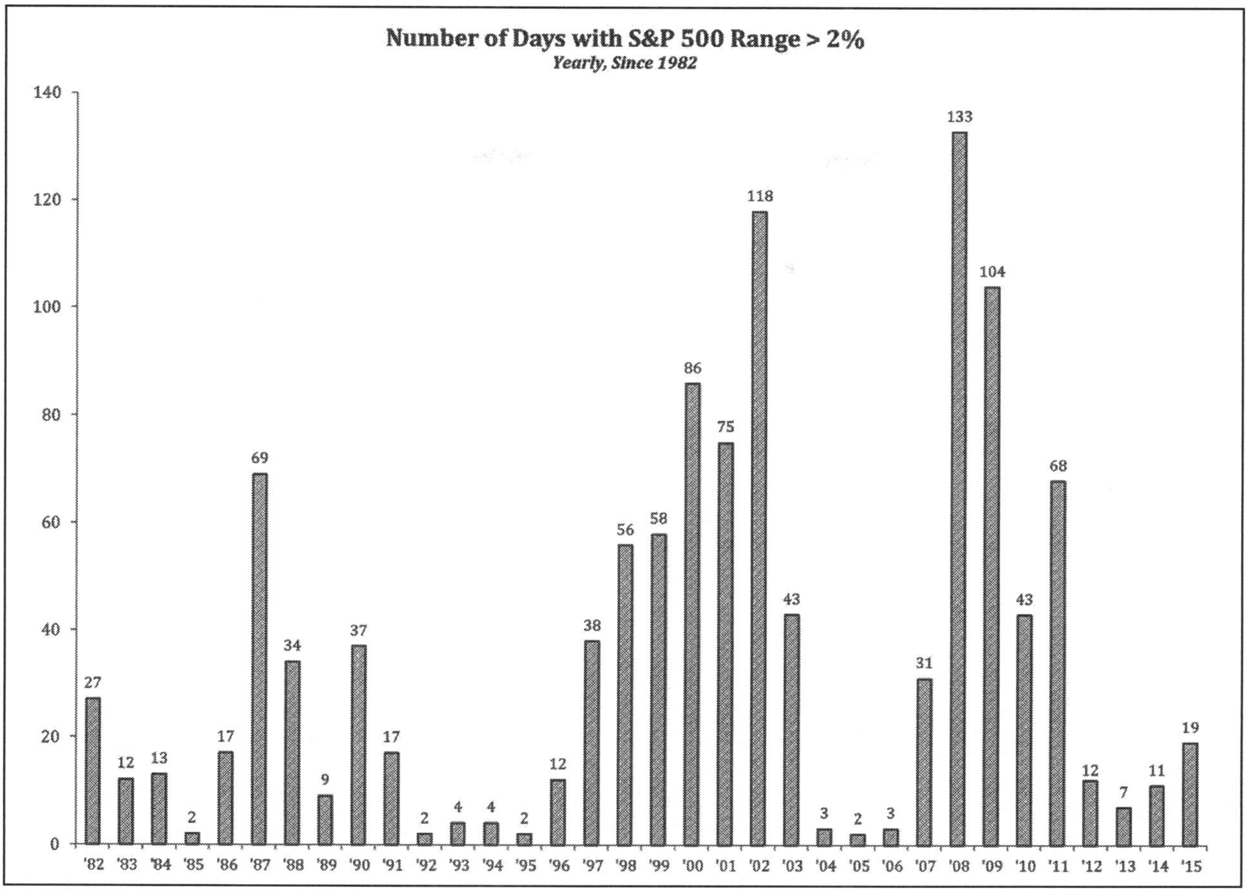

source: *Red Dawn* MGM/UA Entertainment Company (1984) (USA)

# *Lessons for Young People Pursuing a Career on Wall Street*

*Originally Published—October 16, 2015*

Entirely too much time on airplanes and a sentimental nature led me to write a book, My Side of the Street, which was published by St. Martin's Press in May. I wasn't dumb enough to write a book to make money—my first was published about 10 years ago and is now ranked at 2,545,194 on Amazon—I wrote it simply to put between two hard covers some of my impressions from watching this great parade over the past 27 years. I visited my alma mater, Georgetown University, this week to talk about what it was like to build a career on Wall Street. The memories, good and bad, came flooding back, and while I found myself jealous of youth for all the obvious reasons, I also found myself empathetic to the plight of those just starting out. My talk was based largely on the excerpt below:

*A dream factory of a different sort, Wall Street will forever attract young people seeking to make their way in the world and amass their fortunes. For the well connected, getting a job on the ever-expanding behemoth that is Wall Street has grown much easier, so it's not all that difficult to find a seat even when you're just starting out. It's much harder for those who don't know anyone to break in to the great game. But either way, what's really tough is surviving. Surviving the long hours—the travel, the venality of middle management, the siren song of dumb personal investments, and the ever-quickening pace of changes in global finance—with your health and character intact will not be easy. It will require a sense of humor and a perspective that usually develops only after some measure of suffering has been endured. My own struggles to get a job and to build a career on Wall Street have led me to believe that young people should consider the following advice:*

***1. Assume no one will help you until you've accomplished something.*** *All the things you've heard about the large bulge bracket firms' mentorship programs and their concern for your career you will learn upon arrival are absurd. The "recruiting" process may have convinced you that you were highly sought after because your unique skills would allow you, in carefully measured steps, to climb the corporate ladder all the way to the C-suite. Sorry, boys and girls: you're there to do a job that helps the firm make money, pure and simple.*

*If you're unlucky, you'll run into someone who is purposefully trying to derail your career. If you're fortunate, people will leave you alone to privately pursue excellence. The chances are one in a million that someone will actively seek to help you before you've actually achieved something you've had to accomplish on your own. This isn't because people on Wall Street are meanspirited, necessarily; it's because the pace and the stress of most Wall Street jobs leave precious little time for senior people to spare any meaningful time teaching and training those just starting out. This means that career advancement for the young Wall Street professional requires ambition, self-direction, and a thick skin. In a world where everyone these days gets a participation trophy, younger people are having a harder time realizing that no one will look out for their own interests better than they will.*

***2. Focus on achievement rather than status.*** *The prudent man will apply a haircut of 50 percent to any outsized fairy tales of success and money heard around any bar frequented by financial professionals. In any industry largely made up of people of unparalleled competitiveness, it is natural to focus on beating the other guy at his own game. The trick is to figure out what your game is. Most young people on Wall Street care more about getting 21 and having other people know it than simply trying to beat the dealer. This is a recipe for perpetual dissatisfaction even when outsized compensation and status have been achieved. Learn to distinguish between pride and vanity. As Jane Austen pointed out, "Pride relates more to our opinion of ourselves, vanity to what we would have others think of us."*

***3. Learn to live the capital asset pricing model.*** *A foundation of modern finance, the capital asset pricing model (CAPM) attempts to capture the relationship between risk and return. One half of the equation relates to the time value of money, the other half attempts to calculate the return needed to compensate an investor for the risk he's taking. As this relates to a career, the CAPM means, almost by definition, that those earning the highest returns will be the ones who take on the most risk. You may think you have it made because you made it into Morgan Stanley's two-year investment banking training program, but the highest earning member of your graduating class is much more likely to have taken the road less traveled with a company no one's ever heard of or have, ye gods, started his or her own business. A conventional Wall Street career can be both lucrative and satisfying but you should remember that there's a whole big world out there that doesn't care whether you made managing director. Some guy who started his own medical device company in the barn of his parents' farm in Des Moines will be able to buy and sell you ten times over.*

**4. Play to your strengths.** *This should be obvious for any well-educated, well-adjusted adult but it's amazing what can happen when you put a group of highly competitive people together in a survival-of-the-fittest type race to get a Wall Street job. When put in such a circumstance, normally rational people will abandon any thought about what they actually might enjoy doing or, even more importantly, what they might actually be good at when seeking a job in the financial industry. The focus often becomes getting a "better" job than the next guy, a position the mere mention of which conveys responsibility, wealth, and intelligence. Remember, however, that it's not easy to feel smart, wealthy, or important if you're in a job you're ill-suited for in terms of skills or temperament. Tony Bennett is famous for saying that if you do what you love you never have to work a day in your life. Trust me, if you're good at what you do, the money will come. In an industry that isn't trying to cure cancer or put a man on the moon, attitude beats aptitude every time.*

**5. Realize that Wall Street is both large and small at the same time.** *This is less an issue today than it was when I was starting out a generation ago, but it is still common among most young people to assume that Wall Street is basically comprised of the largest money-center banks, mutual funds, and hedge funds. They don't realize that there are literally thousands of firms on Wall Street that might love to hire a bright and enterprising young man or woman who merely wants a chance. Success on Wall Street will always be largely a function of hard work, and of forming future, well-placed connections. Why slug it out among a nest of vipers at a name-brand firm when a smaller company might offer you the chance to make a difference and earn battlefield promotions? While the Street is large enough to accommodate a number of different career interests and paths to success, it should also be remembered that it is an insular industry, especially on the island of Manhattan. Don't make enemies. Take the high road. Be gracious in both success and defeat and remember that your treatment of all people great and small will be remembered, for better or for worse, forever.*

**6. Read.** *For the young person just starting out it's easy to forget, as it says in Ecclesiastes, that there is truly nothing new under the sun. Your ambitions, struggles, failures, anxieties, and successes have all been repeated millions of times in the two hundred thousand years of human existence. The quicker you realize you're not that special and that you've hit life's lottery by being born in a country where peace and freedom are considered givens, the quicker you'll develop the perspective needed to deal with the vast ironies of a life on Wall Street. We read to know that human beings are hopelessly predictable, to know that we're not alone, and to realize that the best and the worst of times don't last. Reading is essential* *to an understanding that investing will never be reduced to mathematical models, that it is and forever will be a social science. Most important, it should help you steer clear of trouble.*

*Lastly, everyone who seeks a job on Wall Street should have at least a passing familiarity with its social utility, of its vast potential to serve the economy, and of its ability to do good in the world. Then the money you make from year to year might not matter as much and, ironically, you might give yourself a greater chance of attaining and keeping wealth—albeit more slowly.*

Adapted from Chapter 11, Other People's Money, My Side of the Street, St. Martin's Press, 2015.

# *Wealth Without Workers*

*Originally Published—October 30, 2015*

One of the many nice things about having a daily research meeting is that you allow other people to make you smarter somewhat passively. If you're not presenting, you can simply sit back and listen and think. As a sell-sider, this is a luxury as far as investment meetings are concerned. The longer one does this job, the harder it is to simply say nothing in any setting, regardless of the subject. In that way, the job can feel as if it wouldn't be much of a stretch to become a politician or, for those burdened with strict ethical standards, a game show host.

About two weeks ago, Strategas' Chief Market Technician showed a chart in his work that has stimulated a lot of thought about the nature of the modern American economy and the workforce. It showed the fact that the market capitalization of Amazon (AMZN, \$293bn) had exceeded that of Wal-Mart (WMT, \$185bn) for the first time ever (see below). It can be argued that Wal-Mart's concept of the superstore was the most significant disruptive business model to have ever been introduced to the retailing industry upon its founding in 1962. Neither the sole proprietorship nor the traditional department store was immune to the juggernaut that became the big-box retailer. Today, it appears that the falcon has started to hear the falconer. This is not surprising in the context of creative destruction, simply the pace and magnitude of the disruption, especially for labor. Wal-Mart, it should be noted, has 2,200,000 employees worldwide (1.4 million in the United States) while Amazon has 154,000.

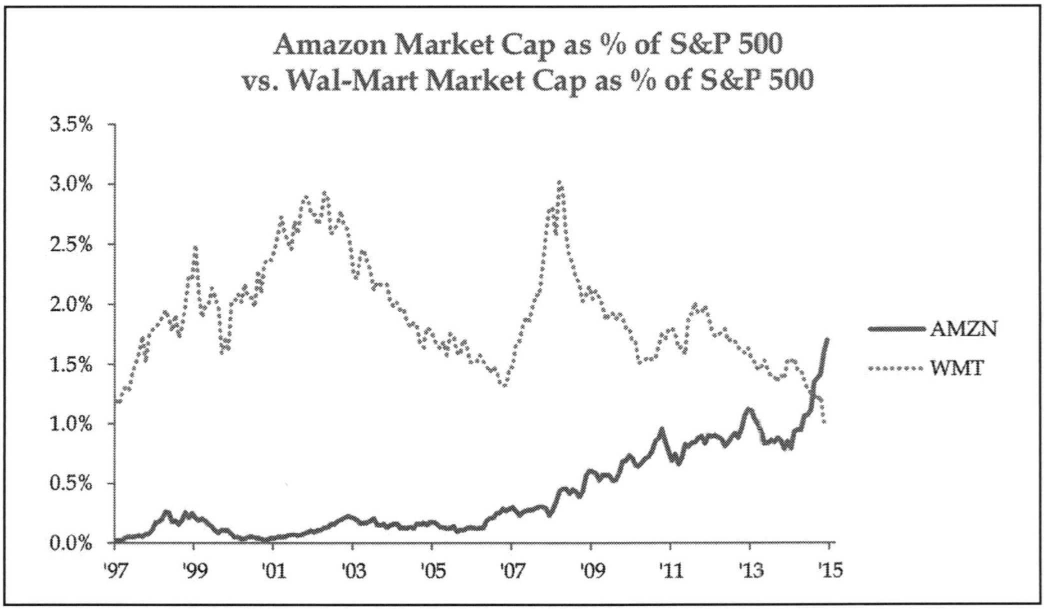

My sense of the impact of such a rapid and meaningful change to society was heightened during my visit to Silicon Valley last week. All of us know that the coasts are and have been significantly different from the rest of America for some time. It can be argued, however, that these differences have grown as the U.S. transitioned from a manufacturing economy to a service-oriented one. (Today, less than 9% of the American workforce plies its trade in manufacturing.) But as the table below shows, the most valuable companies in the U.S. today have relatively few employees. Facebook has an enterprise value of nearly $285 billion with only about 9,000 employees. Similarly, valued companies, like Coca Cola and Comcast have nearly 10 times the number of workers.

**S&P 500 Cos. With Highest Enterprise Value to Employee Count Ratio***

| | Company | EV ($Mil) | Number of Employees | Ratio |
|---|---|---|---|---|
| FB | Facebook | 290,230 | 9,199 | 31.6 |
| GILD | Gilead | 162,365 | 7,000 | 23.2 |
| REGN | Regeneron | 64,390 | 2,925 | 22.0 |
| NFLX | Netflix | 53,458 | 2,450 | 21.8 |
| NAVI | Navient | 130,301 | 6,200 | 21.0 |
| V | Visa | 227,308 | 11,300 | 20.1 |
| ALXN | Alexion | 44,778 | 2,273 | 19.7 |
| CELG | Celgene | 99,538 | 6,012 | 16.6 |
| EOG | EOG | 46,997 | 3,000 | 15.7 |
| VRTX | Vertex | 28,575 | 1,830 | 15.6 |

**S&P 500 Cos. With Lowest Enterprise Value to Employee Count Ratio**

| | Company | EV ($Mil) | Number of Employees | Ratio |
|---|---|---|---|---|
| KSS | Kohl's | 13,460 | 137,000 | 0.10 |
| JEC | Jacobs | 5,570 | 64,000 | 0.09 |
| SPLS | Staples | 6,437 | 79,075 | 0.08 |
| GPS | Gap | 11,440 | 141,000 | 0.08 |
| HOT | Starwood | 12,798 | 180,400 | 0.07 |
| BBY | Best Bu | 8,823 | 125,000 | 0.07 |
| YUM | YUM! | 34,706 | 537,000 | 0.06 |
| DRI | Darden | 8,429 | 148,892 | 0.06 |
| GME | GameStop | 3,407 | 73,000 | 0.05 |
| RHI | Robert Half | 5,938 | 225,000 | 0.03 |

Increasingly it appears as if the markets are placing the greatest value on those companies with the much-diminished needs for people and physical plant. This has broad economic and societal ramifications for everything from commercial real estate to education and politics. The problem ultimately, is that those without specialized skills are finding it increasingly difficult to obtain a job that pays enough to build a family and enjoy a middle class life much less accumulate wealth. While this is good for capital and suggests that margins are likely to stay higher, longer than anyone thought possible, it also suggests that there is likely to be greater friction between capital and labor as time goes on. Populists and politicians will seek to exploit this friction. If we're unlucky, the solution sought will not be to revolutionize our educational system but to fix this inequality by fiat. It is interesting to note that the least regulated sector, Information Technology, is creating the most wealth.

# *Negative Interest Rates, a Modern Policy Error, and the New Bid for Gold*

*Originally Published—February 11, 2016*

> *In the absence of the gold standard, there is no way to protect savings from confiscation through inflation. There is no safe store of value. If there were, the government would have to make its holding illegal, as was done in the case of gold. The financial policy of the welfare state requires that there be no way for the owners of wealth to protect themselves. This is the shabby secret of the welfare statists' tirades against gold. Deficit spending is simply a scheme for the "hidden" confiscation of wealth. Gold stands in the way of this insidious process. It stands as a protector of property rights. If one grasps this, one has no difficulty in understanding the statists' antagonism toward the gold standard.*
>
> *Alan Greenspan, "Gold and Economic Freedom," Capitalism: The Unknown Ideal, 96*

When Chairman Bernanke and the Fed originally embarked upon its' non-traditional form of monetary accommodation, the greatest fear among those who believe in the concept of sound money was not of deflation, naturally, but eventually, of inflation. After all, if central banks could simply print money and have politicians spend it to avoid economic pain what purpose would the free enterprise system serve? Little by little, the Victorian notion of the role of central banks as arbiters of price stability gave way to extra-legal concerns that included economic growth and even "social justice." Paul Krugman and other "new era" thinkers openly ridiculed the potential unintended consequences of the Fed quintupling its balance sheet from $800 billion before Bear Stearns failed in March 2008 to nearly $4.5 trillion today. The frequent victory laps were obnoxiously frequent and frequently obnoxious. But, to be fair, none of the most common anxieties about such easy money came to pass—inflation has stayed stubbornly low to the bewilderment, it turns out, of even the most ardent architects and defenders of the Fed's "new tools." One can't help think about T.S. Eliot's observation that "the last temptation is the greatest treason: to do the right deed for the wrong reason."

The Fed's thinking seemed logical enough—enough monetary accommodation would push up financial asset prices, lower the cost of capital, eventually leading corporations to pursue greater capital expenditures and consumers, who, feeling wealthier, to spend just a little bit more. The problem, it turns out, was that relying only on monetary policy provided the impetus for financial, rather than economic risk taking. Corporations didn't take advantage of the lower cost of capital to build new plants (at least in the U.S.), but to buy back shares. Here, one can blame a regulatory policy on financial institutions that largely sterilized the impact of easy money. In an environment in which the federal government would see no irony in suing J.P. Morgan for the practices Bear Stearns committed, who can blame financial institutions for extending loans to only the most financially sound clients? Despite an embarrassment of riches in excess reserves, the velocity of money has continued to decline. (It should be noted that the average FICO score of a mortgage written in 2015 was 753.) As far as capital spending is concerned, who could blame the average CEO for doing precisely with the company's cash

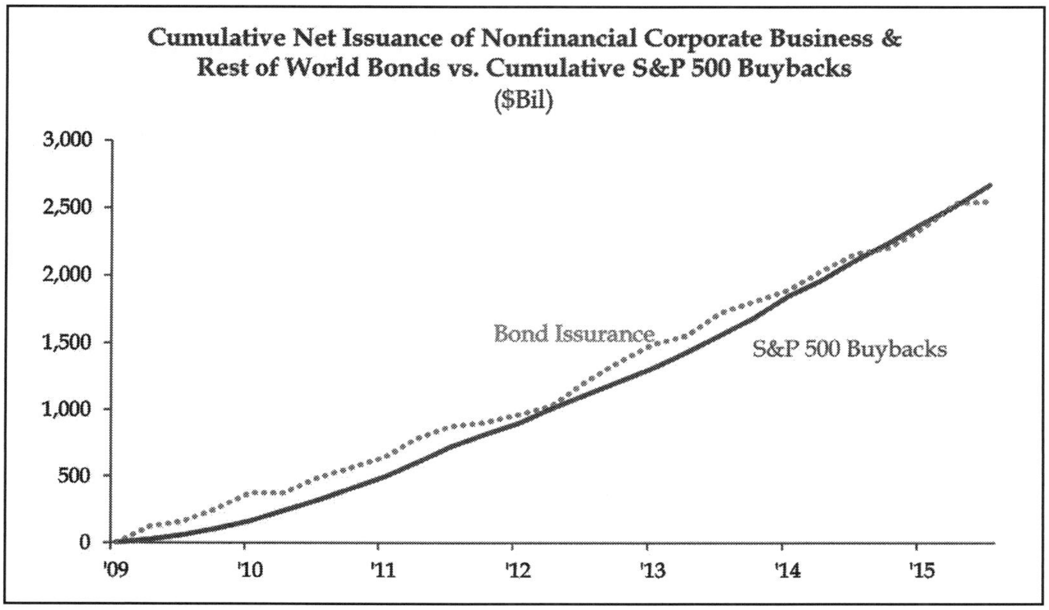

what the market has most handsomely rewarded—share repurchases and other financial legerdemain that was most immediately accretive to earnings. Few nasty questions from investors, or Ye Gods a call from Carl Icahn, are forthcoming after the announcement of a buyback. "A capital spending project that might take three years to pan out? No thanks. Not in this political environment. I may very well be forced to 'spend more time with my family' by that time. And no one wants that, least of all me."

An absence of a cogent fiscal policy that might inspire greater confidence is also to blame. Ask your average group of institutional investors who the Secretary of the Treasury is and you'll be lucky if one in five could tell you within five seconds. That isn't an indictment of the preparedness of investors, but rather an indictment of an Administration that seems to feel as if low rates are a panacea for all that ails the economic system. When all you have is a hammer, everything starts to look like a nail. And so here we are, with a Fed that is in the position of needing to hike rates ("normalize" is the preferred euphemism) when we're already at levels of full employment. In a sense, one could claim that the Fed missed the business cycle. The Fed's attempts are being complicated mightily by the fact that nearly a third of sovereign debt outstanding now sports negative interest rates. In retrospect, watching the dollar rally nearly 21% versus the Euro and 11% versus the Yen since June 2014 was, in effect, a tightening. A continued focus on such academic concepts as the Phillips Curve and NAIRU in the face of declining inflationary expectations and tightening financial conditions today will only put greater pressure on an already fragile financial system and are now starting to be priced into stock prices. The irony again may be that the real economy will

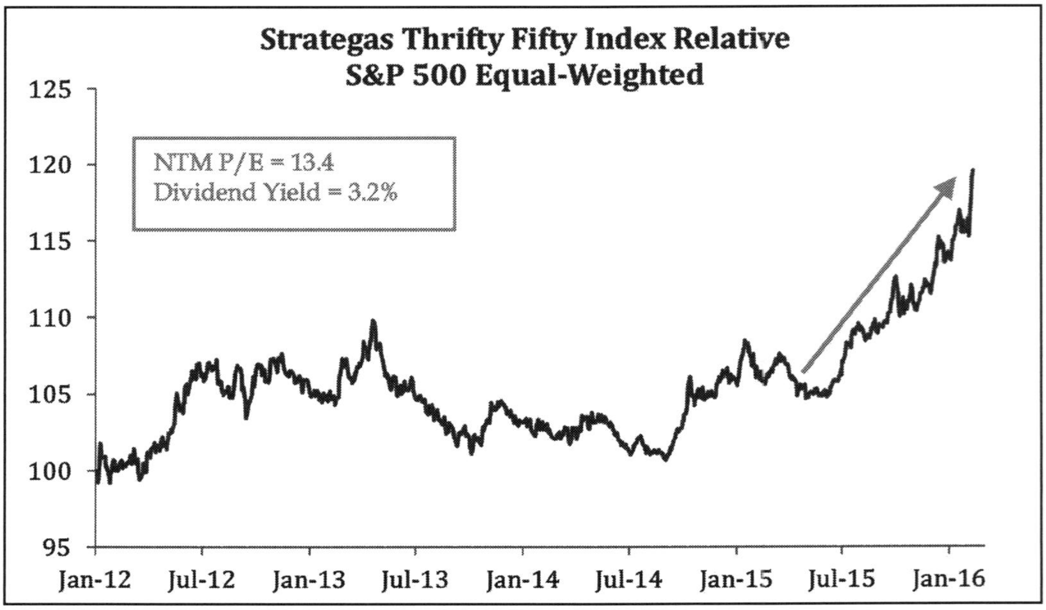

outperform risky assets. At 3.1%, consumer spending grew at its fastest pace in 10 years in 2015. And government spending and tax cuts are likely to add 0.6% to GDP this year.

Enter the current discussion of NIRP or negative interest rate policies. In place by the ECB since 2014 and subsequently adopted by Denmark, Sweden, and Switzerland, Japan joined the party two weeks ago. While not an indication of future policy, it appears that the Fed is flirting with the idea, including NIRP as part of their "severely adverse scenarios" in their 2016 stress tests. This is making an already tense situation for the global financial institutions worse to the extent which it compresses net interest margins, may play havoc with money market funds, and tax savers. Can an asset be considered risk free when one must pay the issuer to own it? In short, there are no risk free assets in countries with negative interest rates. Paradoxically, investors may either need to take greater risks with capital that should be risk free or must save more to meet future spending needs. Neither consequence is consistent with prudent capital allocation or economic growth. Until the Fed restores some of its credibility, it seems likely that the flight to safety will continue. Strategas' Thrifty Fifty basket of stocks that could be reasonably considered proxies for sovereign debt—especially sovereign debt sporting negative interest rates—is likely to continue to outperform. The equally-weighted basket of fifty stocks sports a P/E of 13.4x NTM earnings with a dividend yield of 3.2%. It might not be a bad place to hide until the current flirtation with a new financial crisis passes. A sense of what a hash the alchemists of global central banks have made of things has been the recent bid in the price of gold. It turns out that in a world of negative interest rates, fiat money also yields nothing and costs money to store, just like the yellow metal pejoratively referred to as a barbarous relic. It's also easier to steal.

# *Valeant & the "Platform" Companies of the Past*

*Originally Published—March 18, 2016*

In the 1960s, they were called "conglomerateurs," a group of highly commercial public company CEOs who used their stocks as currency to amass disparate businesses under one roof. The patron saint of the movement was Jimmy Ling, a flamboyant Texan who turned $2,000 into the 14th largest company in the country in a mere 14 years. (It was reported that he first started selling the prospectus of his Ling-Temco-Vought Corporation at the Texas State Fair in 1946.) What was eventually known as LTV Corporation was a patchwork of electronics, meatpacking, aerospace and defense, and sports equipment businesses. Seeing the enormous success of LTV, companies like ITT, Litton Industries, Teledyne, and Textron embraced the conglomerate model as well. Said legendary Wall Street historian John Brooks of Ling "his deals over the succeeding decade were so complex, innovative, and ultimately bewildering that to describe them comprehensibly at book length would be a literary tour de force, and to describe them in a few words impossible."[13] As with most great business adventures, the fuel for the phenomenon was exceptionally easy access to credit and low interest rates, the intellectual justification of the movement—to "diversify risk" during a period of exceptional economic cyclicality—was developed by investment bankers and consultants to satisfy the cupidity of other captains of industry only after the trend was well underway. Typically, the boom fell apart when interest rates started to rise in the 1970s and the expected "synergies" came short of satisfying anxious bondholders.

We mention all this in the context of the current catastrophe-taking place at Canadian drugmaker Valeant (VRX- $29.69). We don't mean to pile on here. As strategists and economists we know nothing about the company and its prospects. Still, as students of financial history, we think it's worth bearing in mind that the conglomerates of yesteryear bear some passing resemblance to today's "platform" companies. Presenting at a Grant's Interest Rate Observer Conference last fall, JHL Capital Group presented a list of stocks with a similar business model trading at lofty valuations. As the data on the next chart shows, the Platform Boom Index, after exceptional outperformance, has slowed its forward progress. Some of the companies look expensive. The potential for wider corporate credit spreads,

13. John Brooks, The Go-Go Years, New York, John Wiley & Sons, pp.165-166.

heavier regulatory scrutiny, and discretion might suggest that Valeant's recent troubles should lead investors to take a closer look at companies growing through serial acquisition.

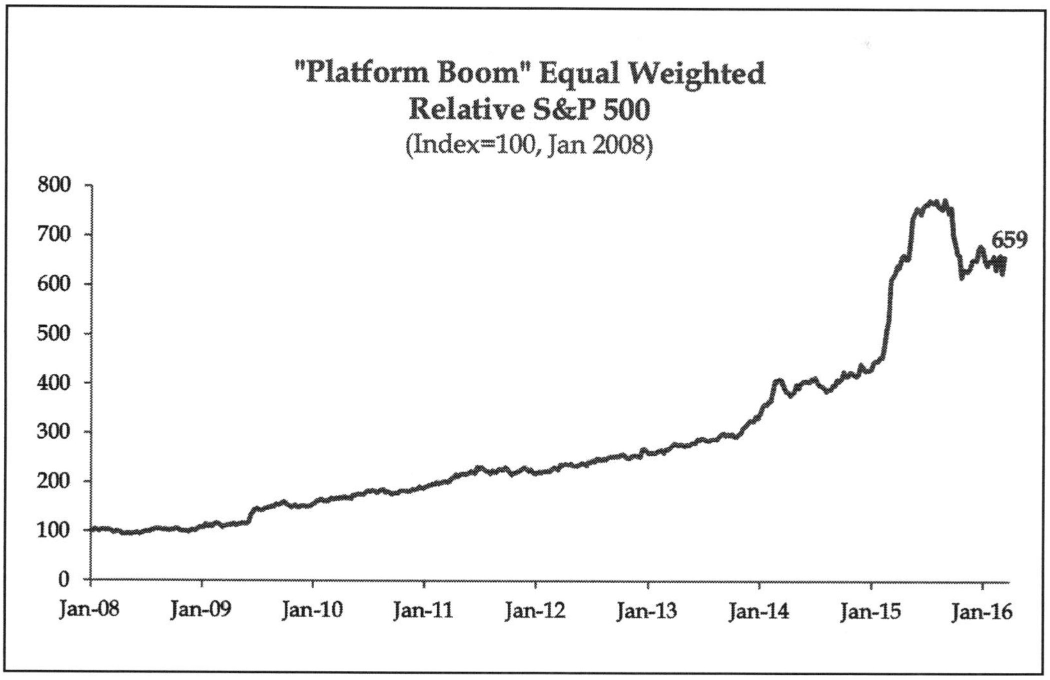


## PLATFORM BOOM CONSTITUENTS

| Ticker | Name | NTM P/E | 2016 Est. EPS Growth | 2016 Est. Sales Growth | Hedge Fund % of Outstanding Shares *(Sorted)* | Market Cap ($Bn) |
|---|---|---|---|---|---|---|
| SPB | Spectrum Brands | 20.5 | 13% | 9% | 69% | $ 6.2 |
| AMAG | AMAG Pharma | 8.9 | 123% | 37% | 40% | $ 0.8 |
| PAH | Platform Specialty | 13.3 | -6% | 35% | 39% | $ 1.9 |
| TDG | TransDigm | 19.3 | 20% | 17% | 33% | $ 11.8 |
| POST | Post Holdings | 38.7 | 159% | 9% | 33% | $ 4.5 |
| HZNP | Horizon Pharma | 6.1 | 25% | 36% | 32% | $ 2.4 |
| VRX | Valeant Pharma. | 3.1 | -6% | -22% | 32% | $ 15.0 |
| KHC | Kraft Heinz | 25.0 | 35% | -3% | 27% | $ 94.8 |
| ENDP | Endo International | 5.5 | 29% | 35% | 20% | $ 7.5 |
| MNK | Mallinckrodt | 6.6 | 9% | 10% | 20% | $ 6.3 |
| JAH | Jarden Corp | 17.7 | 11% | 16% | 19% | $ 12.4 |
| AGN | Allergan | 18.2 | 7% | 13% | 16% | $ 107.8 |
| LBTYA | Liberty Global | 44.4 | 158% | 0% | 15% | $ 9.5 |
| MYL | Mylan N.V. | 9.2 | 15% | 15% | 12% | $ 22.8 |
| AVGO | Avago Tech | 13.2 | 17% | 92% | 9% | $ 58.0 |
| HAIN | Hain Celestial | 18.5 | 7% | 9% | 9% | $ 4.1 |
| PRGO | Perrigo | 13.6 | - | - | 9% | $ 19.1 |
| JAZZ | Jazz Pharma | 10.5 | 17% | 15% | 7% | $ 7.4 |
| CXR | Concordia | 4.8 | 32% | - | 6% | $ 2.1 |
| TMO | Thermo Fisher | 17.2 | 7% | 3% | 4% | $ 55.1 |
| DHR | Danaher | 18.3 | 14% | 11% | 2% | $ 62.7 |
| MDT | Medtronic | 16.4 | 8% | 3% | 1% | $ 107.4 |
| ABI | Anheuser-Busch Inbev | 24.4 | -12% | - | 1% | $ 167.7 |
| ATC | Altice NV | 33.0 | -25% | - | 0% | $ 13.4 |

# *The Ransom of Recession Rick*

*Originally Published—February 5, 2016*

***China Statistics Chief Arrested***

*The head of China's Nat'l Bureau of Statistics was arrested for violations of party discipline, CNN reported. The arrest came just hours after he gave a speech about the risk of capital leaving the country. Financial outflows reportedly topped $650 bil in '15, with some estimates as high as $1 tril. Outflows make it difficult for China to ease the yuan's peg to the dollar in an effort to achieve a soft landing of its slowing economy. IBD, 1/26/16*

Every investment company that has regular research meetings has one—the office gadfly that constantly challenges the house view on everything ranging from its earnings forecasts to the funds available in the 401k plan to the appropriate color to paint the women's bathroom. He (and it's almost always a he) is the proverbial pain in the ass, the fly in the ointment, the monkey in the wrench. Without being overly prejudicial about it, my experience has led me to observe that the majority of these types are bond guys, glass half-empty people in a glass half-full industry. Bond investors have long had the reputation of being ghouls, delighting in bad economic news and occasionally, just like about everybody else I guess, the financial misfortunes of others we feel are undeservedly rich. (And in the lower 48, that is a very long list indeed.)

Rick was a fast-talking, nattily dressed bond salesman from an era when the spreads were wide. A history major in college, he read the paper cover to cover on his commute, and like many Irishmen liked a healthy debate. He was difficult to argue with because he was always prepared and expressed his views with a messianic zeal that would make a Baptist minister weep. Rick could play it a little fast and loose with the facts but, when challenged, would speak faster and throw out more arcana, relevant or not, to support his view. To make him somewhat more colorful was his ability to tempt the uninitiated into sucker bets they had no chance of winning. He once goaded one unsuspecting and exasperated equity salesman into betting Rick on his own height. Within thirty seconds, the poor schlub, realizing that he had been had, just handed Rick a McGarret (that's a 5-0) and walked away, utterly defeated. When the people in the office got tired of arguing with him (which was about 8:15am), he hit the phones like no one you ever saw, regaling his clients with the same colorful stories and arguments. After nine hours a day of listening to the same rap, you might wonder how he got away with it for so long without being left with a mouth full of loose teeth. And here the answer was simple—the man was genuinely funny.

His warnings about the "house of cards" that constituted the global financial system became so frequent that the other salesmen, younger and less experienced, came to deem him "Recession Rick." His litany of financial anxieties were so frequently expressed to anyone within earshot that one enterprising chap constructed a Recession Rick Bingo card to be used in our morning meeting. It looked like this:

**Recession Rick Bingo**

| | | | | |
|---|---|---|---|---|
| Schmoron | Dr. Copper | Mr. Smithers | Corrupt | Odds |
| Elites | China | Credit Spreads | Policy Mistake | Blind |
| Kidnapped | Recession | Bet | Purge | 2s- 10s |
| Tesla | Prix Fixe | Zika Virus | War criminal | Martin Wolf |
| German 10-Year | Curve flattening | Populist | Mr. Market | Bear Market |

In recent months, his favorite bête-noirs were China's alleged growth rate and its policymakers, who he affectionately called "schmorons." Any suggestion that China wasn't already in a deep recession would lead him into paroxysms of stream-of-consciousness utterances that made him look like one of those crazy guys you sometimes see in Manhattan trying to direct traffic in their underwear. After laughing derisively at your stupidity and naïveté, he'd launch into a familiar tirade.

"Do you really believe that? Oil prices are at twelve year lows. Dr. Copper is crashing. Corporate credit spreads are widening. German 10-years yields are 31 basis points. The curve is flattening. The Shenzhen is down 40% from the peak. They're trying to devalue and institute capital controls at the same time. THAT'S IMPOSSIBLE!!! Look at the way they handled the crash in their stock prices. Does that inspire confidence in their ability to centrally plan an economy? Plus they don't have enough women. You know what happens when there's too few women around? That's right—guys get frustrated and antsy and angry. They're building blue water navy at the same time their debt as a percentage of GDP is 232%. Does that sound like a good development to you? Forget about a soft landing, they're in a hard-landing, buddy. Yessirree, no doubt about it. Mr. Market is telling us, so. We're just too blind to see it."

"Rick," I might offer, "as you know, we have a series of single factor regression models that tell us that growth in China should be between 5 and 7 percent this year."

"I reject the data."

"Whaddya mean you reject the data? All data? You have to use something."

"They got to you too didn't they?"

"What? Who?"

"They're commies and liars. I'll bet on my own judgment thank you very much," Rick said self-satisfied. "I'm going to write it up in my daily note to clients. They appreciate someone who celebrates the TRUTH!"

You always learned something talking to Rick but it was exhausting. And so after a long day trying to make heads or tails of an economy and a market that, like Donald Trump, appeared to be breaking all the rules, I was happy to ensconce myself at Nanni's on 46th with my wife, "share" a bottle of Barolo, and have a few laughs.

About halfway through the meal, Alessandro the maître d' walked quickly over to my table and said "Giasone, c'e' una telefonata per te."

"Dai, stai scherzando, vero? Ma come mai..."

"E' molto urgente, lui dice."

"Mannaggia…Bev, I've gotta take this I'll be right back."

I quickly walked past small round tables and the frescos of Procida and the Tyrhennian seascapes to the house phone near the coat check room.

"Hello?"

"Mr. Trennert?"

"Yes. This is he."

"This is Mr. Li of the People's Republic. We have in our possession someone you might know, your Managing Director Mr. Rick," said a man in perfectly accented American English.

"Knock it off willya, Rick. I'm having dinner with Bev. Isn't it enough that I have to hear your bullsh…"

"I can assure you that this is not one of your American pranks. Mr. Trennert. You see the man in the pinstriped grey flannel suit at the first table on the left."

"Yes."

"He will scratch his nose now to assure you that this is not a joke." And just like that an elegant Chinese man eating alone looked at me, scratched his nose, and winked before taking another bite of his angel hair pasta.

"Geez Louise, what did Rick do now? Is he in trouble?"

"Quite. We don't appreciate his skepticism of our official economic numbers. In fact, in our country, such questions are considered crimes."

"Rick is harmless. To be honest our firm isn't that influential. He questions everything, especially when there's money to be made."

"You might find it amusing but we do not. As the Supreme Leader of Strategas you have a responsibility to stop him."

"Skepticism is not a crime in America, sir. Suppose I just call the F.B.I. and have them help me figure this out."

"That would be most imprudent, *Jase*. We know everything about you and Rick, your families, and everything you care about. For instance, your decision to buy a boat last year did little for your FICO score."

That's another thing Dad was right about.

"Is that a threat?" I asked sternly.

"Let us just say that we are starting the re-education process. Tell no one about this conversation in the next 12 hours and you might be able to see Mr. Rick again."

"But how..." In the split second before I heard the phone go dead, I could swear I heard Rick leading his would-be captors in laughter.

Ashen, I hurried back to my table, tried not to alarm my wife, finished dinner, and went home.

After a fitful night's sleep, I awoke early the next day, took my usual route to the office in a cab down Fifth until I arrived at the coffee cart on 46th and Vanderbilt. Without asking, Ahmed placed a large coffee and a hard-boiled egg in a brown paper bag. I gave him two bucks and started my short walk to the office. After five steps, I let out an incontinent yawp as I felt the cold steel of Mohaska between my third and fourth left ribs.

"We're going to take a walk Mr. Trennert. Don't turn around and don't try to run."

"Ok...Is Rick safe?"

"Quite. We had a long night."

"Well, he's one in a million, I'll tell you that," I said trying to lighten the mood.

"Perhaps in your country. In China, when you're one in a million there are fourteen hundred people just like you. And we've never seen anything like him. Our interrogators worked during the Cultural Revolution with some pretty rough characters. After 12 hours of re-education, they came back and told me that they wanted to open up an artisanal cronut shop on the Upper East Side with Mr. Rick. They had doubts about the revolution. In all my years fighting for the people...," his voice trailing. "We mapped his genome. It must be genetic."

"What do we have to do to get him back? What is it you want—money? A retraction?"

"Actually, Mr. Trennert, we would be most appreciative if you just took him back and forgot about the whole incident."

"Uhhhhh, sure. But why didn't you guys just..."

"Make him disappear? We've started to rethink our approach since we joined the SDR. When you have $3.5 trillion in currency reserves you never really have to say you're sorry. Plus, we're superstitious people and we wonder whether this man just might be able to speak from the grave...If you forget about this, no further harm will be done to you or your people."

"Ok. That's a deal."

Three steps later I felt the gun removed from my rib cage. Five steps after that I turned around and saw an empty Vanderbilt Avenue. Relieved, I walked to the office. It was 6:45 am. I turned on the lights and peered into the board room. Rick was sitting there, clear shaven and neat as a pin sipping coffee and reading the *FT*.

"Rick! How are you? Are you ok?"

"Sure, why?"

"Well I thought you were…ummm, kidnapped over your comments about China."

"Oh those fellas? They didn't scare me. I reasoned with them. Unlike the people around here, they actually listened to me. We had a blast. We may open-up a Soulcycle franchise in Williamsburg together after we get back from Vegas."

"Wow." I said stunned. "Well, an expert's anyone from out of town, I guess."

"That's not the quote."

"What? Sure it is."

"Wanna bet?"

"Not really. I'm tired," I said sighing.

"Most people attribute that to Truman or Twain but really that came from the Bible. Luke 14:11, I think. Or Deuteronomy 10. I'm not sure. Give me 3-1 odds and we'll call it a bet. It doesn't matter, I know I'm right. *'No one can be a prophet in their own home town.'* I can't believe you didn't know that."

"Rick?"

"Yeah?"

"How do you feel about making your note this morning about Putin and Russia's oligarchs?"

# *Active Management Fights Back*

*Originally Published—March 11, 2016*

> *And it never failed that during the dry years the people forgot about the rich years, and during the wet years they lost all memory of the dry years. It was always that way.*
>
> John Steinbeck, *East of Eden*

In the course of fifteen years, my old boss, Ed Hyman, taught me many things about the financial services industry. There is one lesson that particularly stands out, however. "In this business," he used to tell us, "never forget that people pay people." This he might say to the research analyst who thought the brilliance of his reports obviated the need for him to get on an airplane and see his customers face to face or to the institutional salesman who, for whatever reason, missed a big a development at an account. At its core, Ed's admonition was a reminder that good fortune breeds competition and competition breeds commoditization. At this point in any business, no one was talented or smart enough to be able to survive without meeting the needs and wants of the *customer*. This is why, at its core, free markets do a better job of allocating scarce resources than other systems devised by human hands. The outsized pay that accompanies jobs in this industry can often lead its stars to believe that their good fortune is either pre-ordained or "secular." Eventually, however, everyone from M&A bankers to sell-side oracles to hedge fund moguls will learn that their fortunes are left largely up to the generosity and consideration of other people based on our skill, experience, and character.

In a political climate that renders it acceptable to despise an entire industry made up of six million people—"Wall Street"—it was nice to see at least one firm, Fidelity, (a client for the purposes of full disclosure) stop the cycle of self-loathing, and celebrate, by way of a television commercial, the importance of the capital markets, of thrift, and of those with the awesome responsibility entrusted to protect and grow it. The ad features portfolio manager Will Danoff and a series of letters and pictures he received from the parents of a newborn about 20 years ago. They chose the Contra Fund as a vehicle to save for their son's college education at the time and wrote to him to tell him so. Mr. Danoff kept the letter and picture of the child taped up to his office wall as a reminder that he was managing more than just "money." It's hard to believe, but Fidelity last launched a television advertising campaign about the same time that baby boy was born. Since then, it seems, most mutual fund companies have celebrated their "process" in advertisements more than the men and women who do battle with Mr. Market every day. Knowing nothing about the mutual fund industry, there may be very good business reasons to eschew the star system that was once so common in the days of Peter Lynch and my good friends Larry Auriana and Hans Utsch (Kaufmann's "tough guy" funds.) But it seems to me that ads based on process will do little to dent the forward progress of other financial instruments, like ETFs, that are simply cheaper. Ultimately, it's important to remember people do pay other people and may pay a little more for the privilege.

For those who hold on to a rather Victorian notion that the capital markets serve free societies and that the industry's role as a fiduciary should be celebrated, the commercial was a breath of fresh air that I hope our other mutual fund clients emulate, at least for a while. There are limits to cynicism, even in a 24-hour news cycle. The commercial hit exactly the right chord and I shared it with my firm immediately after it first appeared on television in early February. I thought it was important, especially for the younger people in my office, to be reminded that, for many of us, this isn't a game. We all need heroes.

# *Nothing "Casual" About Money*

*Originally Published—June 10, 2016*

> *"Dress shabbily and they remember the dress; dress impeccably and they remember the woman." Coco Chanel*

You learn a lot of things when you use your own money to start a company. I learn something new every day, of course, and while I question many of the things I thought I knew for sure a decade ago, I feel more strongly than ever about what it takes to run a financial services company. First, management's greatest responsibility lies in creating the right incentives. Get the incentives right and the need for intensive management oversight declines markedly. Get them wrong and human beings will predictably shock you in their ability to give you precisely what you asked of them regardless of whether it actually benefits the company. Second, the importance of culture in a professional services firm cannot be overestimated, especially after a period in which a "me" generation has been taught to worry about whether they are, at all times, fulfilled on some metaphysical level. An abundance of other people's money has led Wall Street to stop hiring potential partners and to start hiring mercenaries. The potential reputational risks this presents to financial institutions became obvious during the financial crisis.

What instigated this—my latest screed on the devaluation of the perception of finance as a noble profession in this country—was J.P. Morgan's recent announcement to relax its dress code to be more in keeping with times and to compete for "talent" with a variety of FinTech start-ups that appear to be rich in everything—like venture capital money and pretense—with the exception of profits. The memorandum is so tortured and Baroque in its reasoning that it would make Cervantes weep in exasperation. Employees were encouraged to "dress for the client" while simultaneously attempting to draw distinctions between "work casual," "weekend casual," and just plain inappropriate, giving young people, who should be primarily worried about serving their clients and employers, yet something else to worry about. Jamie Dimon's recent trip to Silicon Valley was the genesis of the change, apparently, leading him to conclude that the bank couldn't effectively compete for "talent" in a world of ever-increasing informality. Personally, I view this as simply the latest attempt to extend adolescence that started with the Affordable Care Act, a federal insurance program that allows young people as old as 26 to be covered by their parents for all maladies with the exception of breaking your ass.

I remember my rookie years in this business very well and I can say in complete candor that "talent" as it related to the world of investing was the most manifestly absent feature of my resume. Why Ed Hyman didn't fire me on the spot when I asked him what the difference between what the sell-side and the buy-side was in 1991 remains one of my life's most joyful mysteries. Talent in the investment business, I've come to realize is far more a collection of values like humility, hard-work, and perspective gained from experience than I.Q. In fact, I would argue that, in the history of the financial markets, arrogance has destroyed far more capital than stupidity. At its heart, capitalism works only when companies meet the needs and wants of *other* people. In a world in which the financial media has some odd fetish for stories about Twitter's break room and the largely infantile corporate campuses of Silicon Valley, large banks seem to be doing everything in their power to mask the fact that building businesses that last require back-breaking hard work and seriousness. Of course, in the old days, long before the existence of deposit insurance and a variety of other government backstops that made many banks too big to fail, financial institutions wanted and needed neoclassical buildings of granite and limestone to signal their safety and soundness. With the Fed's balance sheet swelling comfortably to $4.5 trillion, such pretense has gone the way of the straw hat today, allowing normally level-headed executives like Mr. Dimon to buy into the hype that suggests that working at a tech start-up will do more to fulfill their young charges passions and the needs of society at large than banks that progressive politicians now use as a punchline. There is also some implication that taking an extra minute or two to look like an adult would somehow impede the creative process of the super-intelligent being clad in a fleece vest, perhaps the most cliché sartorial choice for a new breed of would-be masters of the universe.

Maybe it's because I'm getting older, but I still carry a briefcase and have eschewed wheelies in favor of military-style shoulder bags for business travel. This is driven in large part by the knowledge that there will be no government guarantees for Strategas if we run into hard times. As a result, the biggest cardinal sin at our shop is taking any client for granted or forgetting that we are surrounded by competitors all-too-happy to take them away from us. For us, dressing like adults is, in part, a defense mechanism. While our true rewards are likely to come in the next life, money is still, like it or not, one of the most important things here on Earth. The only people who don't believe that either rely on kindness of strangers or who have so much of it that they have either never experienced or have forgotten what it's like to get a call from a credit collection agency. Ultimately, we believe that managing other people's money, and serving those that do, is consequential—a solemn commitment to help other people, through thrift and the prudent application of risk, to afford a variety of things that will be important to them in the future—a house, a college education for a child, health care for an aging parent, or even, perhaps, your own break room, replete with foosball tables and "free" snacks and beer.

---

### *GOLDMAN ATTRACTS 250,000 JOBSEEKERS*

*Number of Applications from Students Surges Despite Sector's Poor Image*

*Goldman Sachs attracted more than a quarter of a million applications from students and graduates for jobs this summer, suggesting fears of a "brain drain" in the sector may be exaggerated as banks introduce more employee-friendly policies. Applications globally rose more than 40 per cent since 2012, according to figures given to the Financial Times.*

*Financial Times, June 5, 2016*

---

### *WHY WALL STREET NEEDS TO HIRE YOUNGER STAFF*

*Investment banks are competing fiercely for young talent. Of course, they always did. But in the past, the lure was mostly financial. Now, banks are loudly promising a modicum of quality of life, too. Just last week, UBS told bankers they can take two hours of personal time each week. Credit Suisse has insisted bankers ought to take Friday evenings off unless something important is happening. Morgan Stanley is offering paid sabbaticals. And J.P. Morgan Chase has loosened its dress code to allow employees to wear business-casual attire.... Banks desperately need young people because they are cheaper. The profile of the workforce is changing as investment banks have realized fewer of their highest-paid bankers and traders are crucial for bringing in revenue... The industry even has a word for this: "juniorization." It helps explain how investment banks have cut compensation costs on average 21% since 2009 while cutting staff numbers by just 3%, according to J.P. Morgan analysts.*

*The Wall Street Journal, June 5, 2016*

---

# *Revenge* *<u>on</u>* *the Nerds*

*Originally published—July 2016*

Noogies, titanic wedgies, purple nurples, and wet willies. Anyone of a certain age who attended a large public high school would recognize these activities as the instruments of humiliation the "cool" kids would exact on the kids who were, well, not so cool. Some of these big men on campus peaked in high school, others, through hard work, force of personality, family money, and luck became politically influential and independently wealthy. The "nerds" kept plodding, got good grades, attended the right schools, and achieved graduate degrees. They exacted their revenge later on in a way by becoming professors, politicians, policy advisors, and political commentators. For the past 20 years, they have been able to run the table on debates about a variety public policy initiatives and foreign adventures put forth by political elites on both the left and the right. The cool kids seem to be fighting back, though. Like it or not, Nigel Farage just gave David Cameron a swirlie while Donald Trump pelted the Republican firmament with spitballs from a seat in the back of the classroom for much of the last year. Politically speaking, it seems as if ordinary people are questioning how much they have benefitted from a variety of policies foisted upon them by an intellectual elite that has a degree of job security rarely seen in the private sector. To the extent to which the wisdom of experts is increasingly questioned, there are potentially large implications for the global economy and the markets as it relates to:

**Negative Interest Rates.** It has been reported that the Federal Reserve Board employs 900 PhDs. For some reason that reminds me of my Dad telling me that nothing good ever happens after midnight. (It only took me 20 years figure out that he was right.) Somehow, I feel, nothing good can happen in an organization that employs 900 academics. They tell us that they have plenty of experience with negative interest rates and that zero is just a number. Apparently, no one has told that to savers who feel justifiably queasy about having to pay their government for the privilege of lending them money. All the things that were supposed to happen after the introduction of negative interest rates in Japan went in precisely the opposite direction. The Yen strengthened meaningfully, Japanese bank stocks are down -38%, and Japanese savers are buying safes and hoarding large denomination bank notes. A policy that was designed to get people to take more risk has had precisely the opposite effect and appears to be manifestly deflationary.

**The European Union.** While the concept of the EU derives from the best of intentions—the desire to avoid another land war on the Continent, the truth of the matter is that it has never been politically popular among rank and file voters anywhere. What is easy to forget is that many of the member states are relatively new to the concept of political unification themselves. Italy was unified in 1861. Germany—for the first time—was unified in 1871. For many, feelings of being truly European are most deeply felt during the Ryder Cup. It would be unrealistic to expect people who have little faith in their representatives serving in their own capitals to be more trusting of their representation in Brussels. Only the most optimistic would expect the Brexit vote to be a one-off event in the Union.

**Open Borders.** By history, tradition, and culture, Western democracies have long seen the benefits of globalization and the salutary impact immigration can have on economic growth. But in a world in which people are justifiably nervous about their physical security as well as the sustainability of both the public treasury and their own economic well-being, unconstrained immigration is probably seen now more as a threat than an opportunity. While a politician is unlikely to lose their job based on the issue, those without unique job skills just might. If this is an important issue in the U.S. where the unemployment rate is 4.7%, it shouldn't be surprising that it is an issue in countries with structurally high unemployment.

**"Free" Trade.** By definition, trade with a country that is fixing its currency can't possibly be described as "free." Here again, while globalization has benefitted the C-suite of corporate America, the benefits to the average Joe are more difficult to discern. It is true that everything from tube socks to flat panel television sets are less expensive, but it is also true that the middle class, especially those who aren't college educated, is having a tough time in a country in which only 7% of the workforce is engaged in manufacturing.

**The Yale Model.** Another part of the intellectual orthodoxy of the investment business has been the use of the endowment model and the efficient frontier to meet increasingly unrealistic investment return assumptions. The success of David Swensen and the Yale endowment spawned a cottage industry of industry consultants who were able to convince both the financially sophisticated and unsophisticated alike that it was somehow appropriate to pay 2 and 20 for a product designed to produce returns of LIBOR plus 300. CalPERS decision to divest itself of hedge funds and some of last year's revelations about the hidden fees embedded in some private equity vehicles has led to the reevaluation of the endowment model. While fee compression is nothing new to long-only managers, it is making its dramatic entrance only now in the world of alternatives.

Of course, anyone reading this (or writing it for that matter) has probably benefitted greatly from these firmaments of the intellectual orthodoxies of foreign relations, economics, and finance. Still, it would seem wise, in the current environment, to not take them for granted or to expect them to be permanent. The cool kids have just come back to the cafeteria, want to occupy the best table, and are ready to "trade" their bologna sandwich for the nerds' Del Monte chocolate pudding. Made you look.

# *A Lax Dad's Observations About Politics*

*Originally published—July 2016*

There was a period in the politics of this country in which the term "soccer moms" was used to express the concerns of ordinary women who didn't have the time to worry much about the arcana of public policy but were focused largely on the security of their families. Twenty-five years later the term has largely faded from the taxonomy of political discourse although my circumstances have led me to believe that there is a new constituency to which some attention must be paid—the Lax Dad. At 14, my son cares more about lacrosse than anything else in life as do his fellow "lax bros." This requires their parents to move heaven and earth to coordinate work and family schedules to attend tournaments and practices up and down the Eastern seaboard. The level of commitment this entails can lead one to only two conclusions: parents both love their children and are, also, shockingly insecure about the idea that they could fall behind their peers in an activity that might, if the stars align properly, help them get into college and defray the enormous costs associated with it. My son plays for the Outlaws out of Huntington, Long Island. We are not the most ethnically diverse group of people you're going to meet but we are occupationally diverse. As near as I can tell, the Trennerts are the only Wall Street family involved in the team that lives in Manhattan. The other Lax Dads work in a variety of fields. One owns an auto body repair shop, another is a local lawyer, yet another a fireman. Some have tattoos, others a piercing or two. Bleary-eyed, we spend a lot of time together on the sidelines of lacrosse games talking about a variety of things big and small - like why our sons are addicted to their smart phones, why it's so hard to get them to read, and why they need to be reminded constantly to do the basics—like bathing. More recently I've been intrigued about our inevitable discussions about politics. As a group of people who aren't particularly interested in being politically correct or getting invited to the right cocktail parties on the Upper East Side, the debates are lively and, at times, shockingly and beautifully candid, expressing a diversity of thought on things like gun control and social issues. Where there is little diversity is in the anxiousness that comes with the fact that while we make decent livings on paper, we have to worry constantly about paying an increasingly voracious tax man while also saving for college. We are universally offended by being called bigots for wondering about the impact of largely unconstrained immigration. And we fear, perhaps more than anything else, an opioid epidemic that is finding itself in towns that could be seen as reasonable stand-ins for Mayberry. These Lax Dads are the "unprotected" Peggy Noonan so articulately wrote about a few months ago. The political consultants have largely ignored them the world over and it has been a grievous mistake. The only thing these guys know they can control is their vote in November.

# APPENDIX

## *Memos from the Chairman; Fan Mail; Remembrances*

To: My Colleagues

From: Jason Trennert

Subject: Tough Times—Lehman Fails

Date: September 15, 2008

As you've no doubt seen by now, there are some revolutionary changes taking place on Wall Street that will result in significant layoffs and changes in the way our industry does business. It would be natural to worry about our own future as a small start-up company. I want you all to rest assured that the financial status of Strategas is more than sound and that we have been pleased this year with both the growth in our revenues and the growth in our account base. Of course, we start at zero every day and whatever success we have had tells us little about our future. I am sorry to say that this probably won't be the last time we'll be worried about the markets or the economy. This is the life we have chosen. But in times of stress, I think we should all remember the principles upon which our firm was based—Bonitas, Probitas, Fides—Class, Integrity, Faith. The ancient Greeks believed that fate was a function of character. Ultimately we have no control over commission budgets or the level of the S&P. We only can control our efforts to provide a first class product in a first class way. If we do that, I am confident that we will be able to survive to face both calmer seas and new forms of stormy weather.

Semper Fidelis, Jase

Strategas Research Partners

# Memo

**To:** My Strategas Colleagues

**From:** Jason DeSena Trennert, Managing Partner

**Date:** 01/15/10

**Re:** Embarrassed and Humbled and Angry

---

Few of the 35 people now employed at Strategas know that Don, Nick, and I started this firm to, in part, create a different kind of sell-side firm in the old Wall Street tradition of a partnership that would put its clients first. We wanted to avoid the cliché brokerage firm habit of over-promising and under-delivering services to our clients. Our motto—*bonitas, probitas, fides*[14] and our founding management principles—quality, transparency, and perspective—were meant from the very beginning to guide us on the wonderful journey that has become this company. In short, we were, and still are, insistent that we avoid the appearance of being just another bunch of Wall Street phonies that treat its clients as chattel for the short money achievable in this industry.

And so I was shocked to learn this week that we were being fired by a client that had been in our corner from the very beginning. A great mentor to me and a friend, he somehow got the sense that the amount he was paying us wasn't enough to "move the needle" in getting personal attention from me from time to time. He hadn't been invited to one of our regular luncheons and dinners with investors and he rarely heard from us with value-added ideas one can't find in our reports. Given our friendship and the fact that the amount in question was nearly twice as much as I made my first year out of college, the conversation left me feeling deeply embarrassed and humbled and angry—angry at myself for failing to take care of an important relationship and angry at our organization for missing the signs that led to us to commit the most unpardonable sin of any service

14. Class, Integrity, Faith

business—failing to make its clients feel important and special. In short, he was right. We deserved to be fired.

When I was 24, I "invested" $30,000 in a company out of Ho Ho Kus, New Jersey that I became convinced had found the cure for cancer. The fact that the founder of the firm purported to be a "doctor of medicine" despite an almost shocking disregard for his own health and hygiene and that he instructed me to write a check to his personal checking account in exchange for my membership interest left me unbowed. This was my quick ticket to riches without hard work. After the whole thing was revealed to be a colossal scam, the other suckers and I retained separate legal counsel. Some sued, but my lawyer, a slightly older classmate of mine from Georgetown with wisdom beyond his years, told me to forget it. He thought I should consider the whole affair a form of what he called *rebbe gelt*—a Yiddish term for "money you learn from." Over time, he explained, that $30,000 would pale in comparison to the money I would save by avoiding investments in other "sure things" when I actually had some degree of sustainable wealth later on in life. As it turned out, my aborted quick trip to a life of foreign automobiles and mysterious women seriously depleted the funds I was to use for business school, leading to two long years of Cups of Soup and meaningful debts upon graduation.

The Lord only knows whether we'll be able to get the client we just lost back, but I think we should all consider our recent firing as a form of rebbe gelt—it should serve to save us from the arrogance and hubris of taking one of our clients for granted ever again. Some of you may know that I have decided to forego cigars and hard alcohol during this Lenten season. Trust me when I say this has been harder than it sounds. In the aftermath of this week's sleepless nights, I have decided that I should also commit myself to call every one of our accounts by Easter. For our salesmen, analysts, and traders, the episode should reveal, once again, other persistent devotions:

1) People pay people.

2) It is fool's paradise to believe that you can continue to keep clients without adding value. The firm's written

reports are only a starting point. Our clients have too much to read and they expect us to make it easy for them to determine what is truly important.

3) Never focus on one "important" person at an account to the exclusion of other "important" people. The deeper your reservoir of goodwill at your accounts the stickier your relationship will be.

4) Never assume that just because an analyst has a personal relationship with a client that this absolves you from actively covering the account. The analysts' clients are the firm's clients in *toto* and it can be difficult to give everyone the attention they deserve. Covering the account is the fundamental role of the salesman.

5) We all travel so much that it sometimes feels as if days in the New York office are vacation days. This is a mistake. Remember that one-third of our business derives from accounts on this small island. Our clients here at home deserve the same treatment as those in other parts of the country.

6) Analyst-of-the-Week calls are critically important for both the analyst and the salesman. Our analysts must develop their own relationships with our accounts.

7) If you haven't visited one of your accounts, you aren't covering it. Sales visits without an analyst are a must. The next time you feel like surfing the Internet while eating your salad at your desk, ask yourself whether you shouldn't be visiting a client.

We work in a brutally competitive business in which the difference between success and failure rests with making the extra effort, running out every ground ball, making that one extra phone call, and treating every client relationship as a precious and irreplaceable commodity. ***Regardless of our respective functions at this firm, we are all in client service business. If you feel uncomfortable with that responsibility, Strategas is not the company for you.***

We should all be proud of what we've accomplished in the past 4½ years but we should never forget that this firm only exists to serve its customers. Make me, and yourselves, proud.

Sempre avanti, forti e uniti.

# *Fan Mail*

*Originally Published—October 13, 2014*

A number of years ago I had lunch with Jimmy Dunne of Sandler O'Neill and I asked him what I could expect in running my own firm. He said, "just realize everything will be more—expect more good and more bad." Given the tragedy of 9/11 Sandler had to face, it says a lot about the character of the man to even mention the "more good" part. Still, I've found his warning to be absolutely correct. At any rate, one of the "more bad" parts of the job is occasionally getting unsolicited hate mail from strangers, usually the result of some media appearance where the ratings might be only slightly higher than what the channel would receive by running test patterns. For the most part, these screeds are written by hard money types and financial "preppers" who see all Wall Street professionals as a part of some elaborate conspiracy to debase the currency. I always ignore them. But once a while, one of these notes will get my attention. I received this little chestnut from a fan as I was about to sit down to lunch last weekend:

**From: XXXXXXX [X.XXXXX@bloomberg.net]**
**To: Jason DeSena Trennert (jtrennert@strategasrp.com)**
**Subject: bursting**
**Sent:** Saturday, October 04, 2014 12:34 PM

Dear Mr. Trennert, I'm a long-time subscriber to ISI; I know your work. You are indeed a brilliant analyst; you express your opinions simply, directly. I'm lucky you appear frequently on Bloomberg and in Barron's. But your Barron's photo shows you are clearly eating tons of sugar, rich meats, cakes, processed food (more sugar). Your face, chest, belly look ready to burst. No doubt your physician offers you a variety of medications for the symptoms you suffer from this horrendous diet. You can cut out sugar entirely: for example, a fresh organic Pink Lady apple and a slice of LIGHTLY buttered toast (not sugared) and you'll come to enjoy that as you now do apple pie. Virtually all processed food in supermarkets, soup crackers, things you'd never suspect are highly sugared, have your food shopper read the labels every time. When you eat a rich steak, your body requires sugar to balance. Omit both. No milk, cream, light on butter. Replace meat with fish. The example of how to give up pie for apple and bread gives you the idea of how to exchange junk for healthy, delicious real food. You'll stop having that constant tension caused by the artificial stimulus of sugar, (like kerosene on a fire) you'll sleep deeply, you'll be relaxed and positive. You won't need medications. As simple as that. All a perspicacious, analytic man like you need do is to read about the effects of sugar online. Far more important than what Yellen and Draghi will do.

In a business where they say "if you want a friend, get a dog," it's nice to know other people are looking out for you. It goes without saying that I changed my order from a cheeseburger to a Caesar Salad...And for the record, I cannot yet afford a food shopper.

# *Observations From a Dispirited Notre Dame Fan*

*Originally Published—December 2, 2014*

Late in the fourth quarter, I sent this note to "my" team in December.

> It is known to one and all that I am Golden Domer, having had to adopt a football team after Georgetown lost to Gallaudet repeatedly in the late 1980s. ND beat Miami for the national championship in 1988 and I was hooked. As I watched USC completely embarrass Notre Dame this past Saturday afternoon, I started to reflect on their season and most particularly an almost imperceptible line between success and failure. For those who have productive interests, Notre Dame started out the season 6-0 and arguably beat the second best team in the nation, Florida State, on a blown call late in the 4th quarter. Irish quarterback Everett Golson was being seriously considered as a Heisman Trophy candidate and there was some talk of ND being in the BCS championship. The team is currently 7-5. In the weeks since, a series of shaky holds, unlucky injuries, missed tackles, blown assignments, and bobbled catches and the Irish will be lucky if they make the Famous Idaho Potato Bowl. Golson was benched and Coach Kelly is wondering whether he's going to have to start spending more time with his family. The difference between a 7-5 season and a 10-2 season came down to 10 points total over three games. In all competitive endeavors great and small, victory can be elusive and often comes down on doing the little things right, on concentration, and on confidence. There are 22 trading days left in our "season"—let's make them count. **JDT**

# *Requiem for a Heavyweight—Alex Porter*

*Originally Published—May 2, 2014*

Last Friday I received a sad note from an old friend in the investment business telling me that we lost a great human being, a great intellect, and a great investor on Good Friday to cancer. Alex Porter was a pioneer on Wall Street and worked for the man who invented the concept of the hedge fund, Alfred Winslow Jones. He passed away at 75 at his farm in Davidson, North Carolina. When you reach the age when you start to think about your own mortality, it's always shocking to think that a prominent character from your rookie years might pass from this mortal coil. I had forever thought of him as young and vibrant and his imposing physical size along with shock of blonde and then white hair always led me to believe that he might just be invincible. He ran Porter, Felleman when I was assigned to cover him in 1991 and I'll never forget his patience with a dopey young guy trying to make his way in a difficult business. By chance, I ran into him at the Rizzoli bookstore on 57th the very day I resigned from a firm I had been with for 16 years to start Strategas. He told me then that, as an entrepreneur, "I'd grow up quick" and he was right. Porter Orlin was our sixth client. You never forget the people that help you out when you have nothing to offer them in return.

Although he was too humble to admit it, he was an almost prototypical Renaissance man who could talk sports to the guy on his right with equal ease as with the guy to his left about Scripture or Faulkner at the Tap Room at the New York Athletic Club. He was bereft of pretension. He had a small library attached to his office which featured solely a white rocking chair and bookshelves—electronic communication would never be allowed to sully his need for thought. During one visit, I noticed an odd still black and white picture of Marcello Mastroianni and we then spent thirty minutes talking about the Italian neorealists. During another encounter we somewhat randomly discovered that we shared a favorite Christmas movie—*The Bishop's Wife* with Cary Grant, David Niven, and Loretta Young. Two years later and quite randomly, he sent me a page from the *Gettysburg Journal* that discussed the grace of Grant's character in the film. He pursued all these interests while building a hedge fund that stood the test of time, growing in assets from $360,000 in the 70s to nearly $2 billion today. Julian Robertson chose Alex to be in charge of Tiger's liquidation in the event that Julian was ever unable to fully execute his duties as its General Partner. That's quite a distinction.

He was an avid wrestler and a former star football player at Davidson College. Alex was always encouraging me to stay in shape and, until I was married, it was not difficult to notice that his girlfriends were always younger than mine despite the fact that he was 30 years my senior. For these reasons and many more, Alex Porter has remained a hero for me as a Wall Street fiduciary and as a man. I will miss him.

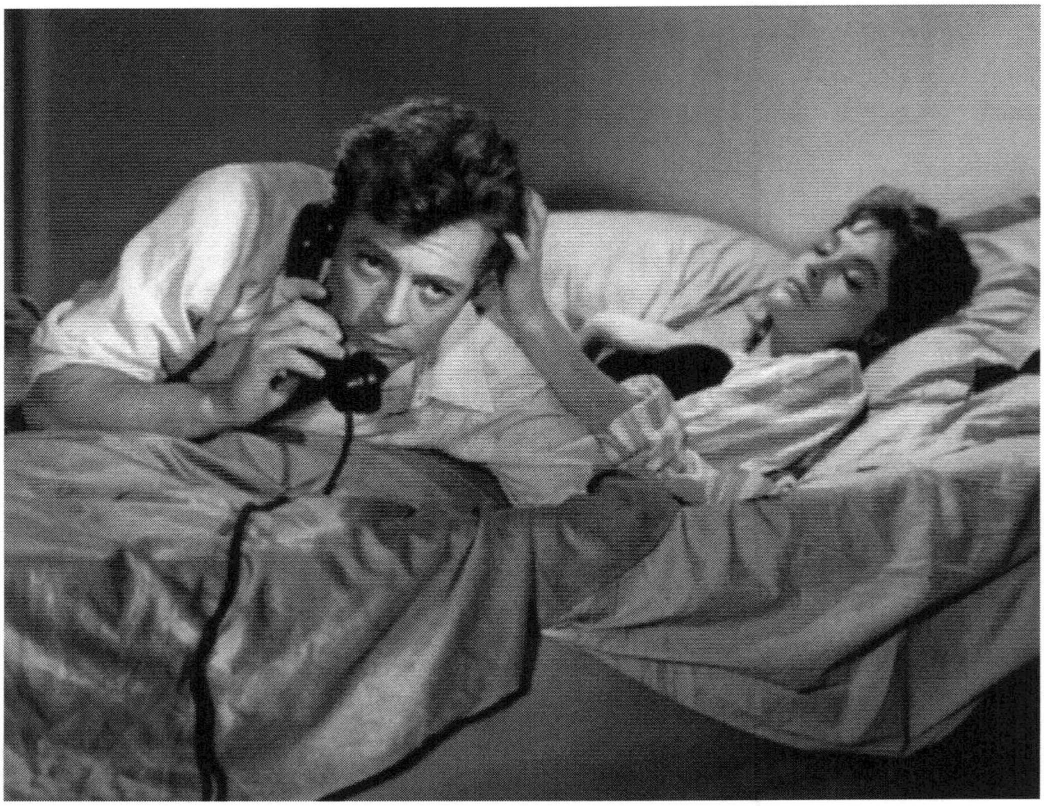

source: *La Dolce Vita* (1960) Riama Film, Gray-Film, Pathé Consortium Cinéma

**SO LONG TO AN OLD FRIEND**

Vince Farrell

Sadly, my friend Vince Farrell passed away last weekend after a long struggle with cancer. He was only 68. Vince was a great investor and an even better guy. We had long been friends and he was one of the earliest supporters of our efforts to establish and grow Strategas. One of the founding partners of Spears, Benzak, Saloman & Farrell, established in 1982, he served as the chief investment officer and portfolio manager for some of the firm's largest clients. Later on, Vince became a portfolio manager for Scotsman Capital and then a ubiquitous market commentator for Soleil Securities and Dominick & Dominick. He also got a great thrill out of being an advisor for Oliver Stone's original *Wall Street* and the sequel *Wall Street: Money Never Sleeps*, where he had a cameo. Vince was one of the best examples I've ever seen of the idea that nice guys can finish first. ***11/21/14***

# ABOUT THE AUTHOR

Jason DeSena Trennert is the Managing Partner of Strategas Research Partners LLC and the Chairman and Chief Executive Officer of the firm's broker-dealer subsidiary, Strategas Securities, LLC. In addition, as Chief Investment Strategist, Mr. Trennert is known as one of Wall Street's top thought leaders on the subject of markets and economic policy. His research pieces are read by leading institutional investors and corporate executives across the globe.

In 2006, Mr. Trennert co-founded Strategas, which originally began with just five employees. Today, the firm employs over fifty research analysts, institutional salesmen, and sales traders at its offices in New York, Washington D.C., and Columbus, Ohio. Prior to founding Strategas, Mr. Trennert was the Chief Investment Strategist and a Senior Managing Director at International Strategy & Investment (ISI) Group where he built and oversaw two of that Firm's most popular research efforts, its Company Surveys and Investment Strategy groups.

Mr. Trennert is a regular guest host on CNBC's "Squawk Box" and "Bloomberg Surveillance" with Tom Keene. His book My Side of the Street was published by St. Martin's Press in 2015.

Of Italian descent, he is devoted to a number of Italian and Italian-American causes and philanthropic activities. He was the Treasurer of La Scuola d'Italia where he headed its investment committee and is a member of the Board of Governors of The Columbus Citizens Foundation.

He is a member of the investment committee of the Rockefeller Brothers Fund and sits on the advisory board at Hollow Brook Wealth Management LLC.

He has an MBA from The Wharton School at the University of Pennsylvania and BS in International Economics from Georgetown University.

Made in United States
Orlando, FL
04 November 2026

90207827R00125